PEACOCK IN THE POISON GROVE

Peacock in the Poison Grove

TWO BUDDHIST TEXTS ON TRAINING THE MIND

The Wheel-Weapon (mTshon cha 'khor lo) &

The Poison-Destroying Peacock (rMa bya dug 'joms)

ATTRIBUTED TO DHARMARAKṢITA

✦

Translated with an introduction
and commentary by

Geshe Lhundub Sopa

Edited and cotranslated by

Michael J. Sweet and Leonard Zwilling

Wisdom Publications • Boston

Wisdom Publications
199 Elm Street
Somerville MA 02144 USA
www.wisdompubs.org

Library of Congress Cataloging-in-Publication Data
Lhundub Sopa, Geshe, 1925–
Peacock in the poison grove : two Buddhist texts on training the mind ; the wheel-weapon (mtshon cha 'khor lo) and the poison-destroying peacock (rma bya dug 'joms) attributed to Dharmarakṣita / translated with an introduction and commentary by Geshe Lhundub Sopa ; edited and cotranslated by Michael J. Sweet and Leonard Zwilling.
p. cm.
Includes bibliographical references and index.
ISBN 0-86171-185-8 (alk. paper)
1. Dharmarakṣita. Theg pa chen po'i blo sbyoṅ mtshon cha 'khor lo. 2. Dharmarakṣita. Rma bya dug 'joms. 3. Spiritual life—Bka'-gdams-pa (Sect) 4. Atiśa, 982–1054. I. Sweet, Michael J. (Michael Jay), 1945– II. Zwilling, Leonard. III. Title
BQ7670.6.L48 2001
294.3/444—dc21 2001025852

ISBN 086171-185-8
2nd Printing
10 09 08 07 06
6 5 4 3 2

Cover design by TL. Interior design by Gopa&Ted2, Inc. Set in Diacritical Garamond 11/14.

Cover photo © Cameraphoo Arte, Venezia
Blockprint of Yamāntaka on page 57 by an anonymous artist; digitized by William Kirtz.
Blockprint of Atiśa on page 187 from the illustrated edition of the *Aṣṭasāhasrikā Prajñāpāramitā* carved by Dingriwa Chokyi Gyaltsen; courtesy of the Tibetan Buddhist Resources Center.

Wisdom Publications' books are printed on acid-free paper and meet the guidelines for permanence and durability of the Committee on Production Guidelines for Book Longevity of the Council on Library Resources.

Printed in the United States of America.

Table of Contents

Printed in the United States
by Baker & Taylor Publisher Services

Preface

THIS BOOK HAS ITS GENESIS in a series of lectures that Geshe Sopa delivered at the Deer Park Buddhist Center in Oregon, Wisconsin over the course of three summer sessions, 1994–96, on the two texts that form its subject, *The Wheel-Weapon Mind Training* and *The Poison-Destroying Peacock Mind Training*. They were chosen in part because of their striking tone and style, which give to their message a special powerful immediacy. These homiletic poems rebuke us for our harmful thoughts and deeds by showing us their inexorable consequences: the sharp wheel-weapon of our negative karma turns fatally back upon ourselves. They exhort us to change our behavior while we are still able, to replace self-centeredness with pure altruism; they invoke the fierce protector Yamāntaka to destroy the primal ignorance that is the root of egotism and thus the cause of all our suffering; and they teach us to become peacock-bodhisattvas, who can transmute the poisonous afflictions of lust, anger, ignorance, envy, and pride into the elixir of emancipation.

We want to express our gratitude to the entire lineage of teachers who have handed down and taught these texts, and to thank those who have helped to make the present book possible: William Kirtz, who was the first to translate *The Wheel-Weapon* into English, has been supportive of this project in a number of ways and provided the image of Yamāntaka that opens part 1 of this book; those who transcribed the tapes of Geshe Sopa's lectures, especially George Propps, as well as Ann Chávez, Suje Own, and James Apple. We are very grateful to Beth Newman for her invaluable editorial assistance and to John Newman and Craig Johnson for critiquing the translation at various stages. We should also like to express our appreciation to David Kittelstrom, E. Gene Smith, and all the staff of Wisdom Publications who have brought this book to fruition. May it be a source of benefit to all living beings.

Historical and Thematic Introduction

Michael J. Sweet and Leonard Zwilling

I: Background

Both *The Wheel-Weapon (mTshon cha 'khor lo) (WW)* and *The Poison-Destroying Peacock (rMa bya dug 'joms) (PDP)* are early examples of the indigenous Tibetan religious literary genre known as *lojong (blo sbyong),* or mind training.[1] This class of literature developed within the Kadampa *(bka' gdams pa)* school, the earliest of the organized Tibetan Buddhist denominations. The school was founded in 1057 by 'Brom ston rgyal ba'i 'byung gnas (1005–64), who based the order on the teachings of his master, the great Indian scholar-saint Dīpaṁkaraśrījñāna, better known as Atiśa (986–1054),[2] whose arrival in western Tibet in 1042 is universally regarded as one of the great landmarks in the history of Tibetan Buddhism. Atiśa had been invited to Tibet by the ruling house of Guge, with the mission of countering the laity-driven pseudotantric antinomianism of the time and reestablishing the celibate monk as the primary model for the religious practitioner. This objective was successfully achieved by his spiritual descendants and remains perhaps his most important legacy. Although he had originally intended to remain in Tibet for only three years, he never returned to India; while making preparations to depart, he met and was impressed by 'Brom, who very likely convinced him of the need to extend his teaching activities to central Tibet. Later, when Atiśa was actually on the road to India, and fighting in Nepal blocked the way, he took this as a convenient pretext to turn back. His return was followed by nine intensive years of teaching in central Tibet, which ended only with his death.[3]

His tantric teaching aside, the Buddhism that Atiśa promulgated in Tibet was essentially a graded approach to the practice of the Mahayana path based on the Mahayana sutras, with a strong emphasis on the cultivation of the "thought intent on enlightenment *(bodhicitta, byang chub kyi sems),*" that is, the fervent aspiration to achieve enlightenment for the sake of all suffering beings.[4] The lojong teachings, which are the means for inculcating and developing the *bodhicitta,* are traditionally regarded as having been introduced to Tibet by Atiśa himself. Within a century of his death there had emerged in certain Kadampa circles a tradition that Atiśa had received special instruction in the cultivation of the bodhicitta from three gurus; Dharmarakṣita, Maitrīyogi,[5] and Dharmakīrti of Suvarṇadvīpa, best known under his Tibetan appellation gSer gling pa, "The Man from the Golden Isle," that is, modern day Sumatra. As the tradition developed, the names of these gurus came to be associated with a group of works that include some of the earliest examples of the mind-training genre—they are: the *WW* and *PDP* attributed to Dharmarakṣita; *The Gyer sGom Vajra Song (Gyer sgom rdo rje'i glu)* attributed to Maitrīyogi; and *The Stages of the Bodhisattva (Sems dpa'i rim pa)* and *The Dharma For Subduing the Barbarian Border Lands (mTha' 'khob 'dul ba'i chos)* attributed to gSer gling pa. The focus of these texts is the thought intent on enlightenment, and they consist of instructions, exhortations, and admonitions *(gdams ngag, man ngag)* of a type that a teacher might give to students to facilitate their practice and understanding. Their language can sometimes be vivid, visionary, and occasionally violent. They are not, however, systematic expositions of the path; this was the province of the other important early Kadampa literary genre, "the stages of the doctrine *(bstan rim).*"[6]

The earliest account of the three-guru tradition is found in the commentary to the well-known *Seven-Point Mind Training (bLo sbyong don bdun ma)* of 'Chad kha ba Ye shes rdo rje (1101–75),[7] written sometime around the mid-twelfth century. Based on the *Root Words of the Mind Training Belonging to the Great Vehicle (Theg pa chen po'i blo sbyong rtsa tshig)* attributed to Atiśa, the text was reorganized and commented on by 'Chad kha ba. For the most part *The Seven-Point Mind Training,* the *WW,* the *PDP,* as well as the other early lojongs, do not differ in their import, but *The Seven-Point Mind Training* is without the tantric and other "baroque" elements found in the others and exclusively follows the nontantric tradition, the so-called *sūtrayāna* or *pāramitāyāna.* In this, 'Chad kha ba and his teachers reflected the generally austere cast of Kadampa teaching imposed by 'Brom, who figures so importantly in the transmission of *The Seven Points,* as well as the trend toward systematic presentations of the Dharma represented by "the stages of the doctrine" literature. From that time forward, *The Seven-Point Mind Training* so came to dominate the teaching of lojong that the two became virtually synonymous, and in the present day its root text has become the most frequently translated Tibetan composition into Western languages. The result of 'Chad kha ba's work, which engendered an immense commentarial literature, was the eclipse of the remaining early lojong literature. When, by the early fifteenth century, the Kadampa had evolved into the Gelukpa—and the old "stages of the doctrine" had become "the stages of the path" *(lam rim)*—mind training, that is, "mind training" as embodied in *The Seven Points,* was assimilated to it. Because the cultivation of the thought intent on enlightenment was at the center of both mind training and the stages of the doctrine/stages of the path, a sharp distinction had never been drawn between them even from the outset. 'Brom himself described mind training as comprising three meditative practices: meditation on impermanence, meditation on love and compassion, and meditation on the two forms of selflessness.[8] These practices would later come to be known as "the three principal aspects of the path" *(lam gyi gtso bo rnam gsum).* By the late eighteenth century two of Atiśa's lojong gurus, Maitrīyogi and gSer gling pa (but not Dharmarakṣita) had been formally incorporated into "the stages of the path" *(lam rim)* lineage,[9] and in the early nineteenth century it would be said that "all the stages of the path beginning with how to serve the spiritual friend are lojong because they are a means for training one's own mind."[10]

2: Dharmarakṣita and the Bodhicitta Guru Tradition

It is likely that the tradition of the three bodhicitta gurus emerged in the lineage of teachers who propagated the text that formed the basis for *The Seven-Point Mind Training.* According to 'Chad kha ba, the point of view represented by *The Seven-Point Mind Training* is that of gSer gling pa, who has always been regarded by tradition, beginning with 'Brom, as having been Atiśa's chief guru; 'Brom is very closely associated with the transmission of gSer gling pa's teachings, culminating in *The Seven Points.* A way of viewing the three-guru tradition is as a part of the process of enhancing 'Brom's stature; Dharmarakṣita and Maitrīyogi were essentially pressed into service as foils for his preferred guru, gSer gling pa.[11]

As for Dharmarakṣita, he is entirely unknown to Indian tradition and whatever we know of him comes exclusively from Tibetan sources. In addition to the aforementioned work by 'Chad kha ba, the most important of the early sources are *The Blue Udder (Be'u bum sngon po)* by Geshe Dol pa, a.k.a. Rog shes rab rgya mtsho, a.k.a. Dol pa dMar zhur pa (1059–1131), and the commentary on it by his pupil Lha 'bri sgang pa (twelfth century).[12] All three know Dharmarakṣita as a guru of Atiśa's and an adherent of a lower vehicle (non-Mahayana) tenet system, the Śrāvaka-Vaibhāṣika *(nyan thos bye brag tu smra ba)*. According to Geshe Dol pa and his pupil, Dharmarakṣita was noteworthy for his compassion, but unlike 'Chad kha ba, they do not know him as a teacher of Mahayana precepts. Lha 'bri sgang pa also reports that Dharmarakṣita had at one time been a Saindhava, a member of a lower-vehicle faction prominent both at Bodh Gaya and Odantapurī, some of whose members were militantly antitantric.[13]

The scriptural and exegetical bases of their teachings are already part of the early bodhicitta guru tradition, with each guru associated with a particular sutra and religious treatise. The sutras and treatises assigned to both Maitrīyogi and gSer gling pa by 'Chad kha ba are easily identifiable from their titles, but this is not so for Dharmarakṣita; the title forms as they appear in 'Chad kha ba and Lha 'bri sgang pa do not permit an identification. In addition, we are also informed that neither text was ever translated into Tibetan.[14] Both 'Chad kha ba and Lha 'bri sgang pa agree that the sutra and the treatise taught an approach to the practice of the Mahayana through the four noble truths; however, Lha 'bri sgang pa observes that "some" associate such an approach with Dharmarakṣita,[15] which in the language of Tibetan polemic indicates that it is a position with which he does not agree. This can only be understood as an explicit criticism of Dharmarakṣita's appropriation by the bodhicitta guru tradition as represented, for example, by 'Chad kha ba.

The legend of how Dharmarakṣita cut off his own flesh and gave it to a sick man as a medicine is an important element of the earliest traditions and is known to our three early sources; this story is repeated or alluded to forever after in association with this guru. In its earliest-known full version, which is that found in *The Blue Udder* commentary, the story is as follows:

> A man whose thigh was afflicted with a fiery smallpox showed it to a doctor who told him he would live if he ate fresh meat but die if he did not. Out of compassion, Dharmarakṣita unhesitatingly cut some flesh from his own thigh and gave it to him, and each then went his own way. When Dharmarakṣita's pain increased, the doctor made a poultice to stop the bleeding. Having learned that his flesh had helped the sick man, Dharmarakṣita was overjoyed. That night he had a dream, and in that dream, a white man appeared who said: "Well done, well done," and passing his hand over the wound, it disappeared. When Dharmarakṣita awoke he saw that the wound had vanished.[16]

If we look at the points of agreement among our three authors, we can discern what is likely to have been the basic Dharmarakṣita tradition—namely, that he was a guru of Atiśa's and a follower of Hinayana tenets, if not an actual Hinayanist, which is just the kind of prosaic information that has every likelihood of being historical fact. Although the flesh-cutting story does form part of the earliest tradition, we cannot say whether it is Indian or Tibetan in origin, but it is typical of the kind of pious tale associated with Indian religious figures, and its original purpose may have been to enhance the prestige of Atiśa's teacher.

As for the flesh-cutting story, it is interesting that even at this early date what had most probably begun simply as an edifying tale was already being treated in a tendentious manner. In the introduction to the story in *The Blue Udder* commentary, we read:

> Now the author shows that through the cultivation of love, compassion, and bodhicitta, conduct becomes pure, and one quickly comes to understand the pure view. [Root text:] "If, with the root of faith, you continually practice the bodhicitta, / Even if you hold to the Vaibhāṣika view / You will quickly understand the true nature of reality *(chos kyi gnas lugs)* / Like the Supreme Lord's guru, who gave his flesh."[17]

That an adherent of a lower-vehicle tenet system could spontaneously come to an understanding of the nature of reality through the practice of love, compassion, and bodhicitta would have resonated with many of the early

Kadampas, for that was just the situation Atiśa encountered in Tibet: monks and laymen who adhered to a lower-vehicle tenet system but followed the Mahayana in their practice. The Kadampas often made the point that the actual distinction between the lower and higher vehicles was not philosophical viewpoint, but practice, specifically the practice of compassion, and this distinction between the vehicles was ascribed to Dharmarakṣita himself in a late nineteenth-century anthology of Kadampa texts and lore.[18] One can easily imagine a teacher using the story to encourage pupils to more fervent practice, or even to advocate for a particular view of the "true nature of reality," and it would appear that this too formed part of the early tradition. At the conclusion of the story, Lha 'bri sgang pa quotes Atiśa as saying: "Because my guru's conduct was pure, by now he will have certainly come to see the truth *(bden pa mthong),*" which for Lha 'bri sgang pa meant the emptiness teaching of Nāgārjuna. However, at the conclusion of 'Chad kha ba's summary of the story, Atiśa says: "Although his point of view was low, by now he will certainly have attained the Great Seal *(mahāmudrā, phyag rgya chen po),*" that is, supreme realization through gnosis of the empty nature of the mind.[19]

The use of the flesh-cutting story to advocate for a particular view is strikingly illustrated in the case of Rinpoche sNe'u zur pa (1042–1118/19), a Kadampa of the second generation.[20] According to one account, he is reported to have said that when Dharmarakṣita awoke from the dream, he found that he had attained understanding of emptiness, and spontaneously began reciting the words of the six major treatises of Nāgārjuna, which he had never heard before.[21] However, in another account, sNe'u zur pa is quoted as saying that the entire story was actually a dream of Dharmarakṣita's, and his resulting insight was that everything was of the nature of mind![22] These differences point to an absence of agreement among the early Kadampas regarding the view to be used in interpreting ultimate reality; that the flesh-cutting story could be pressed into such ideological service is indicative of the prestige attached to the name of Dharmarakṣita at that time. In the thirteenth-century account of the life of Atiśa, *The Extensive Spiritual Biography (rNam thar rgyas pa),* written after the ideological differences among the early Kadampas had been resolved, Atiśa is simply quoted at the end of the flesh-cutting story as saying of Dharmarakṣita: "I am deeply grateful to this guru for the bodhicitta training. Owing to his great compassion he was of great benefit."[23] It would seem that with the philosophical struggle over, the figure of Dharmarakṣita as an ideological counter was no longer needed.

The next group of primary sources dates from approximately the mid-thirteenth to the mid-fourteenth centuries and includes the two major biographies of Atiśa, the aforementioned *Extensive Spiritual Biography,* and *The Famous Spiritual Biography (rNam thar yongs grags).*[24] These works reflect the bodhicitta guru tradition as presented by 'Chad kha ba, with Dharmarakṣita (a) as an adherent of Vaibhāṣika tenets, (b) as Atiśa's instructor in the practice of bodhicitta, which he taught him from the perspective of the aforementioned two unknown texts,[25] and (c) as the hero of the flesh-cutting story.[26] The two histories, however, add a new and significant detail, that Dharmarakṣita was a professor at the monastery of Odantapurī (which may connect him with the aforementioned Saindhavas) with whom Atiśa studied the classical treatises of the lower vehicle for twelve years following his ordination.[27] In addition, both works relate how Atiśa, as Dharmarakṣita's student, had to leave the monastery every seventh day because the monastic code of the monk-bodhisattva forbade him from spending more than seven consecutive days in the company of a follower of the lower vehicle.[28] This, however, would make sense only if Dharmarakṣita was, in fact, a follower of the lower vehicle, and not just a follower of lower vehicle tenets, but a Mahayanist in practice; it is too difficult to believe that Dharmarakṣita taught Atiśa the very heart of Mahayana practice without himself being a Mahayanist. That both biographies include this story indicates that it already formed part of the body of Dharmarakṣita lore and could not be passed over, even though it argued against the figure of Dharmarakṣita that is portrayed elsewhere. As with the aforementioned points of agreement within the earliest sources, this is the kind of detail that is likely to be factual. Both works also inform us that Dharmarakṣita had died prior to Atiśa's departure for Tibet.[29]

It is clear then that by the time the two biographies came to be written there were already two distinct traditions regarding Dharmarakṣita—Dharmarakṣita as bodhicitta guru associated with 'Chad kha ba and the lineage of 'Brom, and Dharmarakṣita as a Hinayanist and professor of Hinayana literature at Odantapurī first partially exposed by Geshe Dol pa and his pupil. The tradition of Dharmarakṣita as bodhicitta guru came to be enshrined as the official view of the Kadampa when *The Famous Spiritual Biography* was incorporated into their official compendium, *The Book of the Kadam (bKa gdams glegs bam).*[30] Nevertheless, despite all the authority behind it even as late as the fifteenth century, the bodhicitta guru tradition had not attained universal acceptance, and the two traditions continued to exist side by side; neither Tsongkhapa in his biography of Atiśa contained in his *Great Stages of the Path* (1403),[31] nor the authoritative history *The Blue Annals* (c. 1480), with its exhaustive biography of Atiśa, mention it; for both, Dharmarakṣita is only Atiśa's instructor in the literature of the lower vehicle at Odantapurī.

With the third and latest body of primary source material we finally come to Dharmarakṣita's authorship of the *WW* and the *PDP*. As we have seen, none of our sources thus far have had anything to say about Dharmarakṣita as an author. The attribution of authorship rests entirely on the colophons to both works as found in the early- to mid-fifteenth century anthology of mind training texts, *The Book of Mind Training (bLo sbyong glegs bam).* In both colophons the author's name is given as "Yogi Dharmarakṣita," a personage otherwise unknown. The identity of Yogi Dharmarakṣita with Atiśa's bodhicitta guru is implied in the placement of the two poems at the head of the works ascribed to the three gurus, and the identification is made explicit in an independent treatise on lojong written by the senior compiler of *The Book of Mind Training,* the eminent Sakya scholar Dkon mchog 'bangs.[32] Doubtless the identification of Yogi Dharmarakṣita with the bodhicitta guru Dharmarakṣita was the tradition Dkon mchog 'bangs inherited from the teachers who passed the texts on to him, but as we know nothing of the history of either the *WW* or *PDP* prior to their incorporation into the collection, we can say nothing definite concerning the tradition of their authorship.

However, the colophons themselves call Dharmarakṣita's authorship into question. In the colophon to the *WW,* Atiśa addresses two verses to the poem's (unnamed) author, whom he praises as his chief guru. It is, however, a commonplace of all the biographies of Atiśa and other Kadampa literature that Atiśa always reverenced gSer gling pa as his supreme guru. Furthermore, the colophon names Atiśa along with his chief disciple 'Brom as the poem's translators; yet the original Sanskrit title is not provided at the beginning of the work as is customary with translations from that language, nor is it included in the canon of translated treatises *(bstan 'gyur),* nor is any work ascribed to a Dharmarakṣita, and the work is not found in the lists of texts in the translation of which Atiśa participated. Thus, it would appear that at some point in the *WW*'s transmission, someone felt the need to provide the work with the colophon he thought it should have, and it is likely that the *WW* was already important and popular enough to warrant the association of Atiśa's and 'Brom's names with it. Again, without any sources for the history of the *WW* prior to circa 1450, we cannot say when the poem began to circulate with its colophon.

The colophon to the *PDP* also casts doubt on the traditional ascription. Here, the colophon is quite short and written in the first person. The author, who styles himself "Yogi Dharmarakṣita," tells us that he wrote the poem in a cave at Black Mountain. This seems somewhat suspect, as Black Mountain *(Kṛṣṇagiri, Ri nag po)* is well known from Atiśa's biographies as the residence of his main tantric guru Rāhulabhadra. While "yogi" often serves as a mere honorific given to any learned and holy person, it is also applied specifically to a tantric practitioner, as appears to be the implication here, yet as we have already seen, the only connection of Dharmarakṣita with the tantra is his possible membership in a group hostile to it. The colophon does not mention Atiśa at all, there is no mention of translators, and again no Sanskrit title is given. As in the case of the colophon to the *WW,* that of the *PDP* gives every appearance of being a later addition.

What then can we say of the person of Dharmarakṣita? Clearly, there are serious problems with the tradition of the three bodhicitta gurus in general, and with the tradition as it relates to Dharmarakṣita in particular. That being the case, the more prosaic tradition represented by Geshe Dol pa, Lha 'bri sgang pa, Tsongkhapa, and *The Blue Annals* seems the more likely; namely, that Dharmarakṣita was a professor at the monastic university of Odantapurī, a follower of the lower vehicle, and an adherent of Vaibhāṣika, with whom Atiśa studied the scriptures and exegetical literature of the lower vehicle following his ordination. In all the biographical literature concerning Atiśa, Dharmarakṣita is the only named teacher with whom he studied the lower vehicle. As such, his name carried sufficient prestige that it could be conveniently appropriated to serve as a foil (like the shadowy figure of Maitrīyogi) for those who advocated the lojong teachings ascribed to gSer gling pa. The ad hoc nature of his incorporation into the bodhicitta guru tradition can be seen in the impossibility of identifying the scriptures associated with him, the convenient absence of Tibetan translations for them, the lack of a lineage tracing his teachings to a divine teacher,[33] and the reported disappearance of his teachings in Tibet at a very early date.[34] As for his authorship of the the *WW* and the *PDP,* these texts were evidently ascribed to him in order to lend them authority and to add to their credibility as works that dated from an early period of the second transmission of the Dharma in Tibet.

3: The Texts

If the ascription of these two works to Atiśa's bodhicitta guru and hence an Indian origin proves problematic, the internal evidence of the texts themselves strongly suggests a Tibetan rather than an Indian provenance. Both works excoriate various kinds of false teachers and gurus, especially those who claim to teach the tantra and the Mahayana, and who pass off their own inventions as the genuine Dharma (for example, *WW* 68, 84, 87–88; *PDP* 50–51). We previously pointed out how this was a significant concern in Tibet about the year 1000 and provided the impetus for the invitation of Atiśa to Tibet in the first place. Moreover, such criticism of non-normative practices was not part of the Indian Buddhist landscape during the time in which these texts would have been composed.

In contrast to its denunciations of those who have strayed too far from the fundamentals of Buddhist belief and practice, the *PDP* itself contains two surprising verses (54–55) in which monastics are urged to give up their vows and kill the enemies of the Dharma, those who are actually destroying the teaching. Such a call to arms would have had deep resonance for Tibetans, who would have understood it as a reference to the assassination of the apostate King gLang dar ma in 842 by the monk dPal rdo rje, a deed celebrated as heroic and praiseworthy.[35] Such fear of the violent destruction of the Dharma would have been out of place in Buddhist circles in northeast India in the tenth and eleventh centuries, when the major challenge to Buddhism was a resurgent but nonviolent Hinduism; the Muslim threat was still two centuries away. In addition, the *WW* (70), like other early lojongs, warns against taking recourse to *mo,* the indigenous Tibetan form of divination, or to Bon, the heterodox form of Tibetan Buddhism.[36] Both poems also refer to native Tibetan classes of demons, the *'gong po* (*WW* 51, 91; *PDP* 50, 76, 81), and the protector deities of the Bon religion under the designation "the dark quarter" (*PDP* 33, 66). In *WW* 32 the poet ascribes the failure of religious rites to backsliding, to the propitiation of the Bon protector deities.

The central simile of both compositions also appears to be indigenously Tibetan. The image is that of the peacock who ingests poisonous plants, particularly "the virulent poison" *(btsan dug)* of aconite, which he "tames" by transmuting it into an elixir responsible for his beauty, just like the bodhisattva who similarly transmutes the afflictions *(nyon mongs)* into the means to accomplish the Buddhist path. In fact, the Tibetan proverb "The poison that nourishes the peacock brings ruin to all others,"[37] closely echoes the opening verses of the *WW.* The ingestion of poisonous plants by the peacock is a stock image in Tibetan poetry, both religious and secular, and in fact the oldest example of it to come to light so far is found in a work on Mahāmudrā from the same period in which our own texts were likely written.[38] However, this trope appears to be entirely foreign to the Sanskrit literary tradition, as well as to Indian folk traditions. Both Buddhist and non-Buddhist Indian literary traditions are quite familiar with the peacock as an eater of poisonous snakes, a theme that goes all the way back to the beginnings of Indian literature in the *Ṛg Veda,*[39] but the Indians, who had firsthand knowledge of peacock behavior, unlike the Tibetans, seem to know nothing of the peacock's ingestion of poisonous plants. The figure of the poison-plant-eating peacock is one that would most certainly have appealed to the Indian imagination and found literary expression; that it is not to be found is strongly suggestive of Tibetan invention. This image resembles those in European medieval bestiaries that present animal behavior that is not based on naturalistic observation but has symbolic significance.

In addition, the mix of Madhyamaka, Mahāmudrā, tantra, and the "Cutting" *(gcod)* teachings that both poems incorporate are strongly suggestive of a Tibetan provenance. Both poems adhere to the Madhyamaka view of emptiness, but, as with the Mahāmudrā, they stress the emptiness of mind, its luminous skylike nature, inherent purity, and the need to leave it to its natural state (*WW* 116, *PDP* 35, 84). It is interesting in this connection that Atiśa is reported to have said that Dharmarakṣita had eventually realized the Mahāmudrā. The tantric influence can be seen in the word the author(s) used for killing or destroying the enemies of the Dharma, *sgrol* or *bsgral,* "to set free, to release," which is "an everyday term of Tibetan tantrism denoting any ritual murder, from that practised by certain tantric orders...to the execution of demons by [a] hero...deity, or a 'sorcerer.'"[40] The "cutting" teachings can be seen in the call to supernatural beings to partake of the offering of the practitioner's body (*PDP* 2–3), and the destruction by Yamāntaka of a personified ego-clinging (*WW* 49–54, *PDP* 76). All these elements are consistent with the Tibetan milieu of the eleventh and twelfth centuries, and the same mix of elements can be found in the closely contemporary compositions of, for example, Machig Labdrön.[41]

Finally, there are a number of stylistic features that clearly show these works to be of Tibetan origin: the device of the refrain, so prominent in the *WW* (10–48, 55–90); the use of reduplicated words for emphasis (*bden bden, sdod sdod, yod yod, snang snang*; *WW* 105, 106, 111); and the employment of an onomatopoeic trisyllable, *chems se chems,* for the sound of thunder (*WW* 55–90; *PDP* 76)—these are all features that are already found in the most ancient Tibetan poetry. There is also to be found in the *PDP* (76, 81) an example of the kind of mutilated Sanskrit characteristic of native Tibetan compositions.

The work whose title we are translating as *The Wheel-Weapon* is actually known under three titles, and the one that is most probably the original one is that found in the title slot at the beginning of the work: *The Wheel-Weapon That Strikes at the Enemy's Vital Spot (dGra bo gnad la dbab pa'i mtshon cha 'khor lo).* The two other titles, which are cover titles, incorporate the words "mind training," as *The Wheel-Weapon Mind Training Belonging to the Great Vehicle (Theg pa chen po'i blo sbyong mtshon cha 'khor lo),* and *The Wheel-Weapon Mind Training That Dharmarakṣita Gave to Atiśa (Dha rma ra kṣi tas atiśa la gnang ba'i blo sbyong mtshon cha 'khor lo).* Nowhere in the work itself is there mention of "mind training," and it only came to be denominated as such with the creation of the distinct genre. It is as *The Wheel-Weapon Mind Training (bLo sbyong mtshon cha 'khor lo)* that it is commonly referred to by Tibetans.

The words in the title that are translated as "wheel-weapon" are *mtshon cha,* literally "weapon," specifically one that is sharp and cutting *(śastra),* and *'khor lo,* "wheel" *(cakra).* This object, a discuslike missile, was an actual weapon in the Indian armory: made of iron with a hole in the center to throw it, its edge was either jagged with teeth like a saw or razor-sharp. Though the Tibetans would have been unfamiliar with the real thing, it was known to them through iconography, where it is included among the many weapons held by wrathful deities. Probably the most famous instance of the wheel-weapon in Buddhist literature is as the "razor-edged wheel-weapon" *(khuradhāraṁ cakkāvudham)* that Māra hurled at the Buddha, who was about to reach enlightenment, and that was transformed into a harmless flower canopy.[42] In our work it serves as a metaphor for the teaching of the poem, which, like a wheel-weapon, cuts through to the vital point of the enemy, egotism. It also relates to a central theme of the text, that present misfortune is the result of evil deeds performed in the past, which, like a sharp-edged discus weapon, turn on oneself, boomerang fashion.[43]

Of all the works attributed to the three bodhicitta gurus, the *WW* must have been considered the most important, given the concerted effort that was made to associate Atiśa and 'Brom with it. It is also the only one of the works ascribed to the three gurus that is furnished with a detailed lineage of transmission from its purported author down to the compiler of the fifteenth-century anthology. While there is no reason to call the lineage into question for the two or three generations preceding the compiler, in the absence of supporting evidence we really can say nothing about the reliability of the transmission prior to that.[44]

As for the *PDP,* the poem as we have it also carries three different titles, *The Poison-Destroying Peacock Mind Training (bLo sbyong rMa bya dug 'joms), The Peacocks' Roaming in the Jungle of Virulent Poison (bTsan dug nags su rma bya rgyu ba),* and *The Elixir Made from Poison (Dug gi bcud len).* The first title, which we have adopted, we may regard as having been devised to serve as a cover title. In actuality, this title is more appropriate to the *WW* in that the image of the poison-to-elixir-transforming peacock is central to that work in a way that it is not to the *PDP* itself. The second title, which is the one found in the traditional title slot at the beginning of the text, is actually taken from the very first line of the *WW.* The third title, *The Elixir Made from Poison,* which is mentioned within the text of the poem itself, is far more relevant to the work's contents and it seems most likely that this was the original title. This title refers to the fact that many Indian and Tibetan medicines and alchemical elixirs are in fact compounded with poisonous ingredients such as aconite and mercury[45] and the poem analogously maintains that the spiritual elixir of bodhicitta[46] must also have an admixture of the poisons of lust, hatred, and the other afflictions, which have been "subdued" by the bodhisattva to work toward, rather than against, the attainment of enlightenment. All things considered, it appears that the *PDP* was at some point in its transmission "piggybacked" onto the *WW,* owing to the similarity of themes, language, treatment, and central deity. The first line of the *WW* was borrowed to serve as a title to establish a connection between the two works, and a colophon was added.

As we have seen, the *WW* has always been the more important of the two texts, and it is, as far as we know, the only work ascribed to the three gurus that was translated into Mongolian.[47] However, by the early nineteenth century the study and teaching of the *WW* had become so neglected that the Reting Rinpoche bsTan pa rab rgyas (flourished in late eighteenth, early nineteenth centuries) gave a series of lectures on it in 1813 so that "its transmission may not be interrupted."[48] Apparently bsTan pa rab rgya's efforts were to good effect since we see after him a renewed, vigorous interest not only in the *WW,* but in the *PDP* as well. In the late nineteenth century the great Nyingma teacher 'Jam mgon Kong sprul blo gros mtha' yas (1813–99) incorporated the entire *Book of Mind-Training* in its Gelukpa recension, known as *A Hundred Mind-Training Texts (bLo sbyong rgya rtsa),* into his *Treasury of Instructions (gDams ngag mdzod).* This led to the study of the *WW* and the *PDP* among the Nyingmapas, and both of our works are quoted at great length in the major Nyingma commentary on *The Seven-Topic Mind Training* written by Zhe chen rgyal tshab 'Gyur med pad ma rnam rgyal (1871–1926).[49] In addition, the eminent Mongolian Gelukpa polymath bLo bzang rta mgrin, a.k.a. rTa dbyangs (1867–1937), wrote topical outlines *(sa bcad)* to both poems,[50] and the Nyingmapa gLag pa bsod nams chos 'grub (1862–1944) wrote annotations *(mchan)* to the *WW.*[51] In 1976 the first published translation of the *WW* into a Western language appeared under the title *The Wheel of Sharp Weapons;* in 1981 a revised edition was published together with a short commentary by Geshe Ngawang Dhargyey.[52]

While the last hundred years or so have seen a great deal of renewed interest in the *WW* and the *PDP,* it must be admitted that the texts as we have them are in a very poor state. The ascertainably earliest text that we have of the *WW* is that found in the rough account *(zin bris)* of the aforementioned lectures of bsTan pa rab rgyas of 1813.[53] These lecture notes, which cover the entire work, are invaluable both for helping to establish a text of the *WW* and for assisting in the work's interpretation, but it is clear that different versions of the text were already in circulation, as bsTan pa rab rgyas often refers in his lectures to variant readings, some of which are not found in any of the versions known to us. To further complicate the matter, the text as incorporated by Kong sprul contains significant divergences from bsTan pa rab rgyas's text indicative of a separate textual transmission, as does the version of the text as found in *The Book of Mind-Training,* which, unfortunately being available only in a modern edition, is of problematic textual value. As for the text of the *PDP,* it too is in an equally poor state, with the various versions in disagreement with each other. Given the lack of reliable editions, we have simply tried to clear away the obvious errors and other inconsistencies and provide the best texts possible.

4: The Meaning of Lojong

Both of the texts translated and commented on in this volume belong to the genre of religious literature known as lojong. Although it has become customary to render this word as "mental/mind training," a look at the history of the term shows it to be of some complexity. Part of the difficulty in ascertaining its meaning as understood by those who first coined it and used it is that for nearly a century after the death of Atiśa, the lojong instructions were a "hidden teaching" *(lkog chos),* that is, they were taught in the form of oral, not written, instructions imparted by the teacher to his pupil in private, rather than in a public setting as with the stages of the doctrine. We have seen that during the century following Atiśa's death, a process of sifting had taken place and many early lojong teachings had become neglected with the rise to dominance of one particular trend. Consequently, the recovery of the original sense of lojong becomes problematic, but if we look at how the terms that make up this collocation were employed around the time the teachings that come to be known as lojong were introduced, it may be possible to approach the original meaning of the term itself.

Lojong is composed of two words, *lo (blo),* and *jong (sbyong).* In the Tibetan translations of Indian Buddhist literature, *blo* most usually represents the Sanskrit *buddhi,* "intelligence or intellect"; however, it is also occasionally used to render the Sanskrit *manas,* "mind" or "thought."[54] Since the lojong teachings are concerned with the cultivation and development of the thought intent on enlightenment, it is perhaps significant that although the Sanskrit word for "thought" in such contexts is usually *citta* (*sems), manas* is not unknown. Without making too much of this, we should keep in mind the possibility that the term *blo* may have been understood as an abbreviation for "the thought intent on enlightenment."[55]

As for *sbyong,* its basic sense as a verb is "to purify, to cleanse" and as a noun, "purification, cleansing." From these basic definitions, various metaphorical senses have developed that exist alongside them, such as "to study, to train, to practice, to cultivate" and "training, practice, cultivation."[56] It should be recalled that from the very beginnings of Buddhism, purification has been the basic metaphor for spiritual progress, as can be seen, for example, in the title of the great *summa* of Theravāda practice, the *Visuddhimagga*, or *Path to Purity*.[57] In the Tibetan versions of Indian Buddhist texts, *sbyong* is almost exclusively employed in its basic sense as a translation of the Sanskrit *(vi)śodhana,* "purification," as of sin, or of the adventitious defilements that stain pure consciousness. In these contexts *sbyong* is frequently found in combination with *sems,* a synonym, as we have pointed out, of *blo,* as in *sems sbyong,* "purification of the mind, mental purification," in Sanskrit *cittaviśodhana.*[58] It was as "mental purification," *cittaśodhana,* that *blo sbyong* was first rendered into Sanskrit by native Tibetan scholars.[59] The various metaphorical senses do not seem to have been exploited in the translation of Indian texts, and instances of such uses appear rare. One of the few places where the translators did so was in rendering the Sanskrit adjectival compound *cīrṇabuddhi,* "having a trained mind," which was translated as *blo sbyangs.*[60] However, this compound serves solely as an epithet and has no doctrinal content. Apart from this instance, the collocation *blo sbyong* does not seem to be found in the translations of Indian Buddhist texts.

In native Tibetan religious literature, *lojong* is frequently found as a verbal phrase, but here the metaphorical senses predominate and it may variously mean "to study, train the mind in, practice, cultivate, meditate," and so forth, according to context. Clarification of the meaning here may be gained by looking at a similar phrase found in Tibetan compositions, often in the very same contexts as lojong, that is, *blo goms.* In this sense, *goms* is far less ambiguous than *sbyong.* In the translations of Indian Buddhist texts, *goms* for the most part renders the Sanskrit noun *abhyāsa,* "frequent and repeated practice or concentration," and it is regularly used in that sense in Tibetan literature. This accords well with the Tibetan sense of *sbyong* as "training or practice" as a metaphorically frequent and continuous purification or "polishing-up." We have seen that the earliest Tibetan rendition of *blo sbyong* into Sanskrit was as "mental purification," which reflected the canonical usage of *sbyong,* but *sbyong* as *goms,* "frequent and repeated practice," has found its way into modern Tibetan Sanskritization as *manaḥabhyāsa,* and a contemporary Nepali scholar has even attempted to incorporate both senses of *sbyong* as "purification" and "repeated practice" in translating *blo sbyong* as *matiśodhanābhyāsa,* "mental-purification training."[61] This is probably not far from the original understanding of *blo sbyong.* Atiśa, who is credited with introducing the lojong teachings into Tibet seems to have both senses of *śodhana (sbyong)* in mind in the following passage from one of his most important works, *An Instruction Entitled "The Middle: An Open Casket of Jewels."* The subject is "the thought intent on enlightenment":

> Purifying it: one should constantly recall that mind *(sems, citta)* has no beginning from whence it has come, no end to where it goes, and no abiding anywhere; it is colorless, shapeless, unborn from the beginning, not obstructed at the end, empty of own-being, and of the nature of clear light. Or, love, compassion, and the thought directed to enlightenment should be made firm through repeated practice (*goms* [*sic!*]); it should be highly purified, it should be continually recalled at every mental moment; it should be made to continue through recollection, deliberation, proper thinking, and restraint.[62]

It thus appears likely that *blo sbyong* was originally understood along the lines of "mental purification through repeated practice of the thought intent on enlightenment." Lojong then is not just a genre of religious literature, but the defining ideology *(lta ba)* of the Kadampa school itself, just as the Great Perfection *(rdzogs chen)* is for the Nyingmapas, the Great Seal *(phyag chen)* for the Kagyupas, the Paths and Fruits *(lam 'bras)* for the Sakyapas, and the Stages of the Path *(lam rim)* for the Gelukpas.

5: Themes and Imagery

A: Yamāntaka

Yamāntaka is the wrathful form of Mañjuśrī, the Buddha who symbolizes wisdom. His name means "he who brings an end to Yama" or "Yama's Terminator." Yama, the lord of death in Buddhist mythology, symbolizes all evil forces *(bdud)* opposed to the Dharma and its practice.[63] The most wrathful form of Yamāntaka is Vajrabhairava, also known as the solitary *(ekavīra)* Yamāntaka, that is, without a consort.[64] Although the best-known form of this deity has nine heads, thirty-four arms, and sixteen legs, the form as described in the *WW* (50) is the simplest, with one head, two arms, and two legs.[65] In both of our texts, the deity is invoked to crush the demon of ego-clinging although the practitioner is not explicitly directed to identify himself or herself with the deity, as in some other early lojong texts. Yamāntaka rituals involve symbolism that is found in our texts, such as his destruction of demons using the sharp wheel-weapon (discussed above), as well as annihilating mantras (*WW* 53, 55–91, *PDP* 76, 82).[66]

B: Transforming Poison into Enlightenment

One of the striking features of our texts, in contrast to the mainstream lojong tradition based on *The Seven-Point Mind Training* and its commentaries, is the central theme of using the mental poisons and afflictions *(kleśa)* as a means to enlightenment, turning them to spiritual ends through the admixture of bodhicitta. This is expressed most explicitly in verses 11–17 of the *PDP,* which show how lust, anger, ignorance, envy, and pride can be used as skillful means, thus reflecting that work's original title, *The Elixir Made from Poison.* Although this theme was to be extensively developed in the tantra, it is already found even in such early nontantric Mahayana treatises as the *Mahāyāna Saṁgraha* and the *Sūtrālaṁkāra.*[67] As for the *WW,* it begins (1–6) by clearly laying out the analogy of the peacock transforming highly toxic black aconite into nourishment as the bodhisattva turns lust and other mental poisons into the elixir of the path. This approach is closely connected to the principle aim of alchemy *(rasāyana),* the transformation of a base substance into a precious one by adding a catalytic agent. The *Gaṇḍavyūhasūtra,* for example, compares turning iron into gold using the residue of heated brass *(rasajāta)* to bodhicitta, which, like the alchemical catalyst mercury *(rasadhātu),* absorbs all the karmic and afflictive obscurations and turns them into the roots of virtue and omniscience.[68] We encounter the same notion expressed in a work on mental purification translated by Atiśa, the *Cittaviśuddhiprakāraṇa* (51): "As copper when touched by mercury turns into pure gold, so the afflictions when touched by pure gnosis become true causes of virtue."[69]

C: Peacocks and Poisons

The beautiful and dramatic tail plumage of the peacock has made it a symbol of majesty and divinity in many cultures, including India, and from early times, we already find in Buddhist literature the bodhisattva compared to a peacock, as for example in the *Bāveru Jātaka.*[70] In the same work we also find the proverbially unclean and cowardly crow[71] used to symbolize the ordinary or spiritually backward individual, as in the *WW* (4). We have already seen that even in the earliest Indian literature, the *Ṛg Veda,* peafowl are believed to have the ability to neutralize poison, although in Indian Buddhist and non-Buddhist lore, this is always connected with snake venom.[72] This belief was based on naturalistic observations of peacocks killing poisonous snakes and being impervious to their poison.

In the *WW* the peacock is specifically credited with the ability to neutralize and use as a nutriment[73] the "virulent poison" of black aconite *(aconitum ferox).*[74] Aconite is a highly toxic plant best known in the West under the name of "wolfsbane." It is an important ingredient in traditional Asian medicine and is used in Tibetan medicine, mixed with other ingredients, as a treatment for, among other ailments, mental illness.[75] However, on the subcontinent it is found only in the Alpine and sub-Alpine regions of the Western Himalayas,[76] and thus its association with peacocks, who live only in temperate climates, becomes problematic. As we have previously remarked, the absence of an association of peacocks with aconite in Indian lore suggests a Tibetan origin for this figure.

D: Dancing on the Head of the Demon

A striking feature of the *WW* is its invocation of Yamāntaka to tear apart and annihilate the demon of ego-clinging, as evoked in the refrain to verses 55–90: "Roar and thunder on the head of the destroyer, false construction! Mortally strike at the heart of the butcher, the enemy, Ego!" This refrain, and the violent imagery in the verses that precede it, would clearly remind a Tibetan reader of one of the climactic scenes in *cham ('chams),* the Tibetan ritual dance dramas performed on important festivals, in which a human figurine *(linga)* representing evils, enemies, demons, and, more philosophically, self-clinging is tied up and stabbed by the actor representing the principal deity, using language similar to that found in our text.[77] Afterward, the figure is dismembered and thrown out of the temple precincts.[78]

A further connection to cham is found in the onomatopoeic word *"chem,"* used in the phrase *chem se chem* ("roar and thunder") in the *WW* refrain; in addition to its primary sense as the sound of thunder, this is the Tibetan way of representing the sound of the clashing of cymbals and relates to the image of dancing on the head of the demon of egocentricity[79] just as the fierce protector deities in the ritual dramas vanquish the evil demons by dancing on their heads to the accompaniment of cymbals. Some of these rituals were performed during the New Year's *(smon lam)* ceremonies in Lhasa before 1959; during the performance, dough images *(torma)* representing evil influences were trampled, burned, and beaten, to the accompaniment of musical instruments, especially cymbals.[80] This New Year's ritual is also viewed in a more metaphysical sense as the annihilation of ignorance in the fire of wisdom, and the destruction of the enemies of the Dharma (although their conscious principles *(rnam shes)* are sent to the Realm of Ultimate Truth *(chos dbyings)*.[81]

The close parallels between the *WW* and ritual performances are probably to be ascribed to the dramas being based on religious rituals, and not the other way around; in the *cham,* an exclusively Tibetan genre that cannot be dated earlier than the thirteenth century, the internal meditative rituals are "mimed" by the masked actors.[82] Nevertheless, both may derive from common sources, as the lojong may be said to enact an internal, psychological drama.

Another parallel is found in the rituals of "Cutting" *(gcod),* a tantric meditation in which one's body is symbolically offered to the wrathful goddess Vajrayoginī to be cut apart and devoured. This meditative practice, derived from Mahāmudrā sources roughly contemporary with the origins of lojong,[83] involves the trampling of Yama, symbolic of egotism and death, by the dancing adept, as well as the attainment of the knowledge of emptiness and compassion as the result.[84] Other features of "Cutting" that are found in our works are the invitation to the beings of the three worlds, including many types of demonic forces (*PDP* 60–62), and making a food offering of one's body and mind (*PDP* 2–3). This theme of invitation and offering in the *PDP* is shared with another of the early lojongs, *The Gyer Sgom Vajra Song.*

E: Conceptual Construction

One of the most important themes of the two poems is that of conceptuality, conceptual construction, or imagining *(rtog pa)* and its role in the process of bondage and liberation. It is symbolized in the *PDP* as a palace (77), and more significantly as a king (83) who must be overthrown (85). In the *WW*, conceptual construction runs through the refrain (55–90) as "the destroyer" who is so powerful that the ferocious protector Yamāntaka must be invoked to destroy it. The way that conceptuality figures in both works is grounded squarely in Mahayana Buddhism, particularly in the body of works known as The Five Treatises of Maitreya, as the ultimate mechanism by which we come to be in spiritual bondage. This is brought about in three ways: firstly, conceptuality divides up the realm of experience—sensual, ideational, and material—into a perceiving subject and a perceived object, that is, it imposes a dualism upon "the data," a dichotomy that is ultimately false. Together with this, it imposes categories and labels upon subject and object, such as "person," "self," "car," "building," "virtue," "computer," and so forth; even "samsara" and "nirvana." This labeling and categorizing is not in itself pernicious, as otherwise there would be no way to make sense out of anything. It is, however, in its third aspect that it is truly dangerous, for what it does is impose a false reality upon the referents of its labels and categories, a false reality of independent existence, of stability and permanence, most disastrously upon the perceiving subject (*WW* 105–7). This results in ego-clinging and the self-cherishing attitude, leading us to perform the types of action that involve us in continued bondage to the round of birth and death and its attendant suffering. However, since all of this is, in the final analysis, nothing but "imagining," liberation is achieved when reality is seen as it is, as nondual, empty of the false reality imposed upon it, and beyond the created world of "conceptual proliferation" (*WW* 115, 116; *PDP* 31, 85).

F: Anger and Transgression

Harnessing the generally feared but powerful emotion of anger for spiritual purposes is a feature of Buddhism that tends to be ignored or downplayed in many contemporary presentations that emphasize the cultivation of the more prosocial sentiments of compassion, friendliness, and sympathetic joy.

However, in Buddhism, as with Saint Augustine and other Christian writers,[85] there is a distinction drawn between ordinary selfish anger, which must be opposed by the practice of forbearance, and righteous anger, in the service of spiritual ends. The function of anger and aggression in our texts is well described by the late sixteenth, early seventeenth century German Catholic mystic Jakob Böhme: "Man must be at war with himself if he wishes to be a heavenly citizen...fighting must be the watchword, not with tongue and sword, but with mind and spirit, and not to give over."[86] This is the spirit of our lojongs: Once the practitioner has isolated the destructive part of the self that springs from attachment to the view of a real personal identity and a self-cherishing attitude, "the thief who ambushed and deceived me, the hypocrite who deceived me disguised as myself," as the *WW* (49) puts it, he or she proceeds to psychically pulverize and destroy this ultimately false self, turning the full force of his or her rage upon it.

The language of spiritual warfare, which portrays the bodhisattva as putting on armor, going into battle, and being fearless before the host of enemies—particularly notable in the *PDP* (26, 70–75)—is a commonplace of Mahayana Buddhism and often gives our texts the flavor of such Christian contemplative and homiletic works as Thomas à Kempis's *Imitation of Christ* and Erasmus's *Manual of Arms for the Militant Christian (Enchiridion).* However, the *PDP* goes further than most other Buddhist works in recommending actions, such as giving up the monastic vows to actually fight against the enemies of the Dharma (54–56), that appear to contradict conventional Buddhist morality (*WW* 94). The idea that a bodhisattva with a sufficiently high level of selflessness and compassion can commit acts that directly transgress basic Buddhist prohibitions against violence and other unethical behavior, as long as they are for the benefit of others, is found throughout Mahayana literature[87] and illustrated in stories of the Buddha's previous births (see Geshe Sopa's commentary on *PDP* 13). These ideas have clear contemporary implications, for example for Buddhists who are persecuted for their religion and denied freedom to practice it. In a recent interview,[88] His Holiness the Fourteenth Dalai Lama ridiculed the Chinese expectation that Tibetan Buddhists be loyal to the Communist party in words that are reminiscent of the verses cited above: "A religious person should be loyal to the destroyer of religion? How can that happen?" That these views were meant to be put into action in appropriate circumstances is supported by stories about such culture heroes as the bodhisattva dPal rdo rje previously mentioned and Rva Lotsawa, the translator of many important ritual texts dealing with Yamāntaka, who is alleged to have killed thirteen tantric masters, including Marpa's son.[89] Of course, as the text and Geshe Sopa's commentary make clear (see *PDP* 56), such violent actions should be engaged in only by a highly advanced bodhisattva motivated purely by compassion; any anger manifested by the bodhisattva is merely a simulacrum used as a skillful means (*PDP* 13): "With simulated anger you should kill the demonic enemies of the Dharma."

6: A Psychological Perspective

As writers on comparative psychology have noted, the basic paradigm of Buddhist practice as found in standard works such as the *Abhidharmakośa* and the *Visuddhimagga* is similar to that of cognitive psychotherapy. That is, the practitioner becomes aware of unhealthy mental factors (such as the three poisons) and consciously substitutes the reciprocally inhibiting healthy opposite factor, for example, forbearance for anger. Both the *WW* and the *PDP,* in common with other mind-training methods, partially follow this model, which has been compared to allopathic medicine, that is, the treatment of diseases using substances antithetical to the pathogen, such as antibiotics.[90] Where they differ is in their "homeopathic" or tantric revalorization of the "negative" emotions, especially of anger, into means for accomplishing spiritual goals, pre-eminently in the eradication of self-clinging and self-cherishing. Their use of such strong emotions in the service of spiritual development, rather than simply jettisoning them in the more "Hinayanistic" mode of detachment and apathy (in the Stoic sense of *apatheia*), recalls the Freudian conception of sublimating primitive libidinous and aggressive affect into socially useful and creative expression. This idea of sublimation, which has its roots in the concept of alchemical transformation of base metal into gold by the addition of a catalyst, is also the fundamental theme of our texts: through bodhicitta, the "poisonous" emotions of anger and lust are transmuted into an elixir producing the highest happiness for the practitioner and for humanity in general.

Notes to Historical Introduction

1 For a less detailed overview of the historical development of lojong, see Michael J. Sweet, "Mental Purification *(Blo sbyong):* A Native Tibetan Genre of Religious Literature," in José Ignacio Cabezón and Roger R. Jackson, eds., *Tibetan Literature: Studies in Genre* (Ithaca, N.Y.: Snow Lion, 1996), 244–60.

2 The form Atīśa, which is still frequently met with, is not correct, predicated as it is on being a combination of Sanskrit *ati* + *īśa*, "the great Lord." However, this combination is not permitted by the rules of Sanskrit grammar, and the correct etymology likely lies in the Sanskrit *atiśaya,* "eminent, superior," *phul (du) byung (ba)* in Tibetan, which is supported by inscriptional evidence; see H. Eimer, *Berichte über das Leben des Atiśa (Dīpaṁkaraśrījñāna).* Eine Untersuchung der Quellen. (Wiesbaden: Otto Harrassowitz, 1977): 21–22. The Tibetans customarily refer to Atiśa as *jo bo (prabhu)* or "(The) Lord."

3 See David L. Snellgrove, *Indo-Tibetan Buddhism* (London: Serindia Publications, 1987), 187, 479–84.

4 Atiśa summed up his graded approach to the practice of Mahayana Buddhism in the *Bodhipathapradīpa* (Toh. 3947/4465), "A Lamp on the Way to Enlightenment." The bodhicitta is the subject of some of his most important works: for example, the *Cittotpādasaṁvaravidhikrama* (Toh. 3369, 4490), "The Stages of the Ritual for Making the Resolution and Vow to Produce the Thought (Intent on Enlightenment)"; the *Bodhisattvādikarmikamārgāvatāradeśanā* (Toh. 3652, 4477) "Instruction on Entering the Path for the Beginner Bodhisattva," and especially the *Ratnakaraṇḍodghaṭe* [sic] *madhyamanāmopadeśa* (Toh. 3930), "The Instruction Called 'The Middle: An Open Casket of Jewels.'" In this work Atiśa tells us in his own words how Lokeśvara on one occasion, and Tārā and Bhṛkuti on another, appeared to him and exhorted him to cultivate bodhicitta as the quickest means to enlightenment; see *The Peking Tripitaka* (Peking ed.) Vol. 160, 477, plate 3.

5 Or Mitrayogi or Maitreyayogi; the Sanskrit form of his name is not entirely clear from the Tibetan *'jam pa'i rnal 'byor pa.*

6 On the bstan rim literature, see David Jackson, "The *bsTan rim* ('Stages of the Doctrine') and Similar Graded Expositions of the Bodhisattva's Path" in Cabezón and Jackson: 229–43.

7 'Chad kha ba, *bLo sbyong don bdun ma'i 'grel pa* in *bLo sbyong legs bam* (Bir: D. Tsondu

Senghe, 1983), pls. 74–76. Hereafter the *bLo sbyong legs bam* will be referred to by the abbreviation *LBLB.* The Six-Point Mental Training shares a line (l. 12 in the LBLB edition, p. 61) "drive all blame into one thing" *(le lan thams cad gcig la bda')* with the WW (95a).

8 *bKa' gdams kyi skyes bu dam pa rnams kyi gsung bgros thor bu rnams* (New Delhi: Geshe Palden Drakpa, 1983): pl. 14.

9 Tshe mchog gling Yong 'dzin ye shes rgyal mtshan (1711–93), *Byang chub lam gyi rim pa'i bla ma brgyud pa'i rnam pa thar pa rgyal bstan mdzes pa'i rgyan mchog phul byung nor bui'i phreng ba* (New Delhi: Ngawang Gelek Demo, 1970): Vol. 1, pls. 223–35.

10 *Khri Chen Bstan Pa Rab Rgyas Collected Works* (Dharamsala: Library of Tibetan Works and Archives, 1985): Vol. 3, pl. 466. The author's full appellation is Rva sgreng A chi tu no mo han bLo bzang bstan pa rab rgyas. This remark is found in the rough account *(zin 'bris)* of the series of lectures he gave in 1813 on the *WW* written by his pupil bLo bzang 'phrin las rnam rgyal, *Khyab bdag rdo rje 'chang chen po nas blo sbyong mtshon cha 'khor lo'i bshad lung rtsal skabs kyi gsung bshad zin bris gzhan phan myu gu bskyed ba'i bdud rtsi.* This work covers plates 463–595 in the aforementioned volume of bsTan pa rab rgyas's collected works. Hereafter it will be referred to as *TPRG.*

11 The literature supplies numerous comparisons to illustrate the inferiority of Dharmarakṣita and Maitrīyogi to gSer gling pa; the meditative system ascribed to Maitrīyogi by 'Chad kha ba (*LBLB,* pl. 75) is attributed to Dharmarakṣita as well in the *bLo sbyong gsung 'gros ma'i kha skong* of Bya bral ba Dkon mchog rgyal mtshan (fourteenth century) and unfavorably compared to the system of gSer gling pa (*LBLB,* pls. 492–93); in the "frame" to the *Eight-Session Mind Training (bLo sbyong thun brgyad ma)* found in the same collection (pl. 204), it is said that neither Maitrīyogi nor Dharmarakṣita have tombs *(gdung khang),* whereas gSer gling pa has a tomb with a silver umbrella; the other gurus do not receive monthly offerings *(zla mchod)* like him; that upon hearing the names of the other gurus the palms are pressed together at the heart, whereas on hearing the name of gSer gling pa the palms are pressed together on the crown of the head; that recollection of gSer gling pa causes tears to flow, which is not so with the two other gurus. Again, in the *bLo sbyong legs bshad kun 'dus* of Dkon mchog 'bangs (Delhi: N. Topgyal, 1996; pls. 12–14), Atiśa grew confident *(nges shes skyes)* in the bodhicitta from the lojong teachings given to him by Dharmarakṣita, even more so from his studies with Maitrīyogi, but eventually he had to go to gSer gling pa, the lord *(bdag po)* of bodhicitta.

12 *bKa' gdams kyi man ngag be'u bum sngon po'i 'grel pa: A commentary on Dge-bśes Dol-pa śes-rab-rgya-mtsho's Be'u bum sṅon po by Lha 'Bri-sgaṅ-pa* (Bir, H.P.: 1976).

An udder, literally "calf's flask" *(be'u bum)* is a metonym for a book, for like an udder, a book gives nourishment. Geshe Dol pa, the author of *The Blue Udder* root text was a disciple of Po to ba (1031–1105), one of the principal disciples of 'Brom. 'Chad kha ba had also been at one time a pupil of Dol pa; see *The Blue Annals,* tr. by George Roerich (Delhi: Motilal Banarsidass, 1976): Vol. 1, 273.

13 This according to Tāranātha; personal communication from Prof. John Newman, March 2000.

14 *Blue Udder,* pl. 213; *bLo sbyong tshogs bshad ma* by Sangs rgyas sgom pa (1160–1229), in *LBLB,* pl. 295. The title of the sutra is variously given as *Dbyug pa* (or *dbyig pa*) *gsum gyi phreng ba* and the treatise as the *Mdo sde rgyan* or *Skye rabs mdo sde rgyan,* but neither of these titles corresponds to any work extant. The *mdo sde rgyan* should not be confused with the *Sūtrālaṁkāra (mdo sde rgyan)* of Maitreya/Asanga. The *Mahālaṁkārasūtraśāstra* (*Ta-chuang-yen-lun-ching;* Nanjio, 1182) ascribed to Aśvaghoṣa in the Chinese canon is a compilation of stories illustrating karmic retribution—a topic dear to the Kadampas—but it is not a formal treatise.

15 *Blue Udder,* pl. 48.

16 *Blue Udder,* pls. 231–33. 'Chad kha ba gives only a brief account.

17 *Blue Udder,* pl. 231.

18 *Legs par bshad pa bka' gdams rin po che'i gsung gi gces btus nor bu'i bang mdzod* (Bir: The Bir Tibetan Society, 1985), pls. 98, 100. This work was compiled and edited by Don grub rgyal mtshan, a.k.a. Ye shes don grub bstan pa'i rgyal mtshan. Hereafter it will be referred to as gCes btus.

19 'Chad kha ba in *LBLB,* pl. 75.

20 sNe'u zur pa was a pupil of dGon pa pa 'Dzeng dbang phyug rgyal mtshan (1016–82), a direct disciple of Atiśa.

21 dKon mchog 'bangs, pls. 5–6.

22 *gCes btus,* pl. 207. The editor disagrees and believes sNe'u zur pa to be in error.

23 Helmut Eimer, *Rnam Thar Rgyas Pa, Materielen zu einer Biographie des Atiśa.* (Wiesbaden: Otto Harrassowitz, 1979) (2 vols., para. 153). Unless otherwise stated, references to this work are by paragraph number.

24 Although neither biography is dated, *The Extensive* shows distinctly more archaic

features than *The Famous,* especially in its language; see Helmut Eimer (1977) 105, 111, 200.

25 Eimer (1979), para. 62.

26 Eimer (1979), para. 44, 62, 153–55.

27 Eimer (1979), para. 130.

28 Ibid.

29 Eimer (1979), para. 47.

30 The role of Dharmarakṣita as bodhicitta guru is echoed by another work, *The Book of the Kadam,* in which Atiśa praises his "two hero gurus, the Great Adept, the Man of Love (=Maitrīyogi), and Rakṣita who gave his own flesh to another, who bestowed upon me the special generation of the thought intent on enlightenment"; *Biography of Atīśa and His Disciple Hbrom-ston* (Zhô edition), Vol. 1. Reproduced by Lokesh Chandra (New Delhi, 1982), pl. 633.

31 Tsongkhapa's biography is based on the earliest biographical sources for the life of Atiśa. These are the panegyrics *(bstod pa)* of Nag tsho lo tshā ba Tshul khrims rgyal ba (1011–?) written upon Atiśa's death in 1054 *(The Eighty Praises),* and of Paṇḍita Sa'i snying po; see Eimer (1977): 138–45.

32 This is the work referred to in notes 11 and 21 above. dKon mchog 'bangs is the alias of Sems pa chen po gZhon nu rgyal mchog (middle fourteenth to early fifteenth century); the junior compiler of the anthology was his disciple Mus pa chen po dKon mchog rgyal mtshan (1388–1469/71). For additional information on this work, see E. Gene Smith, *University of Washington Tibetan Catalogue,* Part I (University of Washington: Seattle, 1969), 68–69.

33 See Sangs rgyas sgom pa in *LBLB,* pls. 294 ff. See also Eimer (1979), para. 56.

34 Lha 'bri sgang pa informs us that although Atiśa gave extensive instruction to 'Brom on the approach to the Mahayana through the four noble truths, according to Po to ba, 'Brom seldom taught it, and Po to ba himself had never heard them (*Blue Udder,* pl. 213).

35 His assassination of Langdarma is commemorated in ritual drama; see P. H. Pott, 1958, "Een 'Duivels-dans' in Tibet's Grensgebied," *Bijdragen tot de Taal, Land-en Volkenkunde,* 114, 197–209.

36 For example, in *The Stages of the Bodhisattva (Sems dpa'i rim pa)* in *LBLB*, pl. 171.

37 *dug 'di rma bya'i zas yin gzhan rnams 'phung bar byed,* cited in Dan Martin, "The Early Education of Milarepa," *The Journal of the Tibet Society,* Vol. 2, 1982, 71, 76. For other Tibetan proverbs involving peacocks, see Lhamo Pemba, *Tibetan Proverbs* (Dharamsala: Library of Tibetan Works and Archives, 1996), 166–67.

38 "Aconite is the optimal nourishment for the peacock. If others eat it, they will die. If the peacock renounces aconite, it will die," in Dan Martin, "A Twelfth-Century Tibetan Classic of Mahāmudrā, The Path of Ultimate Profundity: The Great Seal Instructions of Zhang," in *The Journal of the International Association of Buddhist Studies,* vol. 15, 1992, 264. Some other examples: in the biography of Atiśa attributed to 'Brom (*LBLB* 21), Atiśa is quoted as saying, "The well-being of the peacock is believed to lie in black aconite" *(rma bya' i bde skyid btsan dug nag na 'dod).* In Sa skya paṇḍita's autocommentary to verse 152 in his popular collection of wise maxims *Legs bshad 'dod dgu 'byung ba'i gter mdzod* (Kalimpong: Sakya Khenpo Sangey Tenzin, 1974), 138, "...its [the peacock's] food is the very fearful great poison, black aconite." The theme is also alluded to in a verse ascribed to the Sixth Dalai Lama, see Per K. Sorenson, *Divinity Secularized: An Inquiry into the Nature and Form of the Songs Ascribed to the Sixth Dalai Lama* (Vienna: Wiener Studien zur Tibetologie und Buddhismuskunde, 1990), 330, 436.

39 *Ṛg Veda* I:191:14 "Three times seven peahens...bear away poison."

40 R. A. Stein, *Tibetan Civilization* (London: Faber and Faber, 1972), 190.

41 Jérôme Edou, *Machig Labdrön and the Foundations of Chöd* (Ithaca: Snow Lion, 1996), 49.

42 *The Jātaka Together with Its Commentary,* ed. by V. Fausbøll (Oxford: Pali Text Society, 1990), Vol. 1, 74. On the "wheel-weapon," see O. H. De A. Wijesekera, 1961, "Discoid Weapons in Ancient India," *Adhyar Library Bulletin,* Vol. 25: 250, 252. According to a Chinese account of the Sui dynasty, it is "a disc the size of a Chinese mirror, with a central perforation and the outer rim jagged like a saw"; see W. E. Begley, 1973, *Viṣṇu's Flaming Wheel: The Iconography of the Sudarśana-Cakra* (New York: New York University Press), 12–13. It may have been thrown using a metal rod or a finger inserted into the central aperture, which seems to be the method referred to in the text (50), or cast like a Frisbee. In his form with nine heads, thirty-four arms, and sixteen legs, Yamāntaka carries a cakra in one of his right hands, and in a ritual text, Yamāntaka is represented as having in his heart a wheel-weapon "without a rim, with countless tips of its spokes whirling fiercely" that cuts to pieces all the obstructing demonic forces; see Stephen Beyer, *The Cult of Tārā: Magic and Ritual in Tibet* (Berkeley: University of California

Press, 1978), 315. The idea, prominent in the poem, of karma as a wheel-weapon that circles back upon the actor, recalls its use as a boomerang by Kṛṣṇa in the *Mahābhārata;* see E. Washburn Hopkins, *Epic Mythology* (1915; reprint, Delhi: Motilal Banarsidass, 1974), 206. The razor-edged wheel-weapon also figures as an instrument of torture in Buddhist literature in stories illustrating karmic retribution; see, for example, the story of Maitrakanyaka in the *Āvadāna Kalpalatā* of Kṣemendra (Calcutta: The Asiatic Society, 1918), Vol. 2, 840–59. The same story in a slightly different form is found in the Pali jātakas (no. 439); see E. B. Cowell (ed.), *The Jātaka or Stories of the Buddha's Former Births* (1895; reprint, Delhi: Motilal Banarsidass, 1990), Vol. 4, 1–4. In the commentary to the *Blo sbyong don bdun ma* by Zhe chen rgyal tshab, the action of this wheel is described as "boring into the middle of the brain" (*klad pa'i dkyil du dbug gin 'dug);* see *The Collected Works of Zhe Chen Rgyal Tshab Padma Rnam Rgyal* (Kathmandu: Shechen Publications, 1994), Vol. 19, pl. 282.

43 Both the forms *mtshon cha 'khor lo* and *mtshon cha'i 'khor lo* are found in our exemplars, sometimes both forms in the same text. The syntactical function of the genitive inflectional particle in the form *mtshon cha'i 'khor lo* indicates an appositional relationship wherein one noun is being described by another. From this point of view, the compound means "a wheel that is a weapon," which is equivalent to the uninflected *mtshon cha 'khor lo.* However, the same particle can also be construed as indicating a "compositional" relationship, indicating that of which something is made, so that from this point of view the compound means "a wheel made of or comprised of sharp weapons." This was the translation settled on by the Dharamsala group who published the first translation of this work under the title *The Wheel of Sharp Weapons;* this interpretation is clearly incorrect.

44 Dharmarakṣita, Atiśa (982–1054), 'Brom (1005–1064), (Po to ba) Rin chen gsal (1031–1105), Sha ra yon tan grags (1070–1141), 'Chad kha ba Ye shes rdo rje (1101–75), (rDo rje) sPyil bu pa (1121–89), Lha chen 'gro ba'i mgon (1186–1259?), 'Od 'jo ba [abbot of Reting], mKhan po dMar ston, mKhan po Shes rab rdo rje, mKhan po Buddharatna, Kṛtiśrīla, rGyal ba bzang po, sNubs chos lung pa Bsod nams rin chen, gZhon nu rgyal mchog dKon mchog 'bangs; *LBLB,* pl. 152–53. *The Stages of the Bodhisattva* ascribed to gSer gling pa has no colophon at all, and *The Gyer sGom Vajra Song* has for its colophon a perfunctory lineage, "Maitreya, Maitrīyogi, Atiśa."

45 See Terry Clifford, *Tibetan Buddhist Medicine and Psychiatry: The Diamond Healing* (1984; reprint, Delhi: Motilal Banarsidass, 1994), 199–200. See also David Gordon White, *The Alchemical Body: Siddha Traditions in Medieval India* (Chicago: University of Chicago Press, 1996), 220–22.

46 This is a common metaphor. See for example Śāntideva's *Bodhicaryāvatāra* 1.10. Hereafter this work will be referred to as *BCA.*

47 *Dharmarakṣida-bar juu atiša-dur soyurqag ünen sudulqu mese-yin kürdün kemegdekü orošiba*; see David M. Farquar, "A Description of the Mongolian Manuscripts and Xylographs in Washington, D.C.," *Central Asiatic Journal,* 1, 1955, #60, 202–3. The title translates as: *The Wheel-Weapon Mind Training Given by Dharmarakṣita to Lord Atiśa.* The Mongolian for "wheel-weapon" (*mese-yin kürdün*) follows the Tibetan version with the sixth-case particle infix, *mtshon cha'i 'khor lo.* The Mongolian version is also described as #294 in Walther Heissig, *Mongolische Handschriften Blockdrucke Landkarten,* in vol. 1 of *Verzeichnis der Orientalischen Handschriften in Deutschland,* Band 1 (Wiesbaden: Franz Steiner Verlag, 1961), 175. The translator of the *Wheel-Weapon* was a student of the second Lcang skya Khutukhtu, Rol pa'i rdo rje, who was born in 1690; see Walther Heissig, *Die Pekinger Lamaistischen Blockdrucke in Mongolischer Sprache: Materialen zur Mongolischen Literaturgeschichte* (Wiesbaden: Otto Harrassowitz, 1954), 108.

48 *TPRG,* pl. 466. Could this have been the commentary that the great nineteenth-century Nyingma yogi Shabkar requested from the incarnation of the second Changkya Khutukhtu? See Matthieu Ricard, *The Life of Shabkar* (Albany: SUNY Press, 1994), 521.

49 See fn. 36.

50 *The Collected Works (Gsung 'Bum) of Rje Btsun Blo Bzang Rta Mgrin* (New Delhi: Lama Gurudeva, 1973), Vol. 1, pl. 325–58.

51 *The Collected Writings of Glag-bla Bsod-nams-chos-'grub* (Delhi: Konchog Lhadrepa, 1997), Vol. 2, pl. 661–738.

52 Dharmarakshita, *The Wheel of Sharp Weapons* (Dharamsala: Library of Tibetan Works and Archives, 1981). The earliest translation of the *WW* into English is William Kirtz's *The Wheel Weapon of Mind Practice,* unpublished M.A. thesis, University of Wisconsin–Madison, 1973.

53 There is also a rudimentary topical outline to the *WW* in the treatise on mind training of dKon mchog 'bangs, plates 234–37. In the list of rare books compiled by A khu rin po che Shes rab rgya mtsho (1803–75), there is an entry for a commentary on *The Wheel-Weapon* by Gung thang dKon mchog bstan pa'i sgron me (eighteenth century) [*MHTL* 11183], but no such work is found in his *gsung 'bum;* in the same list there is an entry for an anonymous recasting of *The Wheel-Weapon* in the form of a story [*MHTL* 11207], about which we know nothing; see Lokesh Chandra, *Materials for a History of Tibetan Literature,* Part 3 (New Delhi: International Academy of Indian Culture, 1963), 518, 519.

54 As, for example, at *BCA* 8.115.

55 On *citta* and *manas*, see Helmut Eimer, *Skizzen des Erlösungsweges in buddhistischen Begriffsreihen* (Bonn: Religionswissenschaftliches Seminar der Universität Bonn, 1976), 104.

56 The parts of the verb *sbyong* are: present, *sbyong;* past, *sbyang(s);* future, *sbyang;* imperative, *sbyongs.* Alongside the transitive form, there is also an intransitive *'byong,* "to be cleansed or purified," with its metaphorical senses of "to be well versed in, to be skilled in." The same ambiguity between "purification" and "training" is also found in the Mongolian translation for *blo sbyong, oyun sudulqu,* where *sudulqu,* like *sbyong,* can be rendered either way, yielding "purification of the mind" or "training the mind."

57 Or, *The Path to Purification,* as rendered by Bhikkhu Ñāṇamoli. However, as the work itself makes clear, the path to this purity is one of cleansing or purification *(vodāna).*

58 The adjective "pure," Sanskrit *viśuddhi,* is usually rendered in Tibetan by *rnam par dag pa.* Some examples of *sbyong* in the sense of purification may be seen in the following titles: *Cittaratnaviśodhanakramanāmalekha* of Guhyajetāri; in Tibetan, *Sems rin po che rnam par sbyang ba'i rim pa zhes bya ba'i spring yig,* "A Letter: 'The Stages of the Purification of the Mind-Jewel,'" or the *Karmāvaraṇaviśodhanavidhibhāṣya* of Atiśa; in Tibetan, *Las kyi sgrib pa rnam par sbyong ba'i cho ga bshad pa,* "An Explanation of the Ritual for the Purification of Karmic Obscurations." Many similar examples may be adduced.

59 By dKon mchog 'bangs in the Sanskritized title of his treatise on lojong. The same idea is expressed in the Sanskritized title of the commentary to *The Seven-Point Mind Training* by the eminent Nyingma teacher Zhe chen rgyal tshab 'Gyur med padma rnam rgyal, where *blo sbyong* is rendered by "stainless mind"—*cittavimāla; Zhe Chen Rgyal Tshab,* Vol. 19.

60 Friedrich Weller, *Tausend Buddhanamen des Bhadrakalpa* (Leipzig: Verlag der Asia Major, 1928): Nos. 160, 171, 548, b637, 728.

61 See Alaka Chattopadhyaya, *Atīśa and Tibet* (Calcutta: Indian Studies Past and Present, 1967), 381. The Nepali translation of Kong sprul's commentary to *The Seven-Point Mind Training* has been published as *Mahāyānasātusūtryamatiśodhanābhyāsa* (Kathmandu: Vyomakusumā Anuvāda Samiti, 1993). See also Alex Wayman, "A Problem of 'Synonyms' in the Tibetan Language: *Bsgom Pa* and *Goms Pa*" in *The Journal of the Tibet Society* 1987, Vol. 7, 51–56.

62 *Ratnakaraṇḍodghaṭe* [sic] *madhyamanāmopadeśa,* Peking Tripitaka Reprint, Vol. 160, 475, pl. 4.

63 See Giuseppe Tucci, *Indo-tibetica III,* Parte 2 (Roma: Reale accademia d'Italia, 1936), 78.

64 Lecture, February 1992, Khensur Thabkay Rinpoche, Deer Park Buddhist Center, Oregon, Wisconsin.

65 On this form, see Alice Getty, *The Gods of Northern Buddhism* (2d. ed., 1928; reprint, Delhi: Munshiram Manoharlal, 1978), 164, and pl. 52a. On the other forms of Yamāntaka, see Benoytosh Bhattacharya, *The Indian Buddhist Iconography* (Calcutta: K. L. Mukhopadhyah, 1968), 166, 252.

66 On the use of mantras in Yamāntaka rituals of annihilation see Beyer, *Cult of Tārā,* 316.

67 *Mahāyāna Saṁgraha* 10.28 11–12; *Sūtrālaṁkāra* 13.11–13.

68 Cited in Prajñākaramati's *Pañjika* on *BCA* 1.10; *Bodhicaryāvatāra of Śāntideva with the Commentary Prajñākaramati* (Darbhanga: Mithila Institute, 1960): 502.

69 Prabhubhai Bhikhabhai Patel, *Cittaviśuddhiprakāraṇa of Āryadeva* (Calcutta: Visva-Bharati, 1949), 27, 65.

70 Jātaka #339, translated in Cowell, *The Jātaka or Stories of the Buddha's Former Births,* Vol. 3, 83–84. See also the *Mahāmora-Jātaka* (#491) in Cowell, Vol. 4, 210–16, in which the future Buddha is born as a golden peacock and preaches the Dharma.

71 The touch of a crow's beak is believed to pollute even a pure substance like water. See the reference in the *bhāṇa, Padmaprābhṛtaka* quoted in M. Ghosh, *Glimpses of Sexual Life in Nanda-Maurya India* (Calcutta: Manisha Granthalaya, 1975), 85.

72 See, for example, the verse quoted in Prajñākaramati's commentary to *BCA* 240: "The snake is born for the purpose of the peacock's happiness; because [the peacock] has become accustomed to poison, poison is an elixir [for him]." The Buddhist peacock goddess, Mahāmayūri, is associated with a magic spell to cure snakebite. See Jampa Panglung, 1980, "Zwei Beschwörungsformeln Gegen Schlangenbiss im Mūlasarvāstivāda-Vinaya und ihr Fortleben in der Mahāmayūrividyārajñi" in *Asiatische Forschungen,* 71:66–71.

73 See *TPRG* on *WW* 96, pl. 469 wherein the peacock "increases the splendor of its body," i.e., the beauty of its plumage, through digesting the essential potency (*bcud*) of the black aconite plant.

74 In the text (*WW* 1 and following) the word *btsan dug,* literally "virulent poison," is used; we give this literal meaning in the translation because of its vividness and its accurate conveying of the sense. However, *btsan 'dug* is universally understood as a metonym for black aconite *(bong nga nag po);* see the entry for *bstan dug* in the *Bod rgya tshig mdzod chen po.*

75 See Clifford, 199–200.

76 See Wilhelm Rau, *Altindisches Pfeilgift* (Stuttgart: Franz Steiner Verlag, 1994), 37–40.

77 See the ethnographic account of such a ritual in Mongolia in Aleksei M. Pozdneyev, *Religion and Ritual in Society: Lamaist Buddhism in Late Nineteenth-Century Mongolia,* ed. John R. Kreuger, trans. Alo Raun and Linda Raun. In *Publications of the Mongolia Society, Occasional Papers,* 10 (Bloomington, IN: Mongolia Society, 1978). These words are recited at the dismemberment of the *linga* (492–93): "This enemy who brought harm to the Three Jewels, who insulted his lama, who execrated the faith, brought suffering to animate beings, who violated his vows, hit him, kill him! Part him from the tengri [divinity] with which he was born; bring him together with the shimnus [evil spirits] who came at the same time as he; separate him from his tengri-father; separate him from his tengri-mother...separate him, letting a rain of sickness, poisonous wounds, and swords pour down on him."

78 See discussion in R. A. Stein (1957), "*Le Linga des Danses Masqueés Lamaiques et La Théorie des Âmes,* in Kshitis Roy (ed.), *Liebenthal Festschrift, Sino-Indian Studies* (Santiniketan: Visvabharati, 1957), 200–234.

79 TPRG, pl. 529.

80 Personal communication, Geshe Lhundub Sopa, August 1994. See also Réne de Nebesky-Wojkowitz, *Oracles and Demons of Tibet* (reprint, Kathmandu, Tiwari's Pilgrims Book House, 1993): 508–511.

81 See Giuseppe Tucci and Walther Heissig, *Les Réligions du Tibet et de la Mongolie,* trans. R. Sailley (Paris: Payot, 1973), 198.

82 R. A. Stein, *Tibetan Civilization,* trans. J. E. S. Driver (London: Faber, 1972), 189, 274.

83 See Edou, 2–3.

84 F. Sierksma, *Tibet's Terrifying Deities: Sex and Aggression in Religious Acculturation* (Mouton: The Hague, 1966), 150. See also the depiction of this gcod meditation in

Giuseppe Tucci, *Tibetan Painted Scrolls* (Rome: La Libreria dello Stato, 1949), Vol. 2, p. 368; Vol. 3, pl. 45.

85 See Lester K. Little, "Anger in Monastic Curses," in Barbara H. Rosenwein (ed.), *Anger's Past: The Social Use of an Emotion in the Middle Ages* (Ithaca, NY: Cornell University Press, 1998), 12–14.

86 Quoted in Peter Ackroyd, *Blake* (New York: Knopf, 1996), 150.

87 See chapt. 10 of the *Bodhisattvabhūmi,* which relates how the Bodhisattva may break any vow to prevent a greater wrong.

88 Interview with Sudip Mazumdar, in *Newsweek,* 6 March 2000, 39.

89 Donald Lopez, "An Interview with Geshe Kelsang Gyatso," *Tricycle,* spring 1998, 67–78.

90 See David Seyfort Ruegg, *Buddha-Nature, Mind and the Problem of Gradualism in a Comparative Perspective* (London: School of Oriental and African Studies, 1989), 131, cited in David Jackson, *Enlightenment by a Single Means* (Vienna: Verlag der Östreichischen Academie der Wissenschaften, 1994), 27, fn. 65. Jackson (26–27) also cites a similar analysis of *pāramitāyāna, tantrayāna,* and *mahāmudrā* in the works of Gampopa.

Introduction to Mind-Training Practice

Geshe Lhundub Sopa

The *Wheel-Weapon* and *Poison-Destroying Peacock* are precious *lojong* or mind-training teachings that will help us to develop bodhicitta, the mind directed toward enlightenment. According to our Tibetan tradition, these works by Dharmarakṣita were brought to Tibet in the eleventh century by Atiśa. Atiśa also taught the stages of the path *(lam rim)* in his *A Lamp on the Way to Enlightenment,* which was later elaborated by Je Tsongkhapa in his unsurpassed commentary, *The Great Stages of the Path.* Mind training and meditation on the stages of the path have the same objective—the attainment of conventional and ultimate bodhicitta—although they are composed in different styles. In this introduction I want to present a brief overview of the stages of the path teachings found in the *Wheel-Weapon* and the *Poison-Destroying Peacock* to help those who wish to practice these mind trainings increase their motivation and understanding.

The Brevity of Life

Before starting on a difficult spiritual path, we need a very good reason for doing so. Atiśa explains this initial motivation in the following verse:

> Life is short and there are many things to learn. Since we have no idea what our lifespan will be, we should eagerly pursue our desired goal, as the swan takes milk from water.

In this verse Atiśa reminds us that while there are so many things we should know, our lifespan is uncertain, so we should take up serious goals and not waste our time with trivial things. To make this point, he uses the metaphor of the swan who takes milk from water, referring to the belief that a swan is able to extract the nourishing milk from a mixture of milk and water, as when milk has been watered down by a dishonest milk vendor.

From this verse we learn that our spiritual practice always begins with remembering the shortness of life. Human life is fairly short; few people live longer than a hundred years or so. In this brief life we have so many desires, so many goals that we want to reach; we want to know so many things, so we try to study and learn, but there are too many things to learn about, since the sphere of knowledge is infinite. We should ask ourselves: "What is truly important in this life? What is it that we really want to know and accomplish?" The purpose of knowledge is to help one to accomplish something of benefit to oneself, but it is impossible to fulfill all one's goals in this brief life. We may hear about extremely long-lived people and hope that, like them, we might have a long life. Yet there is no way to know whether we will live another ten or twenty or fifty years, or even if we will wake up tomorrow morning; we do not have the power to determine how long we will live.

According to Buddhist teaching, the length of life is determined by one's previous karma. The only exception to this is found among those who have obtained power over death, those who are completely free from the impure causes and conditions belonging to cyclic existence. When you are free from them, when you obtain buddhahood or emancipation, then there will be no problem, but as long as you are under the power of karma and the defilements, then you have no real power over your lifespan or what you experience during your life. Despite your earnest desire for long life and happiness, things may turn out differently. Therefore, everything is unknown; you may live another hundred years, or just until tomorrow; there are people who are healthy and happy one hour, and the next hour they are gone—such things happen all the time. Nobody wants this to happen, this is just the way it is. Therefore, it is important that the practitioner's meditation start every day with remembrance of the impermanence of human life. You should ask yourself what is the meaning and purpose of your life and whether there is time to do the things you wish. When you seriously reflect in this way, you become aware that everything is uncertain and thus every moment becomes precious.

The Advantages of Human Life

Śāntideva says:

> It is very difficult to meet with this life of leisure, which can lead to accomplishing the goal of human beings. If you do not use it to your advantage, when will you find this occasion again? (*BCA* 1.4)

According to the Buddha's teaching, this life is not unique, but part of a chain of births stretching back to beginningless time and continuing on after death. Although this present life is temporary, it is linked to future births, and so it belongs to impure cyclic existence *(samsara)*. Yet an impure and imperfect life can be transformed into one that is pure and perfect. There are six different realms of life in cyclic existence, three lower ones and three upper ones. The three realms below the human are those of the hell-denizens, the hungry ghosts, and the animals. The three upper realms are those of humans, the demigods, and the gods. This is all explained in detail in the stages of the path teachings.

In some other religions hell is believed to be permanent and absolute: once you get there, you will never escape. In Buddhism, hell also exists, but not in the same way. Committing certain types of negative physical, verbal, or mental actions will result in a bad life in any of the lower realms, depending on the severity of the negative action; the consequence of the worst actions is a life in the hell realm. When the negative results of the actions that resulted in a birth in a lower realm are exhausted, you can then experience a higher birth depending on past virtuous actions that have not yet ripened. You may then be born into the demigod or god realms, but the best place to be born is among humans, for in the other higher realms, as with the lower realms, there is less chance of achieving the spiritual goal of emancipation, enlightenment, or everlasting peace and happiness. To reach such an objective requires much work and understanding and a long period of training and practice, which can only be accomplished in the human realm.

The actions, or karma, that result in a birth in the higher realms of the demigods and among the worldly and transcendental gods are forms of wholesome and virtuous activity called in Sanskrit *śīla,* meaning pure moral conduct such as refraining from harming others. But it is better to accumulate merit through virtuous activity in order to be born as a human. The human realm is the best for achieving spiritual goals because in the three lower realms you do not have any opportunity to hear Dharma teachings, to understand them, to practice the path to enlightenment, or to obtain freedom from cyclic existence. Many of us do not believe in the existence of the hell and hungry ghost realms because they are not visible to us like the animal realm, but they exist nonetheless. The lives of animals, especially of our pet dogs or cats, may seem happy and pleasant. However, they do not have the mental capacity to gain permanent freedom; they don't have any goals, they don't have any awareness of the past or future, or of virtue or nonvirtue. Because they don't have the capacity for understanding, they will not comprehend even if we try to teach them. It is the same in the hell and hungry ghost realms: once you are born there, it is very difficult to have the opportunity to understand the Dharma.

The gods and demigods in the higher realms have only temporary happiness and peace even with their extraordinarily long lives and subtle bodies and minds that are greatly superior to those of humans. They still lack a certain understanding, and they are dominated by attachment to their own pleasures and enjoyments, which are the results of their previous virtuous actions. Thus, they are not motivated to gain freedom from that life, and even if the buddhas or bodhisattvas were to come to the divine realm to teach them, they would not listen. When the stock of merit responsible for their birth as gods is exhausted, they will likely fall into one of the lower realms from which it is difficult to attain a human life.

Even in the human realm, there are many kinds of lives. Many human lives are not very satisfactory from the point of view of spiritual practice; a person may have poor mental or physical characteristics or live in a bad environment. Such people have little opportunity to meet with spiritual teachers and to hear religious teachings, or to accept and practice such teachings correctly. Not many human beings have this type of opportunity. In Śāntideva's verse, "leisure" does not mean leisure for sleeping or loafing around; it means leisure to meet with the pure spiritual teaching, to understand and practice it physically, mentally, and verbally. Therefore, "leisure" really means the opportunity to encounter and understand the practice of the pure teaching.

When one is born as a human, there are four types of positive qualities needed to accomplish a spiritual goal: (1) being born with a sound mind and body, (2) being born in a place where teachings are available, (3) having a positive attitude, and (4) having a correct view of the teachings. Having a human body along with leisure and positive conditions is precious and rare and difficult to obtain. If you look throughout the world there are many more animals and insects than human beings. Without the proper path you cannot reach the goal of perfect peace and happiness, and this proper path can only be obtained in the human realm when you have leisure and the requisite positive qualities. There are many obstacles to achieving spiritual goals; even just to live and maintain this short life is difficult because we lack independence and freedom.

Serious practitioners begin by looking at their own life. They ask themselves: "What kind of life do I have; is it easy or difficult to find the path to this spiritual goal?" They soon discover that it is unusual to have the opportunity to find the path and that properly qualified teachers are rare, as are the right teachings, such as the stages of the path. The stages of the path have all of the details of the step-by-step practice of meditation, beginning with appreciation of the importance of this human life. We learn that all the positive qualities that we now have are the result of our positive actions and all the negative experiences we have are a result of our negative actions. Being aware of this, we should not misuse this precious life; if we should die without having undertaken spiritual practice, this would be a great waste. This subject is extensively discussed in the mental-training teachings.

This type of fortunate human life is often compared to a great wish-granting jewel that is very difficult to obtain. But what kind of wishes can such a jewel grant? Although it might grant us a lot of money or other luxuries, it will never grant us permanent peace or nirvana. Such a jewel does not have the special attribute that this human life has, the ability to generate future lives of good health and prosperity, and even to generate the life of peace, enlightenment, buddhahood, and nirvana.

Making and Achieving Spiritual Goals

Bearing in mind the shortness and preciousness of human life, you need to determine your objectives. The present moment of life is of the greatest value. You should think: "From this moment until the end of my life, however long that may be, I don't want to waste one moment, because this time is so precious, and once it is gone, all things are gone." Such thoughts are useful and valuable and are like a teacher; they lead you on, they encourage you, and they instigate the special work that you must accomplish without wasting time or energy. Thus, practice begins with thinking about the impermanence of your life situation and the preciousness of this life. When you realize this more and more deeply, you will ponder what you should do from this moment on. You may want to do and be countless different things, but like the swan who extracts the nourishing milk, you should take up only what is essential.

What then is your objective? People have all kinds of goals, mostly pertaining to material desires in the present life. There are some who may consider a good birth in the next life to be the most important, or, on a higher level, they may desire their own emancipation from cyclic existence. Finally, others may want to obtain perfect buddhahood as soon as possible in order to be of benefit to others. Thus, there are higher and lower level spiritual goals. The highest spiritual goal requires that we purify our mind so that it will be completely free from all the obstacles and afflictions that create impure karma. Such karma produces all the varieties of births, which vary according to the nature of the karma; sometimes one is reborn in a miserable life, sometimes in an intermediate one, sometimes in a higher one. These impure lives alternate one after another, around and around; such is the nature of cyclic existence. Therefore, according to Buddhist teaching, one's own impure mind creates all the conditions of cyclic existence: an impure body, suffering, and an impure external environment. Every person has his or her own unique environment; even those who live together in the same country or in one house have different environments. In the same house or place, some people are miserable and others are happy. So we see that misery or happiness is not the result of external conditions, but rather of the mental qualities created by previous karma. Nobody shares their experience with others, even if they are in one family, even if they are identical twins. Even such twins have different minds and experiences. One of them may be peaceful and gentle, the other may have a very bad and hostile attitude; one of them may be physically healthy, the other may have physical problems. Their own individual physical, verbal, and mental actions from their past lives have produced a different result for each of them.

So, from a Buddhist point of view, how do you want to behave in this life, positively or negatively? In past lives you did a mixture of good and bad deeds, but now, with the realization of the preciousness of this life, you understand that what you do now will determine your future. Therefore, a kind, compassionate, and loving mental attitude must be developed, and anger, jealousy, and hatred toward others must be eliminated. This human life has the potential for extreme virtue or vice, and we can hurl ourselves into unfortunate births, into hell or among animals or hungry ghosts, and be stuck there for eons and eons. On the other hand, we can make great positive changes in this short life and develop knowledge and wisdom, especially the wisdom that understands cause and effect and how cause and effect operates within ourselves. When one understands the internal causes of suffering, one tries to pinpoint them and fight against them rather than against external conditions. If you strive hard to develop concentration and meditation, you can replace bad states of mind with the most precious mind of wisdom and compassion. These topics that I have briefly touched on here: (1) the difficulty of obtaining a human birth, (2) the impermanence of human life, (3) the relationship between actions and their results, and (4) the shortcomings of cyclic existence, are discussed in detail in the teachings on the stages of the path. They are also called "the fourfold mind training"or "the fourfold method to reverse our habitual way of thinking."

In examining the goals of human beings from the point of view of Buddhism we can distinguish two main categories: the first is from the point of view of what we want to eliminate, namely, suffering. Our whole life is filled with anxiety about preventing suffering. The second is from the positive point of view of what we want to achieve, that is, peace and happiness. We can wish to eliminate suffering and to achieve happiness for just a limited time, such as in the present life, or permanently. We may wonder if there is any way to end our suffering completely. If we could somehow eliminate its cause, then we would be permanently free from suffering.

Even without considering religious or spiritual aspirations, common sense tells us that what we are looking for is some kind of happiness or peace. All living beings seek happiness or peace throughout their life and look for ways to prevent problems from arising. Even insects and animals run around seeking pleasure, looking for food and shelter, and trying to avoid predators and other dangers. But such objectives are only temporary. This kind of temporary objective is a worldly goal and not a spiritual one. When you practice to reach higher objectives, and not just temporary ones, you realize that problems have a cause, and therefore are not permanent, and that the way to get rid of the problems once and for all is to extinguish their causes. The everlasting peace or happiness that one obtains by doing this is what is meant here as the goal of human beings.

Buddhism, along with all other true spiritual teachings, teaches everlasting peace and happiness. This is the task of religion; otherwise the religion is preaching merely worldly goals for this life alone. We look for temporary physical pleasure from our senses, such as nice things to see, to taste, to hear, and to touch. Such things are worldly goals, which come and go and have no permanent value or capacity to bring lasting peace; they can themselves become a cause of misery. With truly religious or spiritual goals, we are seeking permanent pleasure that would far surpass any temporary pleasure. This is the everlasting happiness that is attained by those that have achieved nirvana or enlightenment.

We have to question whether such eternal goals are really achievable, or are mere words or fantasies. Is it worthwhile to pursue such objectives? We humans have great intelligence and analytical capacity; we have the potential to understand things. Thus, we can ask whether there really is a permanent cessation of the results of negative action, the freedom from repeated births in cyclic existence that we call nirvana or enlightenment. The 84,000 teachings of the Buddha contained in the volumes of Buddhist scriptures show that there is a method to achieve these goals and to completely extinguish the causes of suffering forever.

Karma and the Afflictions

Those whose lives are ruled by their negative actions have no ability to choose where they want to be in cyclic existence; their present lives are the result of their past actions. Birth leads to aging, illness, misery and suffering, and finally to death; these are the results of birth in cyclic existence. According to Buddhist teaching, suffering comes from ourselves, not from other people or from the environment. All of our pleasant and unpleasant experiences in life, including our human bodies, whether healthy or unhealthy, beautiful or ugly, are produced by our own actions. Since that is so, there is really no reason to complain about adverse events. Even if we were to do nothing in this life, our positive or negative actions performed in previous lives would still bring their results into the present, for example, in our being accused or punished unjustly. When actions are performed, they deposit karmic "seeds" in our minds that can produce at a future time the negative or positive results of that action. These karmic seeds are not physical seeds, but a potential for the future. Even a small karmic seed can produce a huge result; you should not think that doing minor wrongs will not harm you. The Buddha uses an analogy in the *Rice Seedling Sūtra,* in which he teaches that planting a small rice seed will produce a lot of rice, and planting a small tree seed will eventually produce a huge tree, with branches, leaves, and fruit, that can provide shade for a hundred wagons. Farmers would not waste their time planting if one seed yielded only another seed; they want their planting to have a high yield. This is the case with external causality; regarding internal moral causality, it is more serious. One small negative physical, verbal, or mental action can produce major results if it is harmful to another. Such an action may produce results that bring the one who has performed it into the hell realms, or otherwise affect that person's present or future lives. Even if we are now living what is considered a good life, such results can still occur from the germination of the seeds of past actions.

"Karma" means action, whether physical, verbal, or mental. In itself, action is not necessarily impure; there are pure and impure, perfect and imperfect actions. Even those who are free from cyclic existence, who are enlightened like the Buddha, still perform actions. Buddhahood does not mean the absence of action; buddhas and other perfect beings perform actions to help other sentient beings. Their actions are so great and perfect that they are like clouds of virtue, raining love and compassion on all sentient beings. The best example of such perfect action is the Buddha Śākyamuni having taught all of the 84,000 teachings found in the Buddhist scriptures.

Impure actions are the cause of negative effects in cyclic existence. What makes an action pure or impure? Impure actions are produced by impure mental disturbances, or afflictions. Basically, these are the three poisons of craving, hatred, and ignorance, and from these many other afflictions are produced, like branches and sub-branches. The impure mental afflictions are like a poison tree with poisonous bark, branches, and leaves. Any actions motivated by the three poisons are impure actions and will result in impure births and other negative consequences. The reason that the teachings of the Buddha are 84,000 in number is that there are reckoned to be a corresponding number of mental afflictions. These afflictions are produced because we are not able to understand and control our mind. Regardless of how comfortable we are, these afflictions are present in our mind. The Buddhist teachings directly or indirectly combat the afflictions produced by the three poisons; they are their antidote, not just temporarily, but permanently. Once we get rid of the afflictions, our actions will be pure.

As long as our actions are guided by the afflictions, we will experience negative karmic results in life after life, and there will be no way of obtaining real peace or happiness. The three poisons can motivate actions such as killing, stealing, and other ways of harming others. Such actions could be motivated by ignorance, craving, or hatred. For example, we might kill an animal out of attachment to its flesh, hide, or tusks. We can also kill people out of attraction or desire, or we might kill them out of hatred, as is usually the case. We might also kill out of stupidity or ignorance, such as thinking that killing is justified because it will have a positive result, as in the story of Angulimāla, who thought that he could gain salvation through killing a thousand people. In the end, he saw his mistaken actions in the mirror of the Dharma; the Buddha's teaching is like a mirror in which you can see the reflection of all your past misbehavior.

Ignorance and Egocentricity

In discussing the mind-training texts, we will be looking at how to overcome ignorance. We can use the word "ignorance" in the ordinary sense of not knowing a fact or the difference between right and wrong, or even for not knowing how to perform a specific task, like cooking. Here we're not referring to the ordinary lack of knowledge, but to a special ignorance that is the primary cause of all our suffering. This ignorance is the misperception of the self, of "I," "me," and "mine."

Whatever we do is done under the power of "I," "me," and "mine," and this is the main source of our problems. How do you perceive this "I" or "me" when, for example, someone verbally attacks you? You become very indignant, angry, and defensive, and feel that your very self is under attack. But is there really any kind of substantial, true self, a real "I" or "me" to be defended? If there is, then such defensive thinking is correct. However, the assumption of a real, substantial self is false, and everything that comes from it is also false, such as wanting the best things for yourself, or feeling anger at people who say bad things about you. Every afflicted thought, such as wanting to hurt another person because of what that individual said or did to you, is produced in connection with a false understanding of the nature of the self, which is the type of ignorance we are discussing here.

One's thoughts concerning "I" and "me" are dominated by the view of a real personal identity, which holds the self as permanent and existing absolutely. We are attached to "my body, my self, my mind" and think we deserve to be cherished or loved by everyone, and we get angry or jealous if we are not. This type of thinking comes from a mistaken notion of the self; this is true ignorance, and is the source of everything we have been talking about: impure actions, rebirth, and cyclic existence. This view of a real personal identity creates the selfish, self-cherishing attitude that gives rise to greed, anger, jealousy, and other negative emotions. Therefore, it is the source of every negative and undesirable thing. Śāntideva said:

> Since all the calamities, fears, and sufferings in the world have arisen from self-clinging, what have I to do with that great demon? (*BCA* 8.134)

This means that in this world, we harm each other and experience both physical and mental suffering, especially fear of the many terrifying things inside and outside ourselves. Every aspect of misery and suffering in this world actually arises from the view of a real personal identity, or the egotistic view. It is the devil in the depths of our mind that thinks: "I alone am the best. I alone am to be cherished, respected, and honored. I must be in control. Those who do not agree with me are evil; maybe they should be destroyed. How nice it would be if they did not exist." Do you have this type of attitude or not? According to Śāntideva, most people in the world do.

With this kind of attitude, you put yourself at the center, you hold "I" or "me" as paramount and feel that everything is "mine," that it belongs to "me," that "I" possess it. This type of thinking starts with "my mind," "my body," and continues from there to "my house," "my family," "my property"; you can have so much "mine" that it can go on and on forever. In his verse Śāntideva is saying that the root cause of attachment and hatred is the egoistic view of a real personal identity. When you have this wrong view of a real personal identity, then you also have what is called "the self-cherishing attitude." This means preferring yourself, your mind and body, to the exclusion of others. Before you hear the Buddha's teaching, you will always be inclined to the egoistic view, the view of a real personal identity. Later, you will see through study that this view is faulty and harmful, but still you will not be able to attack it; you will continue to hold on to that part of your mind and be influenced by it.

There are two aspects to egoism: holding to me and mine, and the self-cherishing attitude. The wrong view of me and mine means holding the "me" and "I" as something central and absolute, inherently present in one's own aggregates. It is holding the belief that within the body and the mind there is an "I" that dominates and owns the mind and body, and that is to be cherished and loved. This is the erroneous view of a real personal identity. We may not usually articulate this in such philosophical terms, but this is the sense in which we experience "I" or "me," as in the case previously cited in which we are accused by someone and become defensive. This is a wrong view that the Buddha often discussed; it is the cause of all the problems of cyclic existence.

When you have this kind of ignorance, you develop the other attitude, that of "self-cherishing," preferring oneself over others. A person may have some love for others, but it is nothing in comparison to self-cherishing. The intensity of your love for yourself does not extend toward anyone else, and even if you feel love for another person, it may be based in sexual desire, which is really a form of attachment, of seeking pleasure for yourself. In this case, you are not loving unselfishly, desiring only the happiness and welfare of others. When you want yourself to have everything that is desirable, you also will have the negative attitude that is the opposite side of the coin, that wants to pile everything undesirable on others.

Even though we realize that the view of a real personal identity and self-cherishing are the real enemy, we look for enemies outside ourselves. If someone insults you, or acts hostile, or does not respect you, or does not greet you or follow you but acts contrarily, in their own way, you usually take them as enemies. So long as you have such an attitude, considering others as the enemy and cherishing only yourself, you will not have peace. However much you try to find peace and happiness, it will elude you. Even if you study religion and read a lot of books and become a great scholar—all of this will just end up serving selfishness, the desire to obtain fame, praise, wealth, and honor for yourself. When you seek such things, you are also inviting anger, hatred, and jealousy, which are their other side, and your mind will be continuously disturbed. The chain of the three poisons is linked to your mind and causes you to act out of attachment, hatred, jealousy, and ignorance, producing the impure karma that drives your entire life.

The real enemy then is within ourselves. You have to look carefully within yourself, using meditation, to find this enemy. When we have attained understanding, we will realize that this evil demon is inside us, and that we have to get rid of this inner enemy in order to resolve our problems. We seek an antidote that will free us from this enemy that has caused us so many problems. The Buddha taught that until we can get rid of this demon of egocentricity, we can have no real peace or happiness.

The Antidote of the Secret Holy Teaching: Exchanging Self with Others

Śāntideva said:

> Whoever wants to save himself and others quickly should practice the holy secret of exchanging self and others. (*BCA* 8.120)

This practice is called the holy, secret teaching; it is not for everyone, and it is quite difficult. To actually practice it is to practice at a very high level; your mind becomes much more tamed, subdued, and controlled than it is in its usual state of self-centeredness. Ordinarily we are completely dominated by the kind of self-centered attitude that only wants pleasure and enjoyment for ourselves and is willing to exploit others for that purpose. Such a person can hurt or harm others to suit his or her own purposes, with complete indifference. This teaching cannot be utilized by such self-centered people; even if they encounter it, they will be completely discouraged and will not believe that such a thing is possible.

To follow the holy secret teaching is a great Mahayana practice. "Holy" refers to the most sacred kind of practice, here that of exchanging self with others. The self-cherishing attitude is the target or enemy of this practice; it is what ought to be combated. Exchanging self with others involves cherishing others in order to help them, concerning yourself with their problems and misery, wanting to relieve their problems, and wishing them joy, happiness, peace, and every desirable thing; in short, having the same goals for others as we have for ourselves. Usually it is others whom we would rather see miserable and suffering, and ourselves in possession of everything desirable; this has to be completely changed, which means a complete shift of focus. We must be willing to take onto ourselves from others any misery, suffering, problem, or difficulty. The things to which we are the most attached—peace, happiness, success, enjoyment, personal possessions—we should want to give to others, to share these things. To have real happiness and joy through this powerful practice—this is the true holy teaching.

Cherishing others gives you the ability to take others' problems as your own, and to give to others from your heart all that is precious to you. Of course, it is easy to talk about it or to understand what the words mean. But most people will think: "Can I do this? How can one do it? Who would want to do it? There is no way for it to be done." For this reason, the person who tries to practice this, to do what ought to be done, should not tell anyone about it, but should keep it hidden for the time being. When your mind reaches the point of becoming ready to do all these things effectively, then you will diligently use skillful methods to carry them out. Otherwise, people who are not ready to hear about this teaching may become discouraged when you speak about it, and develop doubts and wrong views, thinking that you are talking rubbish.

There are many Mahayana Buddhist teachings that are called "secret." "Secret" here does not refer to only wanting to share something with a favorite person and otherwise keeping it to yourself, which is the selfish way to keep things secret—this is not that kind of secret. Here, "secrecy" applies to certain spiritual teachings and practices. When a person is not ready and you speak to them about such things, then instead of benefitting them, there will be major negative results, as I have just discussed. When this kind of thing happens, there is danger because such negative mental attitudes are powerful; they will create strong negative karma for these people. Therefore, when you perceive such a danger, you should keep silent. That's what secrecy means here.

It is for that reason that great spiritual teachers have kept certain things secret and spoke of other things quite openly. They are like wise parents who, out of love for their children, may not allow them to see, hear, or know certain things because such knowledge would be of no benefit to them and could even cause them great harm. Some things are kept hidden until it is the right time to share them; there is no fault in parents keeping secrets out of love; on the contrary, it's a sign of their great loving-kindness.

It is the same for spiritual teachings; there are many unique Mahayana practices, and certain kinds of tantric practice, that are secret. Such is the case with the Mahayana mental-training practice called "giving and taking." When we meditate on the exchange of self with others, we give everything good to others and take everything bad upon ourselves. First, you do this mentally along with an awareness of breathing out and in. When breathing out, you imagine you are sending forth everything that is desirable, positive, and meritorious, whatever sources of happiness or peace that you possess—you wish that others might have them. Breathing in, you absorb all of the problems, miseries, and sufferings that afflict others and sincerely wish all of it to ripen in yourself, to experience them all yourself. At first, you may practice this only occasionally, but when you reach an advanced level, every moment can easily be a source of merit and virtue. When you try to practice this before you are ready, you may breathe in and think "Maybe some diabolical thing is entering into me—I do not want to do this." Breathing out, you may think that "All my good things are leaving me, I do not want them to go." This type of thing can happen. When you think in such a way, you are not ready to practice giving and taking because your mind has not yet sufficiently matured.

Training and Purifying the Mind

The texts we are studying here deal with mind training and purification, what is called "lojong" in Tibetan. "Lo" means "mind"; here, it refers to a special kind of mind, specifically to the two types of bodhicitta: the conventional and the ultimate. "Jong" means "training," "controlling," and "purifying"; here it principally means to fully train one's mind to develop the great bodhicitta—that is, in addition to the conventional bodhicitta, to develop the great, ultimate bodhicitta of wisdom. If you purify, control, and train your mind with various techniques, it can become perfect and enlightened like the mind of Śākyamuni Buddha, or like the minds of the bodhisattvas and other great spiritual masters. This mind training is necessary; you will not attain an enlightened mind without training, thought, and activity. There are no buddhas who have been enlightened from the very beginning, who have been buddhas forever; they all had to train their minds. We of course believe that many thousands of buddhas exist because all sentient beings have the potential to obtain buddhahood. They all possess the source of buddhahood and enlightenment, that is, their mind, which is essentially like a buddha's mind, naturally and inherently pure. What then is the difference between the buddhas and ourselves? The difference is that the buddhas have destroyed all impure mental factors and replaced them with completely pure, perfect, and virtuous minds and mental factors. Their body also is a perfect body, in harmony with their mind, and their actions are all wholesome and beneficial to others. All of us have the mental capacity to be like that, but our minds are entirely stuck in the mud of the impure mental afflictions—especially ignorance, craving, and hatred.

From these three basic poisons, many other afflictions arise that are created and dominated by ignorance and affected by attachment and hatred. According to the Abhidharma there are 84,0000 mental afflictions. However you count them, there are so many that they are virtually infinite, and all of these afflicted, impure mental states start with ignorance. The nature of these afflicted states is mental disturbance; they are mistaken in their perceptions and conceptions of objects. Grasping at objects under the influence of these afflicted mental states creates a powerful energy that affects the other parts of the mind. The mind, like clean water, is pure by nature, clear and drinkable, but it can become polluted, muddy, and dirty, and in the worst case, a cesspool! However, even a cesspool can still be cleaned because it is essentially pure. The impurities are only a temporary addition to the water, and they can be separated from it through a cleansing process. Once the impurities are removed, the pure nature of water will remain.

The Buddha used another analogy, that of gold that is mixed with dirt, dust, and mud. The nature of the gold is pure, but in this example it is mixed with many impurities. Such a piece of unrefined gold, however, can be skillfully refined, leaving the pure gold. This is essentially what we are doing in our daily practice: clearing the mind of the impure mental states and allowing its pure nature to manifest itself.

I often cite the *Tathāgathagarbhaśāstra,* which demonstrates the essence of Buddha in all sentient beings. "Tathāgatha" means the Buddha, "garbha" means essence, embryo, heart, or seed. Here, I will translate it as "the buddha-essence." In the sutra, the Buddha explains that we all have this buddha-essence, although currently our minds are impure; the effects of this impurity are misery and suffering. Demons, hell-beings, hungry ghosts, animals, and humans have many different kinds of impurities, but every one of these beings has an essential nature that at some point in the future can become a pure, perfectly enlightened mind exactly like the mind of the Buddha, free from all obstacles. Such a mind is created by compassion and loving-kindness; it possesses all positive qualities and is exempt from all negative qualities. Everyone should strive like the Buddha did because everyone has the same basis upon which to develop this mind. Because of the naturally pure essence of mind, we can get rid of negative mental states and purify our minds more and more until we reach the highest purification. The buddha-essence is the basis and potential for this purification.

If the nature of the mind is like this, how then can the mind possess so many afflictions of desire, hatred, jealousy, and so forth? The Buddha said that "the nature of mind is clear light." This does not mean physically clear; it means naturally free of hatred and attachment, and so forth. When the impurities are removed, what is essentially pure is left. In fact, in the same sutra, the Buddha taught that the buddha-essence itself is clear light. The Buddha also taught that the afflictions are not the nature of mind, but are impermanent and adventitious. All these stains, beginning with ignorance and including craving, hatred, jealousy, and all the many other delusions and obstacles, are temporary. They are temporary because they can be removed—the rough ones first, then the intermediate ones, then the most subtle ones. I often use the analogy of cleaning very dirty clothes using water and detergent. It does not matter how much dirt and grease there is; it can even be thicker than the cloth itself—it is still temporary or impermanent. The stains originate from certain causes and conditions; they are not part of the nature of the cloth, and the powerful detergent will be able to remove them one by one, until finally none of the dirt remains. It is like the previous examples of water and gold; the cloth is naturally clean.

Sometimes people get discouraged and think: "This is my nature, there is no way to get rid of my bad qualities." But the fact is that every one of the defilements can be gotten rid of, regardless of how thickly they adhere to the mind. Even if there is a thick layer, you can make it thinner and thinner, step by step, until it is all gone. Thus it is said that all the obstacles are temporary; they do not have an absolute or permanent nature, they do not exist inherently.

In order to realize the true nature of mind, one should meditate on the real nature of things: on emptiness, especially as it applies to the mind and mental factors. The mind has many characteristics conventionally: there are virtues, nonvirtues, obstacles, and so on, but they are all temporary, and thus these negative qualities can be removed. So we see that the one thing that is essential to our spiritual accomplishment is not something external to ourselves (although some external factors can be helpful). It is the restoration of the mind to purity and perfection. With this mind you will have everything you could wish for, and you will achieve everlasting peace and happiness. This happiness will be generated from inside yourself when all obscurations are completely removed and the mind is purified. However much you may try to create pleasure and happiness externally, however many good things you may accumulate, all of that trying will cause the mind to sink further into the mire of craving, hatred, jealousy, and conceit rather than to become purified. Thus we practice concentration, which is watching one's own mind, one's own mentality, one's own personality, with the objective of becoming a good, kind, and compassionate person.

If our mind is confronted by obstacles to becoming such a loving and compassionate person, how can they be removed, what are their antidotes? The different levels of obstacles have to be removed slowly, step by step; they cannot all be removed at once. It takes time and effort, but all this effort will be profitable; the time spent will not be wasted. From a worldly perspective, people think that such an effort will somehow result in a loss. But actually, when you properly understand things from the spiritual point of view, you will see that the waste is in the other direction. Pursuing ordinary sensual pleasures, feeding the senses, and enjoying their objects are a waste because such activities ultimately only make the mind more unhappy. Thus, one should concentrate on mental purification.

How do we accomplish this mental training, this taming? Most religious teachings involve some form of purification, Buddhist practice especially—from the beginning of practicing the pure conduct of monastic discipline up to the highest and most powerful tantric teachings, every practice without exception aims at mental purification. All of the teachings in the hundreds of volumes of the Buddhist scriptures contain nothing that does not directly or indirectly aim toward the purification of the minds of sentient beings. If a person is engaged in purification, but remains under the power of the afflictions, he or she thinks: "I can act and enjoy as I wish, without controlling the mind, just leaving it alone"; this kind of thinking is quite erroneous. As Śāntideva said:

> An untamed elephant does not inflict as much damage as does the wild elephant of the mind, which can send one into the Avici hell. (*BCA* 5.2)

That is, the untamed mind-elephant does far greater harm than any actual mad elephant, because it will bring punishments and injuries in this life and also cause you to be thrown into hell in the next life. This is one of the fundamental concepts of mind training and purification. Śāntideva also said:

> In this way, you should make an effort to be mindful that this mad mind-elephant not be untied from the great post of reflecting on the Dharma. (*BCA* 5.40)

How is the mind-elephant to be tamed? When an elephant trainer has secured the animal to a post with a strong chain, he can train it using positive and negative reinforcement. Eventually, the elephant can be tamed, and then he will do almost anything that the trainer wants. We see this at the circus, where the elephants obey commands to sit, to get up, to pick the trainer up with their trunk, and many other tricks. So even a wild elephant can become peaceful and gentle. Similarly, the wild elephant of the mind can be tied to the post of the Dharma, through meditation and teaching, and it should not be untied or loosed; you should make great effort to keep your mind "tied" to the Dharma.

The Two Types of Bodhicitta

Mind training is accustoming the mind to the two types of bodhicitta, or thought directed to enlightenment: the conventional and the ultimate. For conventional bodhicitta, which is emphasized in both the *Wheel-Weapon* and the *Peacock,* the main target is our egoism and selfishness, seeing how it arises, how it dominates us, and how it hurts both ourselves and others in life after life. People who act out of anger and hatred and do bad things should be pitied; they should be the objects of our compassion. They do not know what they are doing, nor do they have the power to act morally; they are dominated by their own inner enemy, which causes them to suffer and act in an insane way. Such people need our love and compassion.

You should not think that by caring about others you will gain some kind of worldly advantage; that type of thinking is wrong. Śāntideva said that if you have food, clothing, or material things, you should give them to those who are poor and need our help; bodhisattvas will even give their bodies to those who are in need (*BCA* 8.125). It is wrong to think: "I only have one of these and if I give it to someone else, I won't have it for myself, and I will suffer by not having it." Such an attitude considers only one's own happiness and not that of others; it is a diabolical way of thinking. When you are eating food or drinking or even getting dressed, you should not solely enjoy the food, drink, or clothes, but also think with love and compassion of all the living beings who lack these things. You should think about what you can give to truly needy people, and you should restrict your own consumption. This is thinking in a self-sacrificial way, for the benefit of others. It is like the way a most loving and kind mother would feel toward her only child, loving that child a hundred times more than she loves herself; this is a divine mental state.

Once you have this kind of attitude, loving and helping others under its influence will bring only good things with it. Even though you will not want respect and honor for yourself, you will get it, since people will naturally respond to you in that way. On the other hand, if you desire honor and respect for yourself, than you will not get it, and you will become frustrated and angry. Therefore, when this attitude of exchanging self with others spontaneously arises each day, without effort, it becomes the antidote for self-cherishing. That is the real bodhisattva mind, the divine attitude, the mind of a great being.

The other type of bodhicitta is ultimate bodhicitta. This is the understanding of the true nature of self, that is, emptiness: the reality that nothing has an absolute, independent, true nature. It is necessary to understand the nature of the "self," the "me," and the "mine." When you realize that "me" and "mine" have some relative existence but do not exist as you usually imagine them to, the view of a real personal identity will continually diminish and finally vanish. Getting rid of the view of a real personal identity is freeing oneself from the principal element of ignorance. These two aspects, the wisdom of understanding emptiness and the method of acting with love and compassion, are the heart of Buddhist teachings.

Generally, all the stages of the path can be considered part of mental training; all religious teachings train the mind. But a few specific teachings show how to meditate directly on conventional and ultimate bodhicitta; these are the short teachings stemming from Atiśa, Dharmarakṣita, and others that can be recalled in the midst of practice and that can powerfully attack the view of a real personal identity. Such teachings are called mental training and purification, lojong. These are, in brief, the reasons for the importance of learning and practicing mind training and its preparatory practices.

The *Wheel-Weapon* and the *Peacock*

The origin of most of the mind-training teachings is found in the writings of Śāntideva, especially the *Bodhicaryāvatāra.* These teachings were eventually transmitted to Atiśa, who also received special teachings on mind training from his gurus Serlingpa, Maitrīyogi, and Dharmarakṣita. The two works we are studying here were composed by Dharmarakṣita, who was a master of Abhidharma, a topic he also taught to Atiśa. Both of these works present very powerful yogic methods for fighting the view of a real personal identity and the self-cherishing attitude, and show how these pernicious views and attitudes arise in everyday life; even if you try to behave well, they can destroy the purity of your motives and bring you to ruin.

In a general sense, mind training can refer to any mental practice or spiritual training, and we can speak of mind training for the beginning level of practitioner, for the intermediate level, or for the higher level. The *Wheel-Weapon* and the *Poison-Destroying Peacock* are special teachings for the advanced practitioner of the Mahayana Vehicle. If you thoroughly learn these mind trainings and use them regularly in your spiritual practice and daily activities, they will enable you to cultivate greater mental and emotional maturity and to bring great benefit for other living beings.

PART ONE

THE WHEEL-WEAPON MIND TRAINING

བློ་སྦྱོང་མཚོན་ཆ་འཁོར་ལོ།

Attributed to Dharmarakṣita

བློ་སྦྱོང་མཚོན་ཆ་འཁོར་ལོ།

༄༅། དཀོན་མཆོག་གསུམ་ལ་ཕྱག་འཚལ་ལོ།

དགྲ་བོ་གནད་ལ་དབབ་པའི་མཚོན་ཆ་འཁོར་ལོ་ཞེས་བྱ་བ།

ཁྲོ་བོ་ཆེན་པོ་གཤིན་རྗེའི་གཤེད་ལ་ཕྱག་འཚལ་ལོ།

1

བཙན་དུག་ནགས་སུ་རྨ་བྱ་རྒྱུ་བ་ན།
སྨན་གྱི་ལྡུམ་ར་ལེགས་པར་མཛེས་གྱུར་ཀྱང་།
རྨ་བྱའི་ཚོགས་རྣམས་དགའ་བར་མི་འགྱུར་གྱི།
བཙན་དུག་བཅུད་ཀྱིས་རྨ་བྱ་འཚོ་བ་ལྟར།།

2

དཔའ་བོ་འཁོར་བའི་ནགས་སུ་འཇུག་པ་ན།
བདེ་སྐྱིད་དཔལ་གྱི་ལྡུམ་ར་མཛེས་གྱུར་ཀྱང་།
དཔའ་བོ་དག་ནི་ཆགས་པར་མི་འགྱུར་གྱི།
སྡུག་བསྔལ་ནགས་སུ་སེམས་དཔའ་འཚོ་བ་ཡིན།།

3

དེ་ཕྱིར་བདེ་སྐྱིད་དང་དུ་ལེན་པ་ཡི།
སྡར་མའི་དབང་གིས་སྡུག་ལ་སྐྱོ་བ་ཡིན།
སྡུག་བསྔལ་དང་དུ་ལེན་པའི་སེམས་དཔའ་དེ།
དཔའ་བའི་སྤོབས་ཀྱིས་རྟག་ཏུ་བདེ་བ་ཡིན།།

The Wheel-Weapon Mind Training

Homage to the Three Jewels.

The Wheel-Weapon That Strikes at the Enemy's Vital Spot

I bow down to the Great Wrathful One, Yamāntaka.

1

When the peacocks roam the jungle of virulent poison, the flocks take no delight in gardens of medicinal plants, no matter how beautiful they may be, for peacocks thrive on the essence of virulent poison.

2

Similarly, when the heroes roam the jungle of cyclic existence, they do not become attached to the garden of happiness and prosperity, no matter how beautiful it may be, for heroes thrive in the jungle of suffering.

3

Therefore, it is due to cowardice that persons avidly pursue their own happiness and so come to suffer; and it is due to heroism that bodhisattvas, willingly taking the suffering of others onto themselves, are always happy.

4
ད་འདིར་འདོད་ཆགས་བཙན་དུག་ནགས་དང་འདྲ།
དཔའ་བོ་རྨ་བྱ་ལྟ་བུས་འཆུན་པར་འགྱུར།
སྐྱུར་མ་བྱ་རོག་ལྟ་བུའི་སྲོག་ལ་འཆི།།

5
རང་འདོད་ཅན་གྱིས་དུག་འདི་ག་ན་འཆུན།
ཉོན་མོངས་གཞན་ལའང་དེ་བཞིན་སྦྱར་བ་ན།
བྱ་རོག་ལྟ་བུར་ཐར་པའི་སྲོག་ལ་འབབ།།

6
དེ་ཕྱིར་སེམས་དཔའ་རྨ་བྱ་ལྟ་བུ་ཡིས།
དུག་གི་ནགས་དང་འདྲ་བའི་ཉོན་མོངས་རྣམས།
བཅུད་དུ་སྒྱུར་ལ་འཁོར་བའི་ནགས་སུ་འཇུག།
དང་དུ་བླངས་ལ་དུག་འདི་གཞོམ་པར་བྱ།།

7
ད་ནི་རང་དབང་མེད་པར་འཁོར་བ་ཡི།
བདག་ཏུ་འཛིན་པ་བདུད་ཀྱི་ཕོ་ཉ་འདི།
རང་འདོད་སྐྱིད་འདོད་རོ་དང་ཕར་ཕྲོལ་ལ།
གཞན་དོན་དཀའ་སྤྱད་དང་དུ་བླང་བར་བྱ།།

4
Now here, desire is like a jungle of virulent poison:
the hero, like the peacock, masters it; the coward,
like the crow, perishes.

5
How can persons concerned only with their own desires
master this poison? If they involve themselves in the other
afflictions as well, it will cost them their chance
for emancipation, just like the crow.

6
Thus the bodhisattva roams like the peacock in the forest of cyclic existence, converting the afflictions, which are like a jungle of virulent poisons, into an elixir. Willingly embracing the afflictions, the hero shall conquer the poison.

7
The ego-clinging of the helpless wanderer in cyclic existence is the messenger of the devil. Distance yourself from the savor of selfishness and hedonism, and willingly embrace hardship for the sake of others.

8

ལས་ཀྱིས་བདས་ཤིང་ཉོན་མོངས་གོམས་པ་ཡི།
རིས་མཐུན་སྐྱེས་དགུ་རྣམས་ཀྱི་སྡུག་བསྔལ་རྣམས།
སྐྱིད་འདོད་བདག་གི་སྟེང་དུ་སྤུང་བར་བྱ།།

9

གལ་ཏེ་རང་འདོད་འཁྲི་བ་ཞུགས་པའི་ཚེ།
ཟློག་ལ་རང་གི་བདེ་སྐྱིད་འགྲོ་ལ་སྦྱིན།
ཇི་ལྟར་བདག་ལ་འཁོར་གྱིས་ལོག་སྒྲུབ་ཚེ།
རང་གི་གཡེང་པས་ལན་ཞེས་སློང་ཆོམ་བསྒྲེང་།།

10

ལུས་ལ་མི་བཟོད་ན་ཚ་བྱུང་བའི་ཚེ།
འགྲོ་བའི་ལུས་ལ་གནོད་པ་བསྐྱལ་བ་ཡིས།
ལས་ངན་མཚོན་ཆ་རང་ལ་འཁོར་བ་ཡིན།
ད་ནི་ན་ཚ་མ་ལུས་རང་ལ་བླང་།།

11

རང་གི་སེམས་ལ་སྡུག་བསྔལ་བྱུང་བའི་ཚེ།
ངེས་པར་གཞན་གྱི་སེམས་རྒྱུད་དཀྲུགས་པ་ཡིས།
ལས་ངན་མཚོན་ཆ་རང་ལ་འཁོར་བ་ཡིན།
ད་ནི་སྡུག་བསྔལ་མ་ལུས་རང་ལ་བླང་།།

8

May the sufferings of all beings, who, like myself, are driven
by their karma and their habituation to the afflictions,
be heaped upon me, the hedonist.

9

When I become enmeshed in selfishness, I will offer my own
happiness to living beings so as to counteract it. In the same way,
should a companion be ungrateful to me, I will be content
in knowing that this is in retribution for my own inconstancy.

10

When my body falls prey to terrible sickness,
it is the weapon of my own evil deeds turned upon me
for injuring the bodies of living beings. From now on,
I shall take all sickness upon myself.

11

When my mind falls prey to suffering, it is surely the weapon
of my own evil deeds turned upon me for troubling the minds
of others. From now on, I shall willingly take all suffering
upon myself.

12
རང་ཉིད་བཀྲེས་སྐོམ་དྲག་པོས་གཟིར་བ་ན།
ཁྲམ་དང་རྐུ་འཕྲོག་སེར་ན་བྱས་པ་ཡིས།
ལས་ངན་མཚོན་ཆ་རང་ལ་འཁོར་བ་ཡིན།
ད་ནི་བཀྲེས་སྐོམ་མ་ལུས་རང་ལ་བླང་།།

13
དབང་མེད་གཞན་གྱིས་འཁོལ་ཞིང་མནར་བའི་ཚེ།
དམན་ལ་སྡང་ཞིང་བྲན་དུ་བཀོལ་བ་ཡིས།
ལས་ངན་མཚོན་ཆ་རང་ལ་འཁོར་བ་ཡིན།
ད་ནི་ལུས་སྲོག་གཞན་གྱི་དོན་དུ་བཀོལ།།

14
མི་སྙན་ཚིག་རྣམས་རྣ་བར་བྱུང་བ་ན།
ཕྲ་མ་ལ་སོགས་ངག་གི་ཉོངས་པ་ཡིས།
ལས་ངན་མཚོན་ཆ་རང་ལ་འཁོར་བ་ཡིན།
ད་ནི་ངག་གི་སྐྱོན་ལ་སྨད་པར་བྱ།།

15
གང་ཡང་མ་དག་ཡུལ་དུ་སྐྱེས་པ་ན།
མ་དག་སྣང་བ་རྟག་པར་བསྒོམས་པ་ཡིས།
ལས་ངན་མཚོན་ཆ་རང་ལ་འཁོར་བ་ཡིན།
ད་ནི་དག་སྣང་འབའ་ཞིག་བསྒོམ་པར་བྱ།།

12

When I am tormented by extreme hunger and thirst,
it is the weapon of my own evil deeds turned upon me
for swindling, stealing, and acting miserly. From now on,
I shall willingly take all hunger and thirst upon myself.

13

When I am powerless and suffer enslavement, it is the weapon
of my own evil deeds turned upon me for despising my inferiors
and enslaving them. From now on I shall make slaves of my body
and my life for the sake of others.

14

When insulting remarks assault my ears, it is the weapon
of my own evil deeds turned upon me for my verbal offenses
of slander and so forth. From now on I shall condemn
my own verbal faults.

15

When I am reborn into an impure land, it is the weapon
of my own evil deeds turned upon me for always cultivating
impure vision. From now on, I shall cultivate only pure vision.

16
ཕན་ཞིང་མཛའ་བའི་གྲོགས་དང་བྲལ་བའི་ཚེ།
གཞན་གྱི་འཁོར་རྣམས་བདག་གིས་ཁ་དྲངས་པས།
ལས་ངན་མཚོན་ཆ་རང་ལ་འཁོར་བ་ཡིན།
ད་ནི་གཞན་དག་འཁོར་དང་དབྲལ་མི་བྱ།།

17
དམ་པ་ཐམས་ཅད་བདག་ལ་མི་དགའ་ན།
དམ་པ་བོར་ནས་གྲོགས་ངན་བསྟེན་པ་ཡིས།
ལས་ངན་མཚོན་ཆ་རང་ལ་འཁོར་བ་ཡིན།
ད་ནི་ངན་པའི་གྲོགས་རྣམས་སྤང་པར་བྱ།།

18
སྒྲོ་སྐུར་གཞན་གྱིས་སྡིག་བསྒོག་བྱུང་བའི་ཚེ།
རང་གིས་དམ་པ་རྣམས་ལ་སྨད་པ་ཡིས།
ལས་ངན་མཚོན་ཆ་རང་ལ་འཁོར་བ་ཡིན།
ད་ནི་གཞན་ལ་སྒྲོ་སྐུར་སྨད་མི་བྱ།།

19
མཁོ་བའི་རྫས་ལ་ཆུད་ཟོས་བྱུང་བའི་ཚེ།
གཞན་གྱི་མཁོ་བ་ཁྱད་དུ་བསད་པ་ཡིས།
ལས་ངན་མཚོན་ཆ་རང་ལ་འཁོར་བ་ཡིན།
ད་ནི་གཞན་གྱི་མཁོ་བ་བསྒྲུབ་པར་བྱ།།

16

When I am separated from helpful and loving friends,
it is the weapon of my own evil deeds turned upon me
for luring away others' companions. From now on I shall
not separate others from their companions.

17

When all the holy ones are displeased with me, it is the weapon
of my own evil deeds turned upon me for casting them aside
and resorting to bad companions. From now on I shall
renounce bad companions.

18

When others sin against me by exaggeration or deprecation,
it is the weapon of my own evil deeds turned upon me for reviling
the holy ones. From now on I shall not revile others by exaggeration
or deprecation.

19

When my material necessities waste away, it is the weapon
of my own evil deeds turned upon me for scorning others'
necessities. From now on I shall provide for others' necessities.

20
སེམས་མི་གསལ་ཞིང་སྙིང་མི་དགའ་བའི་ཚེ།
སྐྱེ་བོ་གཞན་ལ་སྡིག་པ་བསགས་པ་ཡིས།
ལས་ངན་མཚོན་ཆ་རང་ལ་འཁོར་བ་ཡིན།
ད་ནི་གཞན་གྱི་སྡིག་རྐྱེན་སྤང་བར་བྱ།།

21
བྱ་བ་མ་གྲུབ་སེམས་རྩ་འཁྲུག་པའི་ཚེ།
དམ་པའི་ལས་ལ་བར་ཆད་བྱས་པ་ཡིས།
ལས་ངན་མཚོན་ཆ་རང་ལ་འཁོར་བ་ཡིན།
ད་ནི་བར་ཆད་ཐམས་ཅད་སྤང་བར་བྱ།།

22
གང་ལྟར་བྱས་ཀྱང་བླ་མ་མ་མཉེས་ཚེ།
དམ་པའི་ཆོས་ལ་ངོ་ལྐོག་བྱས་པ་ཡིས།
ལས་ངན་མཚོན་ཆ་རང་ལ་འཁོར་བ་ཡིན།
ད་ནི་ཆོས་ལ་ངོ་ལྐོག་ཆུང་བར་བྱ།།

23
སྐྱེ་བོ་ཡོངས་ཀྱིས་ཁ་ལོག་བྱུང་བའི་ཚེ།
ངོ་ཚ་ཁྲེལ་ཡོད་ཁྱད་དུ་བསད་པ་ཡིས།
ལས་ངན་མཚོན་ཆ་རང་ལ་འཁོར་བ་ཡིན།
ད་ནི་མི་བསྲུན་པ་ལ་འཛེམ་པར་བྱ།།

20

When my mind is unclear and my heart is sad, it is
the weapon of my own evil deeds turned upon me
for causing others to sin. From now on I shall renounce
contributing to others' sinning.

21

When I am deeply troubled over my lack of success,
it is the weapon of my own evil deeds turned upon me
for hindering the work of the holy ones. From now on
I shall renounce all hindering.

22

When my guru is displeased with me no matter what I do,
it is the weapon of my own evil deeds turned upon me
for acting duplicitously toward the holy Dharma. From now
on I shall reduce my duplicity toward the Dharma.

23

When everyone contradicts me, it is the weapon
of my own evil deeds turned upon me for belittling shame
and modesty. From now on, I shall avoid rough behavior.

24
འཁོར་རྣམས་འདུས་མ་ཐག་ཏུ་འགྲུས་པའི་ཚེ།
སྡུག་གཤིས་ངན་པ་ཕྱོགས་སུ་བཙོངས་པ་ཡིས།
ལས་ངན་མཚོན་ཆ་རང་ལ་འཁོར་བ་ཡིན།
ད་ནི་གང་ལའང་མི་གཞི་ལེགས་པར་བྱ།།

25
ཉེ་ཚང་ཐམས་ཅད་དགྲ་བོར་ལངས་པའི་ཚེ།
བསམ་པ་ངན་པ་ནང་དུ་བཙུག་པ་ཡིས།
ལས་ངན་མཚོན་ཆ་རང་ལ་འཁོར་བ་ཡིན།
ད་ནི་ཕུག་སྐྱོ་སྒྱུ་ནམ་ཆུང་བར་བྱ།།

26
བད་གཅོང་སྐྲན་དང་དམུ་ཆུས་ན་བའི་ཚེ།
ཁྲིམས་མེད་དཀོར་ལ་བག་མེད་འབགས་པ་ཡིས།
ལས་ངན་མཚོན་ཆ་རང་ལ་འཁོར་བ་ཡིན།
ད་ནི་དཀོར་འཕྲོག་ལ་སོགས་སྤོང་བར་བྱ།།

27
གློ་བུར་འགོ་ནད་ལུས་ལ་ཐེབས་པའི་ཚེ།
དམ་ཚིག་ཉམས་པའི་བྱ་བ་བྱས་པ་ཡིས།
ལས་ངན་མཚོན་ཆ་རང་ལ་འཁོར་བ་ཡིན།
ད་ནི་མི་དགེའི་ལས་རྣམས་སྤོང་བར་བྱ།།

24
When there is disagreement as soon as my companions gather,
it is the weapon of my own evil deeds turned upon me for peddling
my discontent and evil disposition everywhere. From now on
without any ulterior motive, I shall behave well toward all.

25
When all my kin become my enemies, it is the weapon
of my own evil deeds turned upon me for harboring
evil thoughts. From now on I shall reduce my deceit
and guile.

26
When I am sick with consumption or edema, it is the weapon
of my own evil deeds turned upon me for unlawfully and
indiscriminately stealing others' wealth. From now on I shall
renounce plundering others' wealth.

27
When my body is suddenly struck by contagious disease,
it is the weapon of my own evil deeds turned upon me
for committing acts that corrupted my vows. From now on
I shall renounce nonvirtuous acts.

28
ཤེས་བྱ་ཀུན་ལ་བློ་གྲོས་རྨོངས་པའི་ཚེ།
བཞག་ཏུ་འོས་པ་ཆོས་ལ་བྱས་པ་ཡིས།
ལས་ངན་མཚོན་ཆ་རང་ལ་འཁོར་བ་ཡིན།
ད་ནི་ཐོས་སོགས་ཤེས་རབ་བསྒོམ་པར་བྱ།།

29
ཆོས་ལ་སྤྱོད་ཚེ་གཉིད་ཀྱིས་ནོན་པའི་ཚེ།
དམ་པའི་ཆོས་ལ་སྒྲིབ་པ་བསགས་པ་ཡིས།
ལས་ངན་མཚོན་ཆ་རང་ལ་འཁོར་བ་ཡིན།
ད་ནི་ཆོས་ཕྱིར་དཀའ་བ་སྤྱད་པར་བྱ།།

30
ཉོན་མོངས་ལ་དགའ་རྣམ་གཡེང་ཆེ་བའི་ཚེ།
མི་རྟག་འཁོར་བའི་ཉེས་དམིགས་མ་བསྒོམས་པས།
ལས་ངན་མཚོན་ཆ་རང་ལ་འཁོར་བ་ཡིན།
ད་ནི་འཁོར་བར་ཡིད་འབྱུང་ཆེ་བར་བྱ།།

31
ཅི་ཙུག་བྱས་ཀྱང་མར་འགྲོར་ཤོར་བའི་ཚེ།
ལས་དང་རྒྱུ་འབྲས་ཁྱད་དུ་བསད་པ་ཡིས།
ལས་ངན་མཚོན་ཆ་རང་ལ་འཁོར་བ་ཡིན།
ད་ནི་བསོད་ནམས་གསོག་ལ་འབད་པར་བྱ།།

28

When my intellect is blind toward all that is worth knowing, it is the weapon of my own evil deeds turned upon me for claiming as the Dharma what ought to be put aside. From now on I shall cultivate the wisdom that comes from study, examination, and meditation.

29

When I am overcome by sleep while practicing Dharma, it is the weapon of my own evil deeds turned upon me for piling up obscurations to the holy Dharma. From now on I shall undergo hardship for the sake of the Dharma.

30

When I delight in the afflictions and am greatly distracted, it is the weapon of my own evil deeds turned upon me for not meditating upon impermanence and the shortcomings of cyclic existence. From now on I shall increase my dissatisfaction for cyclic existence.

31

When things get worse no matter what I do, it is the weapon of my own evil deeds turned upon me for disparaging moral causality and dependent origination. From now on I shall strive to accumulate merit.

32

རིམ་གྲོ་བྱས་ཚད་ལོག་པར་སོང་བའི་ཚེ།
ནག་པོའི་ཕྱོགས་ལ་རེ་ལྟོས་བྱས་པ་ཡིས།
ལས་ངན་མཚོན་ཆ་རང་ལ་འཁོར་བ་ཡིན།
ད་ནི་ནག་པོའི་ཕྱོགས་ལས་བཟློག་པར་བྱ།།

33

དཀོན་མཆོག་གསུམ་ལ་གསོལ་བ་མ་ཐེབས་ཚེ།
སངས་རྒྱས་པ་ལ་ཡིད་ཆེས་མ་བྱས་པས།
ལས་ངན་མཚོན་ཆ་རང་ལ་འཁོར་བ་ཡིན།
ད་ནི་དཀོན་མཆོག་ཁོ་ན་བསྟེན་པར་བྱ།།

34

རྣམ་རྟོག་གྲིབ་དང་གདོན་དུ་ལངས་པའི་ཚེ།
ལྷ་དང་སྔགས་ལ་སྡིག་པ་བསགས་པ་ཡིས།
ལས་ངན་མཚོན་ཆ་རང་ལ་འཁོར་བ་ཡིན།
ད་ནི་རྣམ་རྟོག་ཐམས་ཅད་གཞོམ་པར་བྱ།།

35

དབང་མེད་མི་ལྟར་ཕྱིས་སུ་འཁྱམས་པའི་ཚེ།
བླ་མ་ལ་སོགས་གནས་ནས་བསྐྲད་པ་ཡིས།
ལས་ངན་མཚོན་ཆ་རང་ལ་འཁོར་བ་ཡིན།
ད་ནི་གང་ཡང་ཡུལ་ནས་དབྱུང་མི་བྱ།།

32
When all the religious rites I perform go awry, it is
the weapon of my own evil deeds turned upon me
for looking to the dark quarter for help. From now on
I shall turn away from the dark quarter.

33
When my prayers to the Three Jewels go unanswered,
it is the weapon of my own evil deeds turned upon me
for not believing in buddhahood. From now on I shall rely
on the Three Jewels alone.

34
When conceptual construction rises up as pollution demons and evil spirits, it is the weapon of my own evil deeds turned upon me for sinning against the gods and mantras. From now on I shall crush all conceptual construction.

35
When I wander far from home like a helpless person, it is the weapon of my own evil deeds turned upon me for driving spiritual teachers and others from their homes. From now on I shall not expel anyone from their home.

36
སད་སེར་ལ་སོགས་མི་འདོད་བྱུང་བའི་ཚེ།
དམ་ཚིག་ཚུལ་ཁྲིམས་ཚུལ་བཞིན་མ་བསྲུངས་བས།
ལས་ངན་མཚོན་ཆ་རང་ལ་འཁོར་བ་ཡིན།
ད་ནི་དམ་ཚིག་ལ་སོགས་གཙང་བར་བྱ།།

37
འདོད་པ་ཆེ་ལ་འབྱོར་པས་འཕོངས་པའི་ཚེ།
སྦྱིན་དང་དཀོན་མཆོག་མཆོད་པ་མ་བགྱིས་པས།
ལས་ངན་མཚོན་ཆ་རང་ལ་འཁོར་བ་ཡིན།
ད་ནི་མཆོད་སྦྱིན་དག་ལ་བརྩོན་པར་བྱ།།

38
སྐྱེ་གཟུགས་ངན་ཏེ་འཁོར་གྱིས་བརྙས་པའི་ཚེ།
སྐུ་གཟུགས་ངན་བཞེངས་ཁོང་ཁྲོས་དཀྲུགས་པ་ཡིས།
ལས་ངན་མཚོན་ཆ་རང་ལ་འཁོར་བ་ཡིན།
ད་ནི་ལྷ་བཞེངས་དང་རྒྱུད་རིང་བར་བྱ།།

39
གང་ལྟར་བྱས་ཀྱང་ཆགས་སྡང་འཁྲུགས་པའི་ཚེ།
མ་རུངས་རྒྱུད་ངན་རེངས་སུ་བཅུག་པ་ཡིས།
ལས་ངན་མཚོན་ཆ་རང་ལ་འཁོར་བ་ཡིན།
ད་ནི་རེངས་ཁྲེད་དུང་ནས་དབྱུང་བར་བྱ།།

36
When calamities occur like frost and hail, it is the weapon of my own evil deeds turned upon me for not properly guarding my vows and moral conduct. From now on I shall keep my vows and moral conduct pure.

37
When I, a greedy person, lose my wealth, it is the weapon of my own evil deeds turned upon me for not giving charity or making offerings to the Three Jewels. From now on I will zealously make offerings and give charity.

38
When my companions mistreat me for being ugly, it is the weapon of my own evil deeds turned upon me for venting my rage by erecting ugly images. From now on I shall erect images of the gods and be slow to anger.

39
When lust and hate are stirred up no matter what I do, it is the weapon of my own evil deeds turned upon me for hardening my malevolent, evil mind. Obstinacy, from now on I shall totally extirpate you!

40
སྒྲུབ་པ་གང་བྱས་དམིགས་སུ་མ་སོང་ཚེ།
ལྟ་བ་ངན་པ་ཁོག་ཏུ་ཞུགས་པ་ཡིས།
ལས་ངན་མཚོན་ཆ་རང་ལ་འཁོར་བ་ཡིན།
ད་ནི་ཅི་བྱེད་གཞན་དོན་ཉིད་དུ་བྱ།།

41
དགེ་སྦྱོར་བྱས་ཀྱང་རང་རྒྱུད་མ་ཐུལ་ཚེ།
ཚེ་འདིའི་ཆེ་ཐབས་དང་དུ་བླངས་པ་ཡིས།
ལས་ངན་མཚོན་ཆ་རང་ལ་འཁོར་བ་ཡིན།
ད་ནི་ཐར་པ་འདོད་ལ་བསྒྲིམ་པར་བྱ།།

42
འདུག་མ་ཐག་ལ་བརྟགས་ཤིང་འགྱོད་པའི་ཚེ།
ཁྲེལ་མེད་གསར་འགྲོགས་མཐོ་ཁ་འགྲིམས་པ་ཡིས།
ལས་ངན་མཚོན་ཆ་རང་ལ་འཁོར་བ་ཡིན།
ད་ནི་གང་ལའང་འགྲོགས་ལུགས་གཟབ་པར་བྱ།།

43
གཞན་གྱི་མུག་སྐྱོས་རང་ཉིད་བསླུས་པའི་ཚེ།
རང་འདོད་ང་རྒྱལ་ལྟོགས་འདོད་ཆེས་པ་ཡིས།
ལས་ངན་མཚོན་ཆ་རང་ལ་འཁོར་བ་ཡིན།
ད་ནི་གང་ལའང་མངོན་མཚན་ཆུང་བར་བྱ།།

40
When none of my practices reach their goal, it is the weapon of my own evil deeds turned upon me for internalizing a pernicious view. From now on, whatever I do shall be solely for the sake of others.

41
When I cannot control my own mind even though I engage in religious activity, it is the weapon of my own evil deeds turned upon me for concentrating on my own aggrandizement in the present life. From now on I shall concentrate on the desire for liberation.

42
When I despair as soon as I've sat down and reflected, it is the weapon of my own evil deeds turned upon me for shamelessly flitting about from one new friend of high status to another. From now on I shall be serious about my friendships with everyone.

43
When I am deceived by others' cunning, it is the weapon of my own evil deeds turned upon me for increasing my selfishness, pride, and insatiable greed. From now on I shall markedly reduce all of them.

44
ཉན་རང་ཆགས་སྡང་གཡོས་སུ་སོང་བའི་ཚེ།
བདུད་ཀྱི་སྐྱོན་རྣམས་སྙིང་ལ་མ་བསམས་པས།
ལས་ངན་མཚོན་ཆ་རང་ལ་འཁོར་བ་ཡིན།
ད་ནི་འགལ་རྐྱེན་བརྟགས་ནས་སྤང་བར་བྱ།།

45
བཟང་བྱས་ཐམས་ཅད་ངན་དུ་སོང་བའི་ཚེ།
དྲིན་ལན་ཐམས་ཅད་ལོག་པར་བཅལ་བ་ཡིས།
ལས་ངན་མཚོན་ཆ་རང་ལ་འཁོར་བ་ཡིན།
ད་ནི་དྲིན་ལན་སྤྱི་བོས་བླང་བར་བྱ།།

46
མདོར་ན་མི་འདོད་ཐོག་ཏུ་བབ་པ་རྣམས།
མགར་བ་རང་གི་རལ་གྲིས་བསད་པ་ལྟར།
ལས་ངན་མཚོན་ཆ་རང་ལ་འཁོར་བ་ཡིན།
ད་ནི་སྡིག་པའི་ལས་ལ་བག་ཡོད་བྱ།།

47
ངན་སོང་རྣམས་སུ་སྡུག་བསྔལ་སྨྱོང་བ་ཡང་།
མདའ་མཁན་རང་གི་མདའ་ཡིས་བསད་པ་ལྟར།
ལས་ངན་མཚོན་ཆ་རང་ལ་འཁོར་བ་ཡིན།
ད་ནི་སྡིག་པའི་ལས་ལ་བག་ཡོད་བྱ།།

44

When I am sidetracked by attachment or aversion while studying
or teaching, it is the weapon of my own evil deeds turned upon me
for not considering my own devilish faults. From now on I shall
examine these impediments and abandon them.

45

When all the good I've done turns out badly, it is the
weapon of my own evil deeds turned upon me for repaying
kindness with ingratitude. From now on I shall very
respectfully repay kindness.

46

In short, when calamities befall me, it is the weapon
of my own evil deeds turned upon me, like a smith killed
by his own sword. From now on I shall be heedful
of my own sinful actions.

47

When I experience suffering in the wretched states of existence,
it is the weapon of my own evil deeds turned upon me, like a
fletcher killed by his own arrow. From now on I shall be heedful
of my own sinful actions.

48
ཁྲིམ་གྱི་སྡུག་བསྔལ་ཐོག་ཏུ་བབ་པ་ཡང་།
བསྐྱངས་པའི་བུ་ཚས་ཕ་མ་བསད་པ་ལྟར།
ལས་ངན་མཚོན་ཆ་རང་ལ་འཁོར་བ་ཡིན།
ད་ནི་རྟག་པར་རབ་ཏུ་འབྱུང་བར་རིགས།།

49
དེ་ལྟར་ལགས་པས་དགྲ་བོ་བདག་གིས་ཟིན།
འཇབས་ནས་བསླུས་པའི་ཆོམ་རྐུན་བདག་གྱིས་ཟིན།
རང་དུ་བརྫུས་ནས་བསླུས་པའི་ཟོག་པོ་ནི།
ཨེ་མ་བདག་འཛིན་འདི་ཡིན་ཐེ་ཚོམ་མེད།།

50
ད་ནི་ལས་ཀྱི་མཚོན་ཆ་ཀླད་ལ་འཁྱུར།
ཁྲོས་པའི་ཚུལ་གྱིས་ལན་གསུམ་ཀླད་ལ་བསྐོར།
བདེན་གཉིས་ཞབས་བརྒྱད་ཐབས་ཤེས་སྤྱན་མིག་གདངས།
སྟོབས་བཞིའི་མཆེ་བ་གཙིགས་ལ་དགྲ་ལ་བསྣུན།།

51
དགྲ་བོ་གཟིར་བའི་རིག་སྔགས་རྒྱལ་པོ་ཡང་།
འཁོར་བའི་ནགས་སུ་རང་དབང་མ་མཆིས་པར།
ལས་ཀྱི་མཚོན་ཆ་ཐོགས་ནས་རྒྱུག་པ་ཡི།
བདག་འཛིན་འགོང་པོ་ཞེས་པའི་གདུག་རྩུབ་ཅན།
རང་གཞན་ཕུང་དུ་འཇུག་པའི་དམ་ཉམས་ཁུག།

48
When the sufferings of the householder befall me, it is the weapon of my own evil deeds turned upon me, like parents killed by their cherished son. From now on it is right for me to leave worldly life forever.

49
Since that's the way it is, I seize the enemy! I seize the thief who ambushed and deceived me, the hypocrite who deceived me disguised as myself. Aha! It is ego-clinging, without a doubt.

50
Now, O Yamāntaka, raise the weapon of action and spin it furiously over your head three times. Spread far apart your feet, which are the two truths, open wide your eyes of method and wisdom, and bare your fangs of the four powers and pierce the enemy!

51
O King of Spells who torments the enemy, summon that vow-breaker who is destroying me and others, that savage called "Ego-Clinging, the Enchanter," who, brandishing the weapon of action, runs uncontrollably through the jungle of cyclic existence.

52
ཁུག་ཅིག་ཁུག་ཅིག་ཁྲོ་བོ་གཤིན་རྗེ་གཤེད།
རྒྱོབ་ཅིག་རྒྱོབ་ཅིག་དགྲ་བདག་སྙིང་ལ་བསྣུན།།
ཕུང་བྱེད་རྟོག་པའི་མགོ་ལ་ཆེམས་སེ་ཆེམས།
དགྲ་བདག་གཤེད་མའི་སྙིང་ལ་མཱ་ར་ཡ།།

53
ཧཱུྃ་ཧཱུྃ་ ཡི་དམ་ཆེན་པོ་རྫུ་འཕྲུལ་སྐྱེད།
ཛཿ ཛཿ དགྲ་བོ་འདི་ནི་དམ་ལ་ཐོགས།
ཕཊ་ཕཊ་ཆིང་བ་ཐམས་ཅད་བསྒྲལ་དུ་གསོལ།
ཚཤིག་ཚཤིག་འཛིན་པའི་མདུད་པ་བཅད་དུ་གསོལ།།

54
ཚུར་བྱོན་ཡི་དམ་ཁྲོ་བོ་གཤིན་རྗེའི་གཤེད།
འཁོར་བའི་ལས་ཀྱི་འདམ་རྫབ་སྦྱོར་བ་ཡི།
ལས་དང་ཉོན་མོངས་དུག་ལྔའི་རྒྱལ་པ་འདི།
ད་ལྟ་ཉིད་དུ་ཤག་ཤག་དབྲལ་དུ་གསོལ།།

55
ངན་སོང་གསུམ་དུ་སྡུག་ལ་བསྐྱལ་གྱུར་ཀྱང་།
བྲེད་མི་ཤེས་པར་རྒྱུ་ལ་རྒྱུག་པ་ཡི།
ཕུང་བྱེད་རྟོག་པའི་མགོ་ལ་ཆེམས་སེ་ཆེམས།
དགྲ་བདག་གཤེད་མའི་སྙིང་ལ་མཱ་ར་ཡ།།

52

Call him, call him, wrathful Yamāntaka! Beat him, beat him, pierce the heart of the enemy, Ego! Roar and thunder on the head of the destroyer, false construction! Mortally strike at the heart of the butcher, the enemy, Ego!

53

Hūṃ! Hūṃ! O great tutelary deity, produce your miraculous apparitions! Dza! Dza! Bind the enemy tightly! Phaṭ! Phaṭ! I beseech you to release me from all fetters! Shig! Shig! I beseech you to cut the knot of clinging!

54

Approach, great tutelary deity Yamāntaka. I beseech you at this very moment to rip to shreds this leather sack of actions and the five poisonous afflictions that mire me in the mud of worldly action.

55

Although it has brought me suffering in the three wretched states of existence, not knowing enough to fear it, I rush to its cause. Roar and thunder on the head of the destroyer, false construction! Mortally strike at the heart of the butcher, the enemy, Ego!

56
སྐྱིད་འདོད་ཆེ་ལ་དེ་རྒྱུ་ཚོགས་མི་གསོག
སྡུག་སྲན་ཆུང་ལ་འདོད་ནག་ཧམ་སེམས་ཆེ།
ཕུང་བྱེད་རྟོག་པའི་མགོ་ལ་ཆེམས་སེ་ཆེམས།
དགྲ་བདག་གཤེད་མའི་སྙིང་ལ་མཱ་ར་ཡ།།

57
འདོད་ཐག་ཉེ་ལ་སྒྲུབ་ལ་བརྩོན་འགྲུས་ཆུང་།
བྱ་བྱེད་མང་ལ་གང་ཡང་མཐར་མི་འཁྱོལ།
ཕུང་བྱེད་རྟོག་པའི་མགོ་ལ་ཆེམས་སེ་ཆེམས།
དགྲ་བདག་གཤེད་མའི་སྙིང་ལ་མཱ་ར་ཡ།།

58
གསར་འགྲོགས་ཆེ་ལ་ཁྲེལ་གཞུང་ཕྱི་ཐག་ཆུང་།
ལྟོ་འདུན་ཆེ་ལ་རྐུ་འཕྲོག་འཚོལ་འགྲོ་རེམ།
ཕུང་བྱེད་རྟོག་པའི་མགོ་ལ་ཆེམས་སེ་ཆེམས།
དགྲ་བདག་གཤེད་མའི་སྙིང་ལ་མཱ་ར་ཡ།།

59
ཁ་གསག་གཞོགས་སློང་མཁས་ལ་ཞེ་སྨུག་ཆེ།
བསླུ་བསོག་རེམ་ལ་ཡོད་ཀྱང་སེར་ནས་བཅིངས།
ཕུང་བྱེད་རྟོག་པའི་མགོ་ལ་ཆེམས་སེ་ཆེམས།
དགྲ་བདག་གཤེད་མའི་སྙིང་ལ་མཱ་ར་ཡ།།

56

Although my desire for comfort is great, I don't accumulate its causes. Although my tolerance for suffering is small, my desire and greed are great. Roar and thunder on the head of the destroyer, false construction! Mortally strike at the heart of the butcher, the enemy, Ego!

57

Although that which I desire is near at hand, my effort to achieve it is small. Although my projects are many, none of them are completed. Roar and thunder on the head of the destroyer, false construction! Mortally strike at the heart of the butcher, the enemy, Self!

58

Although I have many new friendships, my modesty and friendships are of short duration. Although I freeload off of others, I eagerly pursue those who pilfer. Roar and thunder on the head of the destroyer, false construction! Mortally strike at the heart of the butcher, the enemy, Ego!

59

Although I am skilled at flattery and asking for things indirectly, my despair is great. Although I assiduously amass things, miserliness binds me. Roar and thunder on the head of the destroyer, false construction! Mortally strike at the heart of the butcher, the enemy, Ego!

60

ཀུན་ལ་བྲུས་པ་ཆུང་ལ་སྨུག་ཡུས་ཆེ།
རང་ལ་ཁྲེར་ཁ་མེད་ལ་ཇམ་པོ་ཆེ།
ཕུང་བྱེད་རྟོག་པའི་མགོ་ལ་ཆེམས་སེ་ཆེམས།
དགྲ་བདག་གཤེད་མའི་སྙིང་ལ་སྨྲ་ར་ཡ།།

61

སློབ་དཔོན་མང་ལ་དམ་ཚིག་འཁུར་ཤེད་ཆུང་།
སློབ་མ་མང་ལ་ཕན་འདོགས་སྐྱོང་རན་ཆུང་།
ཕུང་བྱེད་རྟོག་པའི་མགོ་ལ་ཆེམས་སེ་ཆེམས།
དགྲ་བདག་གཤེད་མའི་སྙིང་ལ་སྨྲ་ར་ཡ།།

62

ཁས་བླངས་ཆེ་ལ་ཕན་པའི་ཉམས་ལེན་ཆུང་།
སྙན་པ་ཆེ་ལ་བརྟགས་ན་ལྷ་འདྲེས་ཁྲེལ།
ཕུང་བྱེད་རྟོག་པའི་མགོ་ལ་ཆེམས་སེ་ཆེམས།
དགྲ་བདག་གཤེད་མའི་སྙིང་ལ་སྨྲ་ར་ཡ།།

63

ཐོས་རྒྱ་ཆུང་ལ་སྟོང་སྐད་ཐད་ཁམ་ཆེ།
ལུང་རྒྱ་ཆུང་ལ་མི་རྟོགས་དགུ་ལ་རྟོགས།
ཕུང་བྱེད་རྟོག་པའི་མགོ་ལ་ཆེམས་སེ་ཆེམས།
དགྲ་བདག་གཤེད་མའི་སྙིང་ལ་སྨྲ་ར་ཡ།།

60

Although whatever I have done has been insignificant, I am swollen with pride. Although I have no reputation, my hunger for it is great. Roar and thunder on the head of the destroyer, false construction! Mortally strike at the heart of the butcher, the enemy, Ego!

61

Although my preceptors are many, my ability to keep my vows is small. Although my disciples are many, I give little time to help and look after them. Roar and thunder on the head of the destroyer, false construction! Mortally strike at the heart of the butcher, the enemy, Ego!

62

Although my promises are many, my practical assistance is minimal. Although my fame is great, if it were examined, the gods and demons would put me to shame. Roar and thunder on the head of the destroyer, false construction! Mortally strike at the heart of the butcher, the enemy, Ego!

63

Although my learning is scant, my penchant for empty verbiage is great. Although the extent of my religious instruction is slight, I pretend to understand everything. Roar and thunder on the head of the destroyer, false construction! Mortally strike at the heart of the butcher, the enemy, Ego!

64
འཁོར་གཡོག་མང་ལ་འཁུར་མཁན་སུ་ཡང་མེད།
དཔོན་པོ་མང་ལ་རྒྱབ་རྟེན་མགོན་དང་བྲལ།
ཕུང་བྱེད་རྟོག་པའི་མགོ་ལ་ཆེམས་སེ་ཆེམས།
དགྲ་བདག་གཤེད་མའི་སྙིང་ལ་མཱ་ར་ཡ།།

65
གོ་ས་མཐོ་ལ་ཡོན་ཏན་འདྲེ་བས་ཆུང་།
བླ་མ་ཆེ་ལ་ཆགས་སྡང་བདུད་ལས་རྔུབ།
ཕུང་བྱེད་རྟོག་པའི་མགོ་ལ་ཆེམས་སེ་ཆེམས།
དགྲ་བདག་གཤེད་མའི་སྙིང་ལ་མཱ་ར་ཡ།།

66
ལྟ་བ་མཐོ་ལ་སྤྱོད་པ་ཁྱི་ལས་ངན།
ཡོན་ཏན་མང་ལ་གཞི་མ་རླུང་ལ་ཤོར།
ཕུང་བྱེད་རྟོག་པའི་མགོ་ལ་ཆེམས་སེ་ཆེམས།
དགྲ་བདག་གཤེད་མའི་སྙིང་ལ་མཱ་ར་ཡ།།

67
ཞེ་འདོད་ཐམས་ཅད་རང་གི་ཕུགས་སུ་ཞུགས།
གྲོགས་སྐོར་ཐམས་ཅད་དོན་མེད་གཞན་ལ་བྱེད།
ཕུང་བྱེད་རྟོག་པའི་མགོ་ལ་ཆེམས་སེ་ཆེམས།
དགྲ་བདག་གཤེད་མའི་སྙིང་ལ་མཱ་ར་ཡ།།

64
Although my companions and underlings are numerous, not one is dependable. Although I have many masters, not one is a reliable protector. Roar and thunder on the head of the destroyer, false construction! Mortally strike at the heart of the butcher, the enemy, Ego!

65
Although I have high status, my merit is less than an evil spirit's. Although I am a great religious teacher, my passions are grosser than a demon's. Roar and thunder on the head of the destroyer, false construction! Mortally strike at the heart of the butcher, the enemy, Ego!

66
Although my view is lofty, my behavior is worse than a dog's. Although my good qualities are many, their basis is carried off by the wind. Roar and thunder on the head of the destroyer, false construction! Mortally strike at the heart of the butcher, the enemy, Ego!

67
All desires enter into me and I blame all my quarrels on others for no reason. Roar and thunder on the head of the destroyer, false construction! Mortally strike at the heart of the butcher, the enemy, Ego!

68

ངར་སྒྲིག་གྱོན་ནས་སྤུང་སྐྱོབ་འདྲེ་ལ་ཞུ།།
སྡོམ་པ་བླངས་ནས་སྤྱོད་ལམ་བདུད་དང་བསྟུན།
ཕུང་བྱེད་རྟོག་པའི་མགོ་ལ་ཆེམས་སེ་ཆེམས།
དགྲ་བདག་གཤེད་མའི་སྙིང་ལ་མཱ་ར་ཡ།།

69

བདེ་སྐྱིད་ལྷ་ཡིས་བྱིན་ནས་སྡུག་འདྲེ་མཆོད།
འདྲེན་པ་ཆོས་ཀྱིས་བྱས་ནས་དཀོན་མཆོག་བསླུ།
ཕུང་བྱེད་རྟོག་པའི་མགོ་ལ་ཆེམས་སེ་ཆེམས།
དགྲ་བདག་གཤེད་མའི་སྙིང་ལ་མཱ་ར་ཡ།།

70

རྟག་ཏུ་དགོན་པར་བསྡད་ནས་གཡེང་བས་ཁྲེར།
དམ་ཆོས་གཙུག་ལག་ཞུས་ནས་མོ་བོན་སྐྱོང་།
ཕུང་བྱེད་རྟོག་པའི་མགོ་ལ་ཆེམས་སེ་ཆེམས།
དགྲ་བདག་གཤེད་མའི་སྙིང་ལ་མཱ་ར་ཡ།།

68

Although I have put on the saffron robe, I appeal to evil spirits for protection. Although I have taken religious vows, my behavior is demonic. Roar and thunder on the head of the destroyer, false construction! Mortally strike at the heart of the butcher, the enemy, Ego!

69

Although the gods give me happiness, I worship evil spirits.
Although the Dharma guides me, I deceive the Three Jewels.
Roar and thunder on the head of the destroyer, false construction!
Mortally strike at the heart of the butcher, the enemy, Ego!

70

Although I have always resorted to secluded places, I am carried away by distraction. Although I request instruction in the holy Dharma and the religious sciences, I cherish divination and shamanism.
Roar and thunder on the head of the destroyer, false construction!
Mortally strike at the heart of the butcher, the enemy, Ego!

71
རྒྱལ་ཁྲིམས་ཐར་ལམ་བོར་ནས་ཕ་ཁྲིམ་འཛིན།
བདེ་སྐྱིད་རྒྱ་ལ་ཕོ་ནས་སྡུག་ལ་སྟེག།
ཕུང་བྱེད་རྟོག་པའི་མགོ་ལ་ཆེམས་སེ་ཆེམས།
དགྲ་བདག་གཤེད་མའི་སྙིང་ལ་མྣར་ར་ཡ།།

72
ཐར་པའི་འཇུག་ངོགས་བོར་ནས་ས་མཐའ་འགྲིམ།
མི་ལུས་རིན་ཆེན་རྙེད་ནས་དམྱལ་ཁམས་སྒྲུབ།
ཕུང་བྱེད་རྟོག་པའི་མགོ་ལ་ཆེམས་སེ་ཆེམས།
དགྲ་བདག་གཤེད་མའི་སྙིང་ལ་མྣར་ར་ཡ།།

73
ཆོས་ཀྱི་འགྱུར་ཁྱད་བཞག་ནས་ཚོང་ཁེ་སྒྲུབ།
བླ་མའི་ཆོས་གྲྭ་བཞག་ནས་གྲོང་ཡུལ་འགྲིམ།
ཕུང་བྱེད་རྟོག་པའི་མགོ་ལ་ཆེམས་སེ་ཆེམས།
དགྲ་བདག་གཤེད་མའི་སྙིང་ལ་མྣར་ར་ཡ།།

74
རང་གི་འཚོ་བ་བཞག་ནས་འདུ་སྒྲོ་འཕྲོག
རང་གི་ཕ་ཟས་བཞག་ནས་གཞན་ལ་རྐུ།
ཕུང་བྱེད་རྟོག་པའི་མགོ་ལ་ཆེམས་སེ་ཆེམས།
དགྲ་བདག་གཤེད་མའི་སྙིང་ལ་མྣར་ར་ཡ།།

71

Forsaking the moral path to liberation, I cling to my home. Pouring my happiness into the water, I run after suffering. Roar and thunder on the head of the destroyer, false construction! Mortally strike at the heart of the butcher, the enemy, Ego!

72

Turning away from the gateway to liberation, I wander in remote places. Despite acquiring the precious jewel of a human body, I wind up in hell. Roar and thunder on the head of the destroyer, false construction! Mortally strike at the heart of the butcher, the enemy, Ego!

73

Putting aside the particulars of spiritual development, I engage in business. Leaving my guru's school, I idle about the town. Roar and thunder on the head of the destroyer, false construction! Mortally strike at the heart of the butcher, the enemy, Ego!

74

Abandoning my own livelihood, I plunder others' property. Forsaking my parents' food, I rob others of sustenance. Roar and thunder on the head of the destroyer, false construction! Mortally strike at the heart of the butcher, the enemy, Ego!

75
ཨེ་མ་སྙོམ་སྲན་ཆུང་ལ་མདོན་ཞེས་རྗོ།
ལམ་སྣ་མ་ཟིན་དོན་མེད་རྐང་པ་མགྱོགས།
ཕུང་བྱེད་རྟོག་པའི་མགོ་ལ་ཆེམས་སེ་ཆེམས།
དགྲ་བདག་གཤེད་མའི་སྙིང་ལ་མྣར་ར་ཡ།།

76
ཕན་པར་བསླབ་ན་སྡང་སེམས་དགྲ་རུ་འཛིན།
མགོ་སྐོར་བསླུ་ན་སྙིང་མེད་དྲིན་དུ་གཟོ།།
ཕུང་བྱེད་རྟོག་པའི་མགོ་ལ་ཆེམས་སེ་ཆེམས།
དགྲ་བདག་གཤེད་མའི་སྙིང་ལ་མྣར་ར་ཡ།།

77
ནང་མིར་བརྟེན་ན་སྙིང་གཏམ་དགྲ་ལ་འཆད།།
ཕེབས་པར་འགྲོགས་ན་ཁྲེལ་མེད་གློ་སྙིང་རྐུ།
ཕུང་བྱེད་རྟོག་པའི་མགོ་ལ་ཆེམས་སེ་ཆེམས།
དགྲ་བདག་གཤེད་མའི་སྙིང་ལ་མྣར་ར་ཡ།།

78
ཀོ་ལོང་དམ་ལ་རྣམ་རྟོག་སུ་བས་རགས།
འགྲོགས་པར་དཀའ་ལ་གཤིས་ངན་རྒྱུན་དུ་སློང་།
ཕུང་བྱེད་རྟོག་པའི་མགོ་ལ་ཆེམས་སེ་ཆེམས།
དགྲ་བདག་གཤེད་མའི་སྙིང་ལ་མྣར་ར་ཡ།།

75

Aha! Although my endurance for meditation is small, my precognition is sharp. Though I have not realized even the beginning of the path, I run around to no purpose. Roar and thunder on the head of the destroyer, false construction! Mortally strike at the heart of the butcher, the enemy, Ego!

76

When someone gives me useful advice, my hostile mind takes that person for an enemy. When someone deceives me, I repay that heartless one with kindness. Roar and thunder on the head of the destroyer, false construction! Mortally strike at the heart of the butcher, the enemy, Ego!

77

I tell my intimate friends' secrets to their enemies. I shamelessly take advantage of my acquaintances. Roar and thunder on the head of the destroyer, false construction! Mortally strike at the heart of the butcher, the enemy, Ego!

78

My frustration is intense and my thoughts are coarser than everyone else's. I am hard to get along with and I continually provoke others' bad character. Roar and thunder on the head of the destroyer, false construction! Mortally strike at the heart of the butcher, the enemy, Ego!

79
བཙོལ་ན་མི་ཉན་ཟློག་ན་གནོད་པ་སྐྱེལ།
བསྟུན་ན་མི་འདུད་རྒྱང་ན་རྩོད་པ་འཚོལ།
ཕུང་བྱེད་རྟོག་པའི་མགོ་ལ་ཆེམས་སེ་ཆེམས།
དགྲ་བདག་གཤེད་མའི་སྙིང་ལ་མྣྲ་ར་ཡ།།

80
བཀའ་སློ་མི་བདེ་རྟག་པར་འགྲོགས་པར་དཀའ།
ཡོག་ཐུག་མང་ལ་རྟག་ཏུ་འཛིན་པ་དམ།
ཕུང་བྱེད་རྟོག་པའི་མགོ་ལ་ཆེམས་སེ་ཆེམས།
དགྲ་བདག་གཤེད་མའི་སྙིང་ལ་མྣྲ་ར་ཡ།།

81
མཐོ་དམན་ཆེ་ཞིང་དམ་པ་དགྲ་རུ་འཛིན།
འདོད་ཆགས་ཆེ་བས་གཞོན་ནུ་དང་དུ་ལེན།
ཕུང་བྱེད་རྟོག་པའི་མགོ་ལ་ཆེམས་སེ་ཆེམས།
དགྲ་བདག་གཤེད་མའི་སྙིང་ལ་མྣྲ་ར་ཡ།།

82
ཕྱི་ཐག་ཐུང་བས་སྔར་འགྲོགས་རྒྱང་དུ་འཕེན།
གསར་འགྲོགས་ཆེ་བས་ཀུན་ལ་ཁ་བྲོད་འདིངས།
ཕུང་བྱེད་རྟོག་པའི་མགོ་ལ་ཆེམས་སེ་ཆེམས།
དགྲ་བདག་གཤེད་མའི་སྙིང་ལ་མྣྲ་ར་ཡ།།

79

When someone seeks my assistance, I ignore him and secretly cause him harm. When someone agrees with me, I won't concur, but seek quarrels even at a distance. Roar and thunder on the head of the destroyer, false construction! Mortally strike at the heart of the butcher, the enemy, Ego!

80

I do not appreciate advice and I'm always difficult to be with.
Many things offend me and my clinging is always strong.
Roar and thunder on the head of the destroyer, false construction!
Mortally strike at the heart of the butcher, the enemy, Ego!

81

I exalt myself above the high and low and consider holy people my enemies. Because my lust is great, I energetically pursue young people.
Roar and thunder on the head of the destroyer, false construction!
Mortally strike at the heart of the butcher, the enemy, Ego!

82

Because my friendships are of short duration, I cast aside former acquaintances. Because my new friends are many, I lay before them empty promises of enjoyment. Roar and thunder on the head of the destroyer, false construction! Mortally strike at the heart of the butcher, the enemy, Ego!

83
མངོན་ཤེས་མེད་པས་རྫུན་སྐུར་དང་དུ་ལེན།
སྙིང་རྗེ་མེད་པས་བློ་གཏད་སྙིང་ལ་འབྲབ།།
ཕུང་བྱེད་རྟོག་པའི་མགོ་ལ་ཆེམས་སེ་ཆེམས།
དགྲ་བདག་གཤེད་མའི་སྙིང་ལ་མྣ་ར་ཡ།།

84
ཐོས་པ་ཆུང་བས་ཀུན་ལ་སྦྱར་ཚོད་བྱེད།
ལུང་རྒྱ་ཆུང་བས་ཡོངས་ལ་ལོག་ལྟ་སྐྱེ།
ཕུང་བྱེད་རྟོག་པའི་མགོ་ལ་ཆེམས་སེ་ཆེམས།
དགྲ་བདག་གཤེད་མའི་སྙིང་ལ་མྣ་ར་ཡ།།

85
ཆགས་སྡང་གོམས་པས་གཞན་ཕྱོགས་ཡོངས་ལ་སྨོད།
ཕྲག་དོག་གོམས་པས་གཞན་ལ་སྒྲོ་སྐུར་འདེབས།
ཕུང་བྱེད་རྟོག་པའི་མགོ་ལ་ཆེམས་སེ་ཆེམས།
དགྲ་བདག་གཤེད་མའི་སྙིང་ལ་མྣ་ར་ཡ།།

86
སློབ་གཉེར་མ་བྱས་རྒྱ་ཆེན་ཁྱད་དུ་གསོད།
བླ་མ་མ་བསྟེན་ལུང་ལ་སྨོད་པར་བྱེད།
ཕུང་བྱེད་རྟོག་པའི་མགོ་ལ་ཆེམས་སེ་ཆེམས།
དགྲ་བདག་གཤེད་མའི་སྙིང་ལ་མྣ་ར་ཡ།།

83
Having no precognition, I eagerly resort to lying and deprecation. Having no compassion, I snatch away the confidence from others' hearts. Roar and thunder on the head of the destroyer, false construction! Mortally strike at the heart of the butcher, the enemy, Ego!

84
Having studied little, I wildly guess about everything. Since my religious education is slight, I have wrong views about everything. Roar and thunder on the head of the destroyer, false construction! Mortally strike at the heart of the butcher, the enemy, Ego!

85
Habituated to attachment and aversion, I revile everyone opposed to me. Habituated to envy, I slander and deprecate others. Roar and thunder on the head of the destroyer, false construction! Mortally strike at the heart of the butcher, the enemy, Ego!

86
Never studying, I despise the vast teaching. Never relying on a guru, I revile religious instruction. Roar and thunder on the head of the destroyer, false construction! Mortally strike at the heart of the butcher, the enemy, Ego!

87
སྤྱེ་སྤྱོད་མི་འཆད་རང་བཟོ་རྫུན་དུ་སྒྲིག།
དག་སྣང་མ་འབྱོངས་ལབ་ཚད་འབར་ཤ་སྒྲ།
ཕུང་བྱེད་རྟོག་པའི་མགོ་ལ་ཆེམས་སེ་ཆེམས།
དགྲ་བདག་གཤེད་མའི་སྙིང་ལ་མཱ་ར་ཡ།།

88
ཆོས་མིན་ལས་ལ་སྤྱོད་པར་མི་བྱེད་པར།
ལེགས་བཤད་ཡོངས་ལ་སུན་འབྱིན་སྣ་ཚོགས་གཏོང་།
ཕུང་བྱེད་རྟོག་པའི་མགོ་ལ་ཆེམས་སེ་ཆེམས།
དགྲ་བདག་གཤེད་མའི་སྙིང་ལ་མཱ་ར་ཡ།།

89
ངོ་ཚའི་གནས་ལ་ངོ་ཚར་མི་འཛིན་པར།
ངོ་མི་ཚ་ལ་ངོ་ཚའི་ཆོས་ལོག་འཛིན།
ཕུང་བྱེད་རྟོག་པའི་མགོ་ལ་ཆེམས་སེ་ཆེམས།
དགྲ་བདག་གཤེད་མའི་སྙིང་ལ་མཱ་ར་ཡ།།

90
བྱས་ན་རུང་བ་གཅིག་ཀྱང་མི་བྱེད་པར།
མི་རིགས་བྱ་བ་ཐམས་ཅད་བྱེད་པ་ཡིས།
ཕུང་བྱེད་རྟོག་པའི་མགོ་ལ་ཆེམས་སེ་ཆེམས།
དགྲ་བདག་གཤེད་མའི་སྙིང་ལ་མཱ་ར་ཡ།།

87

Instead of explaining the scriptures, I falsely set up my own system. Not having mastered pure vision, I curse and yell. Roar and thunder on the head of the destroyer, false construction! Mortally strike at the heart of the butcher, the enemy, Ego!

88

Without condemning sacrilegious activities, I launch numerous criticisms against all the Buddha's words. Roar and thunder on the head of the destroyer, false construction! Mortally strike at the heart of the butcher, the enemy, Ego!

89

Having no shame about things I should be ashamed of, I am perversely ashamed of the Dharma, which is not something shameful. Roar and thunder on the head of the destroyer, false construction! Mortally strike at the heart of the butcher, the enemy, Ego!

90

No matter what I do, it is never done right; everything I do is inappropriate. Roar and thunder on the head of the destroyer, false construction! Mortally strike at the heart of the butcher, the enemy, Ego!

91
ཨེ་མ་བདག་ལྟའི་འགོང་པོ་འཇོམས་མཛད་པའི།
བདེ་གཤེགས་ཆོས་ཀྱི་སྐུ་མངའ་མཐུ་སྟོབས་ཅན།
བདག་མེད་ཡེ་ཤེས་མཚོན་ཆ་དབྱུག་པོ་ཅན།
ཐེ་ཚོམ་མེད་པར་གླད་ལ་ལན་གསུམ་བསྐོར།།

92
ཧྲམ་སྟོབས་ཆེན་པོས་དགྲ་འདི་བསྒྲལ་དུ་གསོལ།
ཤེས་རབ་ཆེན་པོས་རྟོག་ངན་གཞོམ་དུ་གསོལ།
སྙིང་རྗེ་ཆེན་པོས་ལས་ལས་བསྐྱབ་དུ་གསོལ།
ངེས་པར་བདག་ནི་བརླག་པར་མཛད་དུ་གསོལ།།

93
འཁོར་བ་པ་ལ་དུཿཁ་ཅི་མཆིས་པ།
བདག་འཛིན་འདི་ལ་ངེས་པར་སྤུང་དུ་གསོལ།
གང་ལ་ཉོན་མོངས་དུག་ལྔ་ཅི་མཆིས་པ།
རིགས་མཐུན་འདི་ལ་ངེས་པར་སྤུང་དུ་གསོལ།།

94
འདི་ལྟར་ཉེས་པའི་རྩ་བ་མ་ལུས་པ།
ཐེ་ཚོམ་མེད་པར་རིག་པས་ངོས་ཟིན་ཀྱང་།
ད་དུང་འདི་ཡི་ཁ་འཛིན་གཤེགས་འདེབས་ན།
འཛིན་མཁན་དེ་ཉིད་བརླག་པར་མཛད་དུ་གསོལ།།

91
Aha! You whose strength is that of the ultimate body of the Sugata who conquers the demon of the egotistic view, you wielder of the staff, the weapon of the wisdom of selflessness, turn it over your head three times, without hesitation!

92
I pray you, kill the enemy with your fierce wrath! I pray you, subdue my evil thinking with your great wisdom! I pray you, protect me from my evil actions with your great compassion! I pray you, destroy this Ego once and for all!

93
However much suffering those in cyclic existence may endure, I pray you, heap it surely upon ego-clinging! However many of the five poisonous afflictions anyone may experience, I pray you, heap them surely upon this ego-clinging, which richly deserves them!

94
Although through reasoning I have identified without a doubt all the roots of evil, if you judge that I am still abetting them, I pray you to destroy the holder himself!

95
ད་ནི་ལེ་ལན་ཐམས་ཅད་གཅིག་ལ་བདའ།
སྐྱེ་བོ་ཡོངས་ལ་བཀའ་དྲིན་ཆེ་བར་བསྒོམ།
གཞན་གྱི་མི་འདོད་རང་གི་རྒྱུད་ལ་བླང་།
བདག་གི་དགེ་རྩ་འགྲོ་བ་ཡོངས་ལ་བསྔོ།།

96
དེ་ལྟར་འགྲོ་བ་གཞན་གྱི་སྒོ་གསུམ་གྱིས།
དུས་གསུམ་བགྱིས་པ་བདག་གིས་བླངས་པ་ཡིས།
རྨ་བྱ་དུག་གིས་མདོངས་དང་ལྡན་པ་ལྟར།
ཉོན་མོངས་བྱང་ཆུབ་གྲོགས་སུ་འགྱུར་བར་ཤོག།

97
བདག་གི་དགེ་རྩ་འགྲོ་ལ་སྦྱིན་པ་ཡིས།
བྱ་རོག་དུག་ཟོས་སྨན་གྱིས་སོས་པ་ལྟར།
སྐྱེ་བོ་ཡོངས་ཀྱི་ཐར་པའི་སྲོག་བཟུང་ནས།
བདེ་གཤེགས་སངས་རྒྱས་མྱུར་དུ་ཐོབ་པར་ཤོག།

98
ནམ་ཞིག་བདག་དང་ཕ་མར་གྱུར་པ་རྣམས།
འོག་མིན་གནས་སུ་བྱང་ཆུབ་མ་ཐོབ་པར།
འགྲོ་བ་དྲུག་ཏུ་ལས་ཀྱིས་འཁྱམས་ན་ཡང་།
ཕན་ཚུན་གཅིག་སེམས་གཅིག་གིས་འཛིན་པར་ཤོག།

95
Now, drive all blame onto one thing! I shall cultivate gratitude toward all beings, take into my mind what others abhor, and turn over the roots of my virtue to all beings.

96
Just as the pattern of colors in a peacock's feather is due to poison, may the afflictions be transformed into the aids to enlightenment by my taking on the physical, verbal, and mental deeds of other living beings, past, present, and future.

97
I give the roots of my virtue to living beings so they may be cured, as a poisoned crow is healed by medicine. I dedicate my life to the liberation of all beings so they may quickly achieve the buddhahood of the Sugata!

98
Until I and those who have been my parents have attained enlightenment in the Highest Realm, may we support each other with a single thought, even when wandering about in the six states of existence owing to our actions.

99
དེ་ཚེ་འགྲོ་བ་གཅིག་གི་དོན་དུ་ཡང་།
ཉོན་སོང་གསུམ་དུ་བདག་གིས་ཡོངས་ཞུགས་ནས།
སེམས་དཔའ་ཆེན་པོའི་སྤྱོད་པ་མ་ཉམས་པར།
ཉོན་སོང་སྡུག་བསྔལ་བདག་གིས་དྲངས་པར་ཤོག།

100
དེ་མ་ཐག་ཏུ་དམྱལ་བའི་བསྲུང་མ་རྣམས།
བདག་ལ་བླ་མའི་འདུ་ཤེས་སྐྱེས་གྱུར་ནས།
མཚོན་ཆ་དག་ཀྱང་མེ་ཏོག་ཆར་དུ་གྱུར།
གནོད་པ་མེད་པར་ཞི་བདེ་འཕེལ་བར་ཤོག།

101
ཉོན་སོང་བ་ཡང་མངོན་ཤེས་གཟུངས་ཐོབ་ནས།
ལྷ་མིའི་ལུས་བླངས་བྱང་ཆུབ་སེམས་བསྐྱེད་དེ།
བདག་གི་དྲིན་ལན་ཆོས་ཀྱིས་གཟོ་བར་ཤོག།
བདག་ལ་བླ་མར་བཟུང་ནས་བསྟེན་པར་ཤོག།

102
དེ་ཚེ་མཐོ་རིས་འགྲོ་བ་ཐམས་ཅད་ཀྱང་།
བདག་དང་མཚུངས་པར་བདག་མེད་རབ་བསྒོམས་ནས།
སྲིད་དང་ཞི་བ་རྣམ་པར་མི་རྟོག་པར།
མཉམ་པ་ཉིད་དུ་ཉིང་འཛིན་བསྒོམ་པར་ཤོག།
མཉམ་པ་ཉིད་དུ་རང་ངོ་འཕྲོད་པར་ཤོག།

99

When I enter the three wretched states of existence for the sake of even one living being, may I save him or her from the suffering of that wretched destiny without compromising a great being's way of life.

100

At that very instant, the guards of hell will realize that I am a guru, and their weapons will turn into a rain of flowers. May peace flourish unharmed!

101

Even those in wretched states of existence shall obtain superknowledge and mantras, assume the bodies of gods and men, and generate bodhicitta. In return for my kindness, may they repay me with Dharma practice! Taking me as their guru, may they properly attend me!

102

Then, may all the beings in higher realms also deeply meditate on selflessness, just as I do, cultivating the nonconceptual meditative absorption on the identity of existence and peace. May they recognize this identity!

103
དེ་ལྟར་བྱས་ན་དགྲ་འདི་ཆོམས་པར་འགྱུར།
དེ་ལྟར་བྱས་ན་རྣམ་རྟོག་ཆོམས་འགྱུར་ཏེ།
མི་རྟོག་ཡེ་ཤེས་བདག་མེད་བསྒྲོམ་འགྱུར་ཏེ།
གཟུགས་སྐུའི་རྒྱུ་འབྲས་ཅི་སྟེ་ཐོབ་མི་འགྱུར།།

104
ཀ་ཡེ་དེ་དག་ཐམས་ཅད་རྟེན་འབྲེལ་ཡིན།
རྟེན་འབྲེལ་རྟོགས་པ་རང་ཚུགས་མེད་པ་ཡིན།
ཕར་བསྒྱུར་ཚུར་བསྒྱུར་བརྟན་སྣང་སྒྱུ་མ་ཡིན།
མགལ་མེ་བཞིན་དུ་སྣང་བའི་གཟུགས་བརྙན་ཡིན།།

105
ཆུ་ཤིང་བཞིན་དུ་སྦྲོག་ལ་སྙིང་པོ་མེད།།
ལྦུ་བ་བཞིན་དུ་ཆོ་ལ་སྙིང་པོ་མེད།།
ཁུག་སྣ་བཞིན་དུ་བཏུད་ནས་འཇིག་པ་ཡིན།
སྨིག་རྒྱུ་བཞིན་དུ་རྒྱང་ནས་མཛེས་པ་ཡིན།
མེ་ལོང་གཟུགས་བརྙན་ལྟ་བུར་བདེན་བདེན་འདྲ།
སྤྲིན་དང་ན་བུན་བཞིན་དུ་སྟོད་སྟོད་འདྲ།།

103

Having done so I will crush the enemy. Having done so I will crush conceptual construction. After cultivating selflessness through nonconceptual wisdom, how can I not obtain the causes and effects of the form body?

104

Now hear this! Everything is dependently co-arisen.
Being dependently co-arisen, they are not independent.
Changing this way and that, they are false appearances and illusions;
they are images that appear like a whirling firebrand.

105

Like the plantain tree, life has no inner core. Like a bubble, a lifetime has no inner core. Like a mist, it dissipates upon close examination. Like a mirage, it is beautiful from afar.
Like a reflection in a mirror, it seems as if it were really true.
Like clouds and fog, it seems as if it were really stable.

106
དགྲ་བདག་གཤེད་མ་འདི་ནི་དེ་བཞིན་དུ།
ཡོད་ཡོད་འདྲ་སྟེ་ནམ་ཡང་ཡོད་མ་ཡིན།
བདེན་བདེན་འདྲ་སྟེ་གང་དུའང་བདེན་མ་མྱོང་།
སྣང་སྣང་འདྲ་སྟེ་སྒྲོ་སྐུར་ཡུལ་ལས་འདས།།

107
དེ་ལ་ལས་ཀྱི་འཁོར་ལོ་གང་ཞིག་ཡོད།
འདི་ནི་དེ་ལྟར་རང་བཞིན་མེད་ན་ཡང་།
ཆུ་ཕོར་གང་དུ་ཟླ་བའི་གཟུགས་བརྙན་ཤར།།
ལས་འབྲས་འདི་ནི་བརྫུན་པ་སྣ་ཚོགས་བཀྲ།
སྣང་བ་ཙམ་དུ་བླང་དོར་བྱའོ་ཨང་།།

108
རྨི་ལམ་ཡུལ་དུ་བསྐལ་པའི་མེ་འབར་ཚེ།
རང་བཞིན་མེད་ཀྱང་ཚ་བས་འཇིགས་སྐྲག་ལྟར།
དམྱལ་ཁམས་སོགས་ལ་རང་བཞིན་མེད་ན་ཡང་།
བཙོ་བསྲེགས་ལ་སོགས་འཇིགས་པས་སྐྱང་བར་བྱ།།

106

This butcher, the enemy Ego, is just the same. It seems as if it really exists, but it has never really existed. It seems as if it is really true, but it has never been really true anywhere. It seems as if it is vividly appearing, but it is beyond the realm of affirmation or denial.

107

And as for the wheel of actions, it is just the same: though it lacks an inherent nature, yet it appears, like the reflection of the moon in water. Actions and their consequences are a variegated multitude of falsehoods. Even though they are just appearances, I urge you to embrace virtue and avoid sin.

108

When in a dream a peat fire blazes, we are terrified by the heat, although it is without substance. In the same way, although the hell realms and such are without substance, we fear the smelter's fire and other tortures. As that is so, we should forsake evil actions.

109
ཚད་པས་འབྲུལ་ཆེ་མུན་ནག་ཡོད་མེད་ཀྱང་།
གཏིང་རིང་ཕུག་ཏུ་རྒྱུ་ཞིང་འཚུབ་པ་ལྟར།
མ་རིག་སོགས་ལ་རང་བཞིན་མེད་ན་ཡང་།
ཤེས་རབ་གསུམ་གྱིས་འབྲུལ་པ་བསལ་བར་བྱ།།

110
རོལ་མོ་མཁན་གྱིས་དགྱེས་པའི་གླུ་བླངས་ཏེ།
དཔྱད་ན་སྒྲ་དེའི་རང་བཞིན་མ་མཆིས་མོད།
མ་དཔྱད་ཚོགས་པའི་སྙན་པའི་སྒྲ་བྱུང་ནས།
སྐྱེ་བོའི་སེམས་ཀྱི་གདུང་བ་སེལ་བ་ལྟར།།

111
ལས་དང་རྒྱུ་འབྲས་ཡོངས་སུ་དཔྱད་པ་ན།
གཅིག་དང་ཐ་དད་རང་བཞིན་མེད་ན་ཡང་།
སྣང་སྣང་ལྟ་བུར་ཆོས་ལ་སྐྱེ་འཇིག་བྱེད།
ཡོད་ཡོད་ལྟ་བུར་བདེ་སྡུག་སྣ་ཚོགས་སྤྱོད།
སྣང་བ་ཙམ་དུ་བླང་དོར་བྱའོ་ཨང་།།

112
ཆུ་ཡི་ཐིགས་པས་བུམ་པ་ཁེངས་པ་ན།
ཆུ་ཐིག་དང་པོས་བུམ་པ་མི་ཁེངས་ཤིང་།
ཐ་མ་ལ་སོགས་རེ་རེས་མ་ཡིན་མོད།
རྟེན་འབྲེལ་ཚོགས་པས་བུམ་པ་གང་བ་ལྟར།།

109

In a feverish delirium we may feel as if we are wandering around suffocating in a deep cave, even though there is no darkness at all. In the same way, even though ignorance and the like are without substance, we should get rid of our delusions through the three wisdoms.

110

When a musician plays a melody on a lute, the sound lacks inherent nature, if we analyze it. But when the sweet sounds emerge, their unanalyzed aggregate eases the anguish in people's hearts.

111

When we analyze all causes and effects, they lack inherent nature as either identical or different. Yet phenomena vividly appear to arise and perish, and we experience pleasure and suffering as if they really existed. Even though they are just appearances, I urge you to embrace virtue and avoid sin.

112

When drops of water fill a jar, the first drop does not fill it, nor the last, nor each drop individually. Yet the dependently arisen aggregate fills the jar.

113
བདེ་སྡུག་འབྲས་བུ་གང་གིས་སྨྱོང་བ་ན།
རྒྱུ་ཡི་སྐད་ཅིག་དང་པོས་མ་ཡིན་ཞིང་།
ཐ་མའི་སྐད་ཅིག་སོགས་ཀྱིས་མ་ཡིན་ཀྱང་།
རྟེན་འབྲེལ་ཚོགས་པས་བདེ་སྡུག་སྨྱོང་བར་འགྱུར།
སྣང་བ་ཙམ་དུ་བླང་དོར་བྱའོ་ཨང་།།

114
ཨེ་མ་མ་བརྟགས་གཅིག་པུར་ཉམས་དགའ་བའི།
སྣང་བ་འདི་ལ་སྙིང་པོ་མ་མཆིས་མོད།།
འོན་ཀྱང་ཡོད་པ་ལྟ་བུར་སྣང་བ་ཡི།
ཆོས་འདི་ཟབ་ཏེ་དམན་པས་མཐོང་བར་དཀའ།།

115
ད་ནི་འདི་ལ་མཉམ་པར་འཇོག་པ་ན།
ངེས་པར་སྣང་བ་ཙམ་ཡང་ཅི་ཞིག་ཡོད།
ཡོད་པ་ཅི་ཡོད་མེད་པའང་ཅི་ཞིག་ཡོད།
ཡིན་མིན་དམ་བཅའ་གང་དུའང་ཅི་ཞིག་ཡོད།།

116
ཡུལ་དང་ཡུལ་ཅན་ཆོས་ཉིད་མ་མཆིས་ཤིང་།
བླང་དོར་ཀུན་བྲལ་སྤྲོས་དང་བྲལ་བ་ཡི།
གཉུག་མའི་ངང་དུ་བློ་གྲོས་མ་བཅོས་པར།
ལྷུན་ནེ་གནས་ན་སྐྱེས་བུ་ཆེན་པོར་འགྱུར།།

113
Similarly, when someone experiences their reward of pleasure or pain, it is due neither to the first moment of the cause, nor to the last moment, and so on. Yet the dependently arisen aggregate makes us experience pleasure or pain. Even though they are just appearances, I urge you to embrace virtue and avoid sin.

114
Aha! The appearance that delights our mind, though independent when unanalyzed, definitely lacks an inner core. However, the fact that phenomena appear as if they exist is profound and difficult for the dull-witted to understand.

115
Now, when you are absorbed in meditative equipoise on this, what is there really to a mere appearance? How can either existence or non-existence exist? How can anyone anywhere assert "it is" or "it is not"?

116
Subject and object lack ultimate reality. If your mind remains in its innate nature, uncontrived and shining, free from all discrimination and conceptual proliferation, you will become a great being.

117
དེ་ལྟར་ཀུན་རྫོབ་བྱང་ཆུབ་སེམས་དང་ནི།
དོན་དམ་བྱང་ཆུབ་སེམས་ལ་སྦྱོང་པ་ཡིས།
ཚོགས་གཉིས་བར་ཆད་མེད་པར་མཐར་ཕྱིན་ནས།
དོན་གཉིས་ལྷུན་སྲུམ་ཚོགས་པ་ཐོབ་པར་ཤོག།

དགྲ་བོ་གནད་ལ་དབབ་པ་མཚོན་ཆའི་འཁོར་ལོ་ཞེས་བྱ་བ།

༄༅ འཇིགས་པའི་གཅན་གཟན་སྣ་ཚོགས་རྒྱུ་བའི་ནགས་ཁྲོད་དུ་ལུང་རིགས་དང་རྟོགས་པའི་རྣལ་འབྱོར་པ་དྷ་རྨ་རཀྵི་ཏ་ཆེན་པོ་དེས་བླ་མ་དམ་པའི་གསུང་ལྟར་སྦྱངས་ནས་དུས་ཀྱི་སྙིགས་མ་ལ་འཇིགས་པ་དང་བཅས་པའི་ནགས་ཁྲོད་དུ་ཉམས་སུ་བླངས་པའོ།། དེས་ཨ་ཏི་ཤ་ལ་གནང་ནས། ཨ་ཏི་ཤས་ཀྱང་གདུལ་དཀའ་བའི་སེམས་ཅན་མང་པོ་འདུལ་བའི་ཕྱིར། ཕྱོགས་དང་མི་ཕྱོགས་མཚམས་མེད་པར་ཉམས་སུ་བླངས་ཏེ། རྟོགས་པ་འཁྲུངས་པའི་ཚིགས་སུ་བཅད་པའང་འདི་སྐད་གསུངས་སོ།

ཁོ་བོས་རྒྱལ་སྲིད་སྤངས་ནས་དཀའ་བ་སྤྱད་པའི་ཚེ།
བསོད་ནམས་བསགས་ནས་བླ་མ་མཆོག་དང་མཇལ།
དམ་ཆོས་བདུད་རྩི་འདི་བསྟན་ཆོས་དབང་བསྐུར།
དེང་སང་གཉེན་པོ་ཐོབ་ནས་ཚིག་ཀྱང་བཟུང་།།
གྲུབ་པའི་མཐའ་ལ་ཕྱོགས་རིས་མ་མཆིས་པར།
བློ་གྲོས་བཀྲམ་ནས་ཀུན་ལ་བསླབ་པའི་ཚེ།

117

Thus, by practicing the conventional and ultimate bodhicitta,

and thereby uninterruptedly carrying the two accumulations

through to completion, may I perfectly realize the two aims.

Colophon

In the dense jungle wherein roam many fearful beasts of prey, the great yogi Dharmarakṣita, who understood both scripture and logic, composed *The Wheel-Weapon That Strikes at the Enemy's Vital Spot* according to his holy religious teacher's instruction, and he practiced it in the dark and terrifying jungle of our degenerate age. He bestowed it upon Atiśa, and Atiśa too came to realize it by practicing it disinterestedly for the sake of taming sentient beings who are difficult to tame. Atiśa spoke these verses:

I After I left my royal estate and practiced austerities, I met my supreme religious teacher due to the merit I had accumulated; he taught me this ambrosia of the holy religion and initiated me into it; having obtained the antidote for the present age, I committed it to memory.

II Without partisanship toward doctrinal systems, I opened my mind and studied them all, and although I have understood teachings marvelous and vast, this is the teaching that will bring benefit to this degenerate age.

ཡ་མཚན་དཔག་མེད་བདག་གིས་མཐོང་མོད་ཀྱི།
སྙིགས་མའི་དུས་འདིར་ཆོས་འདིས་ཕན་པར་འགྱུར།། ༢

ཞེས་གསུངས་ནས་། རྒྱ་བོད་ན་སློབ་མ་བསམ་གྱིས་མི་ཁྱབ་པ་མཆིས་པའི་ནང་ནས་བཅོམ་ལྡན་འདས་མ་སྒྲོལ་མ་ལ་སོགས་པ་ཡི་དམ་གྱི་ལྷ་དཔག་ཏུ་མ་མཆིས་པས། ལུང་བསྟན་པའི་སྟོད་དང་ལྡན་པའི་སློབ་མ་ཨུ་པཱ་ས་ཀ་ལ། བོད་མཐའ་འཁོབ་ཀྱི་གདུལ་བྱ་མ་རུངས་པ་འདུལ་བའི་ཆོས་སུ་གནང་བ་སྟེ། ལོ་པཎ་ཡང་རྒྱལ་བ་ཡབ་སྲས་གཉིས་ཀྱིས་མཛད་དོ།།

From among the inconceivably vast number of his Indian and Tibetan disciples, Atiśa bestowed it upon Upāsika ('Brom ston pa), the fit vessel, the disciple who was prophesied by numberless tutelary deities such as Lady Tārā. The teaching was given to tame the dangerous converts of the Tibetan borderlands.

The Conqueror Father and Son [Atiśa and 'Brom] served as pandit and translator.

Commentary on Dharmarakṣita's *The Wheel-Weapon Mind Training*

Geshe Lhundub Sopa

THE ATTITUDE OF MAHĀYĀNA BUDDHISM is one of love and compassion for all beings, as embodied in the bodhisattva's assumption of the responsibility to free them all from misery and suffering and lead them all to enlightenment, regardless of any hardship. But in order to pursue that aim, we have to fight against the major impediment to carrying it out, namely, the view of a real personal identity and the self-cherishing attitude, and seek instead to cherish others. The true target of Mahayana practice is the destruction of these impediments. Therefore, the title of this work is:

The Wheel-Weapon That Strikes at the Enemy's Vital Spot

The first task of this mind training is to identify the real enemy, the demon of ego-clinging and self-cherishing. As long as this demonic attitude dominates you, you will not be a bodhisattva, and both you and others will be harmed by your egocentric behavior. *The Wheel-Weapon* is a weapon of mind training for the purpose of hitting the vital spot, the bull's-eye of the target of our internal enemies. The first step is to identify the vital spot, then aim the weapon and destroy the twin enemies—the view of a real personal identity and the self-cherishing attitude. This is analogous to a skillful woodcutter who knows the exact spot at which to aim his axe to chop down a tree so that it will die and not grow back, or the expert butcher who knows the exact vein to cut to slaughter an animal cleanly and quickly. At the beginning of the text is the dedication, which says:

I bow down to the Great Wrathful One, Yamāntaka.

Yama is the Lord of Death. *Yamāntaka* means "terminator *(antaka)* of Yama." In many sutras and tantras ignorance is considered the most powerful spiritual enemy, and the perfect wisdom that eliminates this enemy is personified by Mañjuśrī, who is depicted with a flaming sword and a book; the flaming sword signifies the wisdom that cuts down the enemy of ignorance. This peaceful form of Mañjuśrī is the manifestation of perfect wisdom, but his wrathful form is Yamāntaka, the terminator of Yama. He is depicted as bearing many types of weapons, which he employs to destroy Yama. This is Yamāntaka's outward form, but in his ultimate form, he is the inseparable combination of the wisdom that realizes emptiness with the highest bliss. In the dedication Yamāntaka is addressed as the Great Wrathful One, but his wrath is not the ordinary anger of deluded beings; actually, he is not angry at anyone, but in fact has great love and compassion toward all sentient beings. It is against spiritual enemies—the view of a real personal identity and the self-cherishing attitude—that his anger is directed. All bodhisattvas can be wrathful in this way, since it is the duty of the bodhisattvas to destroy the sources of misery for sentient beings. The buddhas have the highest form of wrath, because they have destroyed self-cherishing completely. Yamāntaka is a protector of the Dharma, which is why he appears in a wrathful form. He has been praised by Tsongkhapa, who says that everyone has two main enemies: ignorance, which destroys the mind, for which the remedy is the youthful Mañjuśrī carrying the sword of wisdom, and death, which destroys the body, for which the remedy is the wrathful form of Mañjuśrī, Yamāntaka.

The verses in this text are the weapons that will enable us to conquer the causes of our misery and suffering. These weapons have to hit the target; if they do not, we will not succeed in achieving our goal. If you just memorize these verses and recite them without actually reflecting on their meaning and really trying to reduce your view of a real personal identify and self-cherishing attitude, you will get only limited results. At some point in the future you can meditate on these verses, even according to your own understanding, and it will help you to relieve your mental instability and unhappiness. Now we begin our discussion of the verses of the *Wheel-Weapon.*

1 When the peacocks roam the jungle of virulent poison, the flocks take no delight in gardens of medicinal plants, no matter how beautiful they may be, for peacocks thrive on the essence of virulent poison.

2 Similarly, when the heroes roam the jungle of cyclic existence, they do not become attached to the garden of happiness and prosperity, no matter how beautiful it may be, for heroes thrive in the jungle of suffering.

This text begins with the image of peacocks roaming through the jungle deriving no enjoyment from the gardens of medicinal plants around them, but finding nourishment only from the poisonous plants. In the next verse the hero or heroine, that is, the bodhisattva, is compared to the peacock. Impure cyclic existence is like the jungle filled with trees of poisonous afflictions among which the bodhisattvas wander like the peacocks. Bodhisattvas are not attached to cyclic existence, to the beautiful forms and desirable things that are part of this world. Instead of pursuing their own pleasures, bodhisattvas, out of their great love and compassion, take upon themselves the things that bring misery to other sentient beings. Therefore, the bodhisattvas, like peacocks, are nourished by taking up the misery and suffering of sentient beings. Their energy and great deeds flow from the waves of their great love and compassion. Praise, fame, wealth, and other ordinary worldly pleasures are like the beautiful flowers in the medicinal garden; the bodhisattvas do not enjoy these things or become attached to them. On the contrary, suffering or hardship, such as violence or verbal abuse, will never harm them and they will generate even more love and compassion toward people who are under the influence of ignorance and egocentricity.

What do we mean by the bodhisattva being in cyclic existence? Does he or she just fall into it like other sentient beings? The bodhisattva is not in cyclic existence involuntarily because of negative actions and the afflictions—the bodhisattva comes into cyclic existence voluntarily in order to assist the beings there. The buddhas can also appear in cyclic existence in many other manifestations—as rulers, parents, enemies, animals, even as inanimate objects such as trees. However, these are mere manifestations, and thus they are not what they appear to be.

3 Therefore, it is due to cowardice that persons avidly pursue their own happiness and so come to suffer; and it is due to heroism that bodhisattvas, willingly taking the sufferings of others onto themselves, are always happy.

Like the bodhisattvas, we should take others' problems onto ourselves rather than work only for our own benefit. What we really have been doing until now is seeking our own sensual pleasure and enjoyment. We desire the best things only for ourselves, thinking only of "I" or "me" with a strong self-cherishing attitude; this has been our course from beginningless time. We fear the loss of our pleasures and the prospect of suffering, and we are always striving to be free from these worries and anxieties. Since we don't get what we want and we can lose what we have, we are miserable and filled with worries. This is what is meant by "cowardice." Cowardice comes from our view of a real personal identity and our self-cherishing attitude; these notions make us fearful of losing what we have and not getting what we want. We are like someone sitting in the middle of a thorn bush, being pricked all over by the thorns. We are always seeking protection and security, but that search only leads to suffering because we will always have reasons to be frustrated and discouraged. Bodhisattvas have a diametrically opposed attitude; they are heroic and regard even great pain and torture as of no consequence to themselves so long as they are working for the welfare of other living beings, voluntarily taking suffering upon themselves for the sake of others. Heedless of their own sufferings, they are neither discouraged nor unhappy; they have only the wish to remove the suffering of others and grant them happiness. In this way they experience much joy, even though they are not seeking it. This heroic attitude also creates merit that will bring future peace and happiness, eventually resulting in the attainment of enlightenment.

4 Now here, desire is like a jungle of virulent poison: the hero, like the peacock, masters it; the coward, like the crow, perishes.

5 How can persons concerned only with their own desires master this poison? If they involve themselves in the other afflictions as well, it will cost them their chance for emancipation, just like the crow.

"Here" means that you are a bodhisattva, possessed of the courage and compassion developed on the lower levels of practice when you wanted to be quickly liberated from cyclic existence. You first undertook mind training for your own benefit and later for the benefit of others. "Now" refers to the fact that you have been properly trained in the past and are now ready to practice with a courageous bodhisattva attitude.

This type of courage is not produced quickly or easily; it requires extensive training. Once you reach this level, you will be like the heroic bodhisattva who benefits from taking up desire, hatred, and the other poisons of cyclic existence and turns them into love and compassion, just like a peacock, which can digest poisonous plants in the jungle. This is the tantric view that attachment can be turned into part of the Path, leading one more quickly to enlightenment. Poison is harmful in itself, but it can be beneficial if combined with other substances such as herbs, or if certain mantras are used. As you know, there are some medicines that are made from toxic substances. Similarly, the bodhisattva takes the afflictions and digests them, turning them into love and compassion, making them the path to enlightenment. The bodhisattva uses especially the affliction of desire, which is omnipresent here in the jungle of cyclic existence, as a means for the enlightenment of others. However, if ordinary people, whose desire arises from self-interest, try to utilize their desire and the other afflictions, they will be destroyed by them. Destruction does not mean that their present life will necessarily be ruined, but that their potential for emancipation will be lost.

> 6 Thus the bodhisattva roams like the peacock in the
> forest of cyclic existence, converting the afflictions,
> which are like a jungle of virulent poisons, into an elixir.
> Willingly embracing the afflictions, the hero shall
> conquer the poison.

Peacocks feed on poisonous plants; they use the poisons to maintain their bodies and the color and brilliance of their feathers. Similarly, bodhisattvas in the jungle of cyclic existence can feed on the mental poisons of the afflictions, using them as a type of food for their mental development, making the body of their practice strong and powerful. For example, out of attachment to our bodies we endeavor to get enough sleep, exercise, and proper food. A bodhisattva is motivated by the desire to maintain his or her body as a means for benefiting others. The bodhisattva views his or her body as a precious jewel that should be strong and well cared for, and not wasted or destroyed. Sleep, exercise, and good food are necessary since the body must be strong to support a strong mind. When the bodhisattva does these things with the motivation of serving other sentient beings, then every action becomes a noble one; eating a mouthful of food, sleeping, and other things that are done to care for the body become virtuous actions. The bodhisattva motivation turns even small daily tasks into noble activities. Concerning this, I often like to quote from Śāntideva (*BCA* 1.19):

> From now on, though you may doze off or be distracted,
> an uninterrupted stream of merit equal to the sky comes forth.

For example, when a bodhisattva thinks, "I must sleep to maintain my body in order to bring all sentient beings to enlightenment," then his or her slumber will produce great merit for all sentient beings. In this way, with proper motivation, bodhisattvas destroy the power of the poisons of desire, attachment, and other negativities. Bodhisattvas are always aware of the negative aspects of things and are able to transform them into positive means with their wisdom and compassion.

> 7 The ego-clinging of the helpless wanderer in cyclic existence is the messenger of the devil. Distance yourself from the savor of selfishness and hedonism, and willingly embrace hardship for the sake of others.

> 8 May the sufferings of all beings, who, like myself, are driven by their karma and their habituation to the afflictions, be heaped upon me, the hedonist.

Right now living beings in cyclic existence circle uncontrollably from life to life; they have no way out of this cycle. The root cause of this, the messenger of the devil or of evil, is the view of a real personal identity: grasping at a real, unique, permanent "I" or "me." The self-cherishing attitude is like a devil or evil force, and the driving force is usually selfishness, wishing to have only pleasure and enjoyment. Once we realize that these desires and attitudes and our attachment to them are to blame for our continued misery in cyclic existence, we should cast away these mental states. We should willingly and joyfully undertake whatever hardship is necessary for the benefit of others. If you strongly develop such an attitude, no difficulty will cause you to feel anger or impatience toward others. As it says in the *Guru Worship:*

> Because of compassion I will never be discouraged,
> even if I have to remain in Avici hell for the sake of
> one sentient being.

All beings in cyclic existence are pursued by the results of their own actions and habituation to the afflictions of attachment and hatred, and so on; this is what causes their sufferings. Seeing yourself as someone who seeks only pleasure, you should pray to have all the miseries and sufferings of others heaped upon yourself. We should think this way in order to make war against the enemies of ego-clinging and self-cherishing.

> 9 When I become enmeshed in selfishness, I will offer my own happiness to living beings so as to counteract it. In the same way, should a companion be ungrateful to me, I will be content in knowing that this is in retribution for my own inconstancy.

Keeping in mind the previous verses, we should try to employ an unselfish attitude in dealing with specific problems we have with others. Despite carefully guarding against selfishness, if you should regress into wanting everything good only for yourself, you should immediately recognize this as a relapse and work to reverse it. The way to eliminate selfishness is through its opposite—the strong wish to give all good things to others. You can actually give things to others and also develop the mental attitude of sharing everything.

Sometimes, regardless of how sincerely and diligently you try to do good for others and to treat them kindly, they will not appreciate it. Even your own friends or relatives may turn against you and try to harm you. This can cause you to have negative thoughts: "Look how much I did for him and now he is treating me so badly." These types of thoughts can cause powerful anger and hatred. Instead, you should blame their conduct on your own past view of a real personal identity and self-cherishing attitude, which caused you to act wrongly by responding to peoples' kindness with harmful behavior. Even our well-intentioned conduct toward others may be tainted by selfishness, when we expect some praise or respect in return. Once you have realized where the blame lies, you can feel a kind of gratitude or satisfaction that these negative things are happening, since they are beneficial to your practice. Thus, a bodhisattva feels joy and satisfaction in others' ingratitude, rather than anger or impatience.

> 10 When my body falls prey to terrible sickness, it is
> the weapon of my own evil deeds turned upon me
> for injuring the bodies of living beings. From now on,
> I shall take all sickness upon myself.

Whenever disease, pain, or suffering strikes your body, you should realize immediately that this is the result of your having violently injured or harmed other living beings in the past. Such evil past actions become weapons that return and are directed against us. There is a special kind of Yamāntaka meditation in which a sharp weapon is used to destroy negativities. Similarly, here we are talking about a kind of wheel or disc that has a sharp serrated edge that can completely cut things to pieces. This wheel turns back on us, even though we aim it toward others. Metaphorically, our evil actions are such a wheel, and beginning with this verse, the wheel is used in the refrain of many of the following verses. When you experience physical misfortune, you usually feel anger and frustration, thinking, "I am a wonderful person, why is this happening to me?" which only adds mental suffering to your physical pain. Instead, you should understand that you are experiencing this because the wheel-weapon of bad actions that you turned on others is returning and working on you. You should recognize that you acted under the influence of the view of a real personal identity and with a self-cherishing attitude. Once you have that recognition, you can work to change yourself by eliminating them and replacing them with an attitude that cherishes others instead of yourself. When you think in this way, even an illness can be turned into something of value. It can benefit the person who is ill to see the illness as a means of purifying previous bad actions whose results are now coming to fruition, as well as promoting understanding of the destructive nature of unwholesome actions and their effects.

This kind of thinking can be applied to any bad situation, thus turning it into something positive. Reasoning in this way, you will want all the sickness and suffering of the world to come to fruition on yourself and not upon others.

There is a story from the previous lives of the Buddha where the consequence of having performed bad actions takes the form of being tortured by a razor-edged wheel. In ages past, long before the time of Śākyamuni Buddha, there was a merchant who traveled the seas in search of wealth. He had a son, and in those days, a son took up his father's trade. The father died at sea, and when it was time for his son to follow in his footsteps, his mother did not want him to go, fearing he would meet the same fate. When the son was leaving to go to sea, his mother tried to prevent him by lying down in the doorway. The boy was very angry about this; he stepped on his mother's head and went out the door.

After many years at sea, his ship arrived at a strange island inhabited by cannibals, who first welcomed and entertained sailors and later ate them. The young sailor-merchant enjoyed himself with these cannibals, and one day, he decided to take a walk into the jungle. After walking a great distance, he came upon a very large black building that seemed to be made of metal. As he approached it, he heard screaming and crying coming from within. The building did not have windows or doors, but as he was looking around, a huge door suddenly appeared and opened, so he went inside.

After going into the building, he saw that it was full of suffering people. Each person had a wheel attached to their head that was spinning and wounding them, making them scream and cry from the pain. As he looked on this scene, a guard appeared before him; the guard looked like an ordinary person, so he asked him what was happening. The guard told him that this was a type of temporary hell caused by people having stepped on their mother's head. When the young man heard this, he thought, "Uh oh, I have done that to my mother." The instant he thought this, a wheel appeared on his head and began turning, causing him to experience the same suffering and pain as the others.

The young man then thought, "Oh, my bad actions have caused me to suffer by this wheel and I deserve to have this done to me because of what I did to my mother." Then with a very strong compassionate wish he thought, "All of these people have suffered enough. Since I deserve this suffering, may I take all of their wheels on my head and release them from their suffering." When that noble thought came into his mind, all the wheels on people's heads, including his own, disappeared, and the hell disappeared as well. This happened through the power of his compassionate wish for the benefit of others.

It is extremely beneficial to have a strong desire to release all sentient beings from their sickness and suffering and to take their sickness and suffering upon oneself. As Śāntideva says (*BCA* 1.21–22):

> One who has the beneficial thought, "Let me just alleviate the headaches of sentient beings," will gain incalculable merit. What need is there to speak about the person who desires to remove the immeasurable unhappiness of all sentient beings and endow them with infinite merit?

> 11 When my mind falls prey to suffering, it is surely
> the weapon of my own evil deeds turned upon me for
> troubling the minds of others. From now on, I shall
> willingly take all suffering upon myself.

This verse is like the previous one, although here it is applied to mental rather than physical suffering. Mental suffering is also caused by negative past actions, here, disturbing the peace of mind of others; thus, the wheel-weapon is returning now upon you. The essential nature of mind is like the Buddha's mind, completely peaceful and perfect, but there are so many things that can disturb our minds, such as attachment, hatred, fear, anxiety, and bad outside conditions. Sometimes we can even become unhappy apparently for no reason at all. We should reflect that such mental disturbances come from our having disturbed the minds of others, especially our past teachers or gurus, parents, friends, and other beneficial people. Positive or negative actions, with such people as their object, create the most powerful good or bad results; causing such persons physical or mental harm will result in especially bad consequences for us.

> 12 When I am tormented by extreme hunger and thirst, it is
> the weapon of my own evil deeds turned upon me for
> swindling, stealing, and acting miserly. From now on, I
> shall willingly take all hunger and thirst upon myself.

When we experience very powerful hunger and thirst, this is the result of previously cheating others, stealing their goods, and our miserliness in not wanting to share our possessions with others. Such actions and especially selfish and greedy thoughts produce the bad results that we are now experiencing. Again, we should put the blame on our nonvirtuous past deeds or thoughts that produced the present undesirable situation. Thus, we resolve that from now on, not only will we not take others' food and drink, but we will supply these things to those in need. The commentary explains this type of practice in terms of giving and taking *(gtong len),* the breathing meditation practice of taking all the misfortunes of others upon ourselves and giving them all beneficial things.

Each of these verses and the ones that follow relate to our ordinary daily experiences, explaining them in a religiously elevating way as a training for us. People have different capacities; some may derive great benefit from these practices now, but others may only be able to form the good intention to practice this way in the future. In the latter case, you should at least say the words in the form of a prayer. Then in difficult situations, instead of becoming angry, frustrated, or anxious, which is a big waste of time, you can accept the suffering and channel it to good effect.

It says in the *Guru Worship* that "when the animate and inanimate worlds are filled with negative results, all sorts of undesirable things descend on us like rainfall." When such things happen to us, it is necessary that we have an understanding of why they are happening and where they are coming from.

Karma, or action, is both general and individual. General karma refers to actions that were shared with other individuals, such as killing in war; this will bring both a common result in the external world and have repercussions as well for the individual alone. Actions shared with others will bring different results depending upon the involvement of each of the people involved; the results may be heavy, intermediate, or light. A person could be in a situation like a war and not experience any negative consequences, because the person hadn't participated or acted wrongly. Karma is subtle and difficult to understand, because of the complexity of cause and effect.

There is also individual karma, which is unshared with others. Even if one is born into what is considered the most favorable environment in the human world, it does not mean that one will necessarily have an excellent life. Each person has individual experiences based on his or her previous actions. You must have strong faith in karma and its results based on the testimony of the Buddha and the sages: this is what is called "the worldly right view." This right view eliminates anger, jealousy, and other negative emotions when bad things happen. If you don't have the right view, then the view of a real personal identity will cause such negative feelings to increase in intensity and frequency.

> 13 When I am powerless and suffer enslavement, it is the weapon of my own evil deeds turned upon me for despising my inferiors and enslaving them. From now on I shall make slaves of my body and my life for the sake of others.

It is terrible to be in the power of others and under their control, and to be forced into slavery or servitude. When such things happen, it is the result of having despised those who were socially inferior to you and having compelled them by force to act as your servants. This applies not only to human beings, but also to the animals that we force to work for us and that we use for meat and milk. Now, when the weapon of those past actions turns back on yourself, instead of being angry at the people who oppressed you, you should remember that they are also creating consequences that will return upon themselves, and that they will suffer the same fate as you. You should feel compassion toward such persons and wish to take upon yourself all the negative results that they are creating. In addition, you should feel happy that your previous bad actions have ripened. This will help you and the other person, and enable you to feel happy even if you are suffering.

As an example of people who force others into servitude, the commentary refers to local Tibetan rulers, specifically in Tsang, which is my native place. In the past the landlords sometimes made people pay off their debts by performing forced labor, such as building roads or houses or doing work in the fields. This kind of thing happens in many countries, especially in those that are not free, where people are tortured and punished and everyone lives in fear. Yet, you shouldn't hate your oppressors; instead you should blame your own similar past actions, which have led you to your present state of hardship. You can utilize this thinking in your daily life, for example, if you have problems with your boss.

Once you have understood things in this way, you will resolve never to subjugate others, and you will dedicate every aspect of your body, mind, and life to them. By dedicating yourself in this way, you plant seeds that will produce great merit in the field of sentient beings. These things are hard to practice in their entirety, but regular practice can reduce the obstacles and gradually get you closer to the goal; don't be too hard on yourself if your practice isn't perfect—this would not be helpful.

> 14 When insulting remarks assault my ears, it is the weapon of my own evil deeds turned upon me for my verbal offenses of slander and so forth. From now on I shall condemn my own verbal faults.

Actions are divided into acts of the body, speech, and mind, which we call "the three doors." This verse refers to verbal actions, such as remarks that are insulting, offensive, or otherwise cause anger and unhappiness by striking at the heart of our egocentricity. This is a result of our previous verbal misconduct: making divisive comments, gossiping, lying, insulting, any type of sharp words. Sometimes verbal weapons are even more harmful than physical violence; people can remember a hurtful remark for their entire lives. Now, when you are the target of others' bad words, you should, just as before, realize that they are the result of your own past behavior and accept them with joy. If you do this, you won't react in the ordinary way and become angry and upset, and you will be more attentive to your own verbal faults rather than the words of others.

> 15 When I am reborn into an impure land, it is the weapon of my own evil deeds turned upon me for always cultivating impure vision. From now on I shall cultivate only pure vision.

When you are born in an impure and undesirable place, many harmful things can befall you; it could be a miserable, barren place without sufficient food. Or, it could be a generally nice place, but you may be in bad circumstances. From a commonsense point of view such a place is considered impure. This is a result of having accustomed ourselves to impure vision. If we believe things to truly exist in the way that they appear to our perceptions, it will lead us to make judgments about them as good or bad, and to have positive and negative feelings about them. In tantric practice we have to accustom ourselves to pure appearances; even in the beginning, on the developing stage of practice, you meditate on yourself and on your environment as divine, as part of a pure mandala. The mental attitude that views everything as pure is important; it doesn't matter whether this is objectively true, since we can't know that anyway, unless our minds are perfectly pure. It is like Asanga seeing Maitreya's manifestation as a sick dog, or Nāropa first seeing his guru Tilopa appear as an ugly and dirty fisherman. Since our minds are so tainted by various obstacles, our perceptions become completely distorted, just as someone with an eye disease might see everything as yellow or cloudy. Therefore, you shouldn't trust your judgments that certain people are good or bad. We should treat all beings with respect and honor as if they were emanations of buddhas and bodhisattvas: this is cultivating pure vision. By having this attitude even toward someone not worthy of it, you are acting in a wholesome way.

> 16 When I am separated from helpful and loving friends, it is
> the weapon of my own evil deeds turned upon me for
> luring away others' companions. From now on I shall not
> separate others from their companions.

When we have dear or helpful friends we don't want to part from them, and we feel great pain when they leave us. As a result of our negative karma, undesirable things may happen that separate us from those we love. Our dear friends and relations may die, move away, or for other reasons no longer be around us. When these things happen, we suffer sadness and frustration. The root cause of that suffering is our attachment to "my friend, my dear one."

In our practice, again, we should think: "I have committed negative actions in the past, separating people from their friends, disciples from their teachers, or breaking up marriages. As a result of these actions I am now separated from people who help and care for me, from my friends, children, or partners." Recognizing that the fault is with one's own previous bad actions, you should resolve never again to separate friend from friend, disciple from teacher, spouse from spouse, or child from parent. As I mentioned, practicing in this way is helpful in dealing with the loss of those who are close to us, a loss that can otherwise cause us to become depressed or even suicidal.

> 17 When all the holy ones are displeased with me, it is the weapon of my own evil deeds turned upon me for casting them aside and resorting to bad companions. From now on I shall renounce bad companions.

There are times when whatever we do to honor and satisfy our gurus only seems to cause them displeasure. This too is the result of our past negative actions, such as not having respected our teachers, not having listened to their advice or followed their instructions, or having had a bad attitude toward them. Instead of doing what we should have done to please our teachers, we took up with bad companions. These kinds of negative actions can prevent us from meeting a holy teacher, or from being able to follow or please a teacher even if we do meet one. When we talk about bad associates, the principal ones we are referring to are your inner companions; and we are talking about the view of a real personal identity and the self-cherishing attitude that led to the commission of these previous bad actions. On a more mundane level there are those of our friends who are hostile to religious practice and wholesome conduct. Recognizing that your present bad situation is a result of your previous actions, you should vow that from now on you will forsake all bad associations. This does not mean that you should hate such people, but that you will not follow them in a negative direction; instead, you should use love and compassion to help them change in a positive way.

> 18 When others sin against me by exaggeration or deprecation, it is the weapon of my own evil deeds turned upon me for reviling the holy ones. From now on I shall not revile others by exaggeration or deprecation.

If people falsely accuse you or slander you, insinuating that you have certain faults or deprecating your real achievements, it is very easy to get angry and have violent thoughts about these people. Here again, we should recognize that this is the result of our own past actions of slandering or deprecating others, especially holy or excellent people. We should rejoice that this past karma is completed in the present painful result, voluntarily taking upon ourselves the result of others' bad behavior and giving our happiness to them. We should also resolve not to slander or deprecate others in the future.

19 When my material necessities waste away, it is the weapon of my own evil deeds turned upon me for scorning others' necessities. From now on I shall provide for others' necessities.

The material necessities of our lives are things such as food, clothing, and shelter. When we experience their being wasted, destroyed, or stolen, we usually get angry at what seems the immediate cause, such as fire or thieves. However, we should realize that this situation is ultimately caused by our not having respected someone else's property in the past, for example by stealing or destroying it. When we recognize the negative effects such behaviors have on ourselves and others, we should resolve never again to act in this way. Further, we should provide for others as much as possible. If you are generous, you will easily achieve wealth in the future. If you are not charitable, you will not be prosperous in the future; no matter how hard you strive, you will remain in poverty.

20 When my mind is unclear and my heart is sad, it is the weapon of my own evil deeds turned upon me for causing others to sin. From now on I shall renounce contributing to others' sinning.

This verse refers to chronic unhappiness, when you are depressed without a specific reason. At such times, you are unable to think clearly, and if you are meditating you may not be able to visualize properly. This verse especially applies to times when you are trying to direct your mind to religious thoughts or practices. The cause of this type of mental disturbance is your having caused others to be unhappy or frustrated, giving them wrong advice or otherwise creating obstacles to their mental or spiritual well-being. For example, you can make your subordinates angry by forcing them to follow certain rules that you openly violate yourself, and thus stir them up to quarrels or other wrong actions. As in the previous verses, we should accept the consequences of our past actions and vow not to cause others to be disturbed or to act nonvirtuously.

21 When I am deeply troubled over my lack of success, it is the weapon of my own evil deeds turned upon me for

> hindering the work of the holy ones. From now on, I shall renounce all hindering.

Here we are looking at any type of goal that we want to accomplish—in business, school, religious activities, and so on. Sometimes we lack the support of those who can help us, or things turn out exactly opposite to our expectations. As a result of such disappointments, we become very disturbed. The cause of this is that in past lives we hindered good advisers in their projects, acted in contradiction to their instructions, and interfered with them. We must stop doing this and willingly accept the consequences of what we have done.

> 22 When my guru is displeased with me no matter what I do, it is the weapon of my own evil deeds turned upon me for acting duplicitously toward the holy Dharma. From now on I shall reduce my duplicity toward the Dharma.

This verse is similar to previous ones, in that it addresses the mental anguish we feel when our guru is not pleased with us or does not trust us regardless of our efforts. Of course, at such times you should not blame the guru for not appreciating what you have done; that will only create more bad karmic consequences in the future. Instead, you should realize that the current situation is caused by your previous bad actions, especially hypocritical behavior, pretending to respect the teachings externally but covertly acting in the opposite way, such as taking vows in front of your guru but not honoring them. This deception of our teachers and the Dharma is actually a kind of self-deception. As a result of this conduct in the past, gurus and others may not trust you, even without a good reason. You must accept these consequences, and avoid this type of duplicity in the future. Your external behavior and internal attitude should be in harmony. If you can't do that, the next best thing is to be internally gentle and peaceful although your exterior may seem a bit rough.

> 23 When everyone contradicts me, it is the weapon of my own evil deeds turned upon me for belittling shame and modesty. From now on I shall avoid rough behavior.

There are times when everyone talks badly about you, denigrating and turning against you. Even when you do wonderful things, people do not give you credit and they belittle you for faults you don't have. The cause for this is that previously we were shameless; we totally disregarded what other people thought about our bad behavior, and we lacked personal modesty. Recognizing the result of our unsuitable behavior, we should try to reduce or totally eliminate such actions.

> 24 When there is disagreement as soon as my companions gather, it is the weapon of my own evil deeds turned upon me for peddling my discontent and evil disposition everywhere. From now on without any ulterior motive, I shall behave well toward all.

This verse addresses situations in which our followers, students, or associates are unstable and quarrelsome, causing dissension and division among people. Our natural reaction would be to look at their faults; instead, we should look at our own misbehavior, since the present bad situation was caused by our unpleasant personality in the past, acting selfishly without regard or respect for others. We should acknowledge this, feel remorse over the harm our bad actions caused in the past, accept their consequences, and resolve to improve our personality by treating others kindly and earnestly from now on.

> 25 When all my kin become my enemies, it is the weapon of my own evil deeds turned upon me for harboring evil thoughts. From now on I shall reduce my deceit and guile.

At times even those closest to us can slowly turn against us; our dear friends, teachers, neighbors, and relatives can become our enemies. This can cause us great misery and suffering. Again, we must recognize that we caused this by our past actions, by our unsympathetic attitude and negative feelings toward others. Such behavior stems from selfishness, lack of empathy, and insensitivity to others. We should blame ourselves and not others for this situation and resolve to act without deceit and hidden grudges in the future.

When you do this, even if everyone appears to be your enemy, you still will have peace of mind.

In connection with this subject Śāntideva said (*BCA* 4.28–29):

> The enemies hatred, attachment, and so forth have neither arms nor legs; they have neither courage nor wisdom, so how is it that they have enslaved me? Joyfully abiding in my mind they ruin me, and yet I bear it without anger; I should despise such misplaced forbearance!

We should have no patience with the inner enemies that are our afflictions; instead we should want to destroy them. This is the true target of our anger. We should be patient and merciful with others who act wrongly because they are controlled by their inner enemies. You should not be a slave to your own afflictions by reacting to them in kind, for example by responding to their anger with your own. If you are respectful, loving, and patient with such people, realizing that their essential nature is good, it will be very beneficial.

> 26 When I am sick with consumption or edema, it is the weapon of my own evil deeds turned upon me for unlawfully and indiscriminately stealing others' wealth. From now on I shall renounce plundering others' wealth.

When we experience serious chronic illnesses, such as edema, it is the result of powerful past negative actions, although it is difficult to tell exactly where they came from. Among the possible causes is having unlawfully taken possession of property or offerings made to the Buddha, Dharma, and Sangha—the Three Jewels. When offerings are made to the Three Jewels it produces the highest degree of merit. The reverse is also true: to disrespect or injure the Three Jewels produces the greatest demerit. If such actions are done without guilt, or even with pleasure, the negativity of the action is powerfully magnified. This is explained in detail in the Buddhist scriptures. When we get sick, we should realize that it is the maturation of our past negative actions that is to blame and that those actions were propelled by our selfish and egocentric attitudes. Thus, we should resolve never again to lawlessly appropriate the property of the Three Jewels, and we should resolve to take upon ourselves the illnesses of others.

> 27 When my body is suddenly struck by contagious disease, it is the weapon of my own evil deeds turned upon me for committing acts that corrupted my vows. From now on I shall renounce nonvirtuous acts.

This verse is similar to the previous one, but here we are dealing with acute diseases, like a sudden severe headache, rather than chronic ones; these also are the result of past actions, although again it's difficult to tell which ones. Among the causes of illness is the violation of religious vows that you have taken in a solemn manner. In Tibet, when we make such pledges, we sometimes place a vajra on our heads and partake of sacramental liquid to seal such promises. If we carelessly neglect such vows, a serious acute illness can befall us.

> 28 When my intellect is blind toward all that is worth knowing, it is the weapon of my own evil deeds turned upon me for claiming as the Dharma what ought to be put aside. From now on I shall cultivate the wisdom that comes from study, examination, and meditation.

When our minds become dull or blocked from understanding any type of knowledge, especially religious knowledge, it is a result of our past nonvirtuous actions. When you try to analyze what you are studying, you feel mentally dull and are unable to do so. You may try to meditate, or to memorize a text, but you just can't succeed. At that time, your mind is as dull as that of a donkey! The cause of such mental darkness is that in the past we chose what was good for us from a worldly perspective rather than what was in accordance with the Dharma. For example, when there is a choice between a Dharma teaching and a wonderful show, you have to choose which is really suitable; sometimes we choose entertainment over the Dharma. We must understand this and vow to avoid frivolous activities and to apply ourselves to religious teachings from now on so as to gain the wisdom that comes from study, from examination, and from meditation.

> 29 When I am overcome by sleep while practicing Dharma,
> it is the weapon of my own evil deeds turned upon me for
> piling up obscurations to the holy Dharma. From now on
> I shall undergo hardship for the sake of the Dharma.

When we become sleepy during spiritual practices, such as reading the scriptures or commentaries, listening to teachings or meditating, it is a result of negative past actions that obscured or hindered the Dharma. We must show great respect and interest toward the teachings, progressively gaining more understanding and ridding ourselves of barriers to our comprehension of them. We have to make special efforts and endure any hardship in this undertaking. For example, many of the monks at Drepung, Sera, and Ganden monasteries came from distant places like Amdo or Mongolia; in order to reach Lhasa they had to walk for a month or more through difficult, uninhabited areas, enduring heat, winds, hunger, and thirst. They underwent such hardships, even risking death, in order to study the Dharma. Even once they got to the monasteries, there was often not enough to eat, and they had to live in very poor conditions. You should resolve that from now on you will gladly endure any hardship for the sake of the Dharma. We also have to respect embodiments of the Dharma such as the scriptures. In Tibet, we always put Dharma books in a high place, respecting even loose pages, and we had special ceremonies with music, decorations, incense, and a feast when a Kangyur was donated. Respecting and understanding the Dharma creates great positive results, and treating it disrespectfully produces very powerful negative effects in the future.

> 30 When I delight in the afflictions and am greatly distracted,
> it is the weapon of my own evil deeds turned upon me for
> not meditating upon impermanence and the shortcomings
> of cyclic existence. From now on I shall increase my dissatisfaction for cyclic existence.

When our minds are filled with afflictions, like the three poisons, we are not able to keep our minds from wandering; we become so distracted by objects of desire, hatred, and ignorance that we are unable to study the Dharma or to meditate. However, if we think about the impermanence of life, how we are rushing toward death, we will not waste even a moment. Similarly, if we think about the faults of cyclic existence, then we will direct our short life in a purposeful way. We must remember that at the time of death only the Dharma will be of benefit to us. If we are mindful in this way, we won't be distracted by the enticements of the three poisons. We should resolve from now on to renounce cyclic existence, just as a prisoner desperately wants to get out of prison, once aware of all of its faults. If a person gets to enjoy prison, he or she will not want to leave.

The motive for renunciation is impermanence, which is why this subject is taught at the beginning of the *Stages of the Path*. We must behave like farmers who in the fall plow under the stalks of the last crop to fertilize and mulch the soil during the winter so that it will be ready for planting in the spring. Similarly, we need to prepare during this life so that we can have a better life in the future. Just as the stalks of the fall crop are the best fertilizer, the perception of impermanence is the best of perceptions. We must realize that time is short and that we must not waste this precious life. Death is looking right over our shoulder and is ready to take us at any time, separating us from all we love and sending us on to the next birth. Therefore, we must spend as much time as possible preparing ourselves by studying the Dharma and acting virtuously. People can be complacent; often they are impelled to Dharma practice only when they become sick or meet with terrible losses, such as seeing the devastation of a major war, and thus are forced to become more aware of impermanence.

31 When things get worse no matter what I do, it is the
weapon of my own evil deeds turned upon me for
disparaging moral causality and dependent origination.
From now on I shall strive to accumulate merit.

This verse addresses the situation in which everything goes against you; no matter what you do—in your personal, business, or spiritual life—you are unable to succeed in anything. This type of misery is the result of disregarding the laws of karma and cause and effect and performing nonvirtuous activities that harm others. Therefore, you should resolve from now on to be patient with others, behave virtuously, and understand the laws of reality, the truth of suffering and its cause. If we strive to do only what is right, not to harm any sentient beings, and to work for their benefit, we must expect to meet many hardships, which, however, we should look upon as opportunities to practice patience. From now on, we should keep in mind karma and its results and act accordingly.

> 32 When all the religious rites I perform go awry, it is the
> weapon of my own evil deeds turned upon me for looking
> to the dark quarter for help. From now on I shall turn
> away from the dark quarter.

There are times when the religious rituals we perform for special objectives such as better health or material advancement do not turn out as we hoped—in fact, things get even worse. This is not the fault of your guru, the buddhas, the Dharma protectors, other objects of your prayers, or the religious practices themselves. Rather, it is the result of your previous actions, especially having trusted in evil spirits and other dark forces. When you meet with the results of such practices, you should turn away from reliance on the dark quarter.

> 33 When my prayers to the Three Jewels go unanswered, it is
> the weapon of my own evil deeds turned upon me for not
> believing in buddhahood. From now on I shall rely on the
> Three Jewels alone.

This verse is similar to the previous one; it concerns people who are praying unsuccessfully to the Three Jewels. You may wonder why your requests were not fulfilled and blame the Three Jewels; such thinking is wrong. You should realize that the fault is only your own; it is the result of having acted negatively in the past regarding the Three Jewels in which we take refuge: the Buddha, Dharma, and Sangha. The Buddha is the perfect teacher; the Dharma is the pure teaching; and the Sangha is the assembly of religious persons. The actual refuge is to have faith in the Dharma, understanding reality, giving up nonvirtuous actions, and performing wholesome actions. Acting in the opposite way implies that you lack faith in the Buddha and his teaching and disrespect the Sangha, the best helpers to Dharma practice. Realizing the effects of your past lack of faith in the Three Jewels, you should resolve to have faith in them from now on. To take refuge in the Three Jewels is to entrust your life to the Three Jewels. They are called jewels because they are rare and superior and have the highest qualities. For example, when you have a serious illness you want the best doctor, medical treatment, and nurses or assistants. For our spiritual illness, the Buddha is the best doctor, the Dharma is the most effective medicine, and the Sangha is the best nurse and spiritual friend to be followed and imitated. But just as the best doctor and medicine and nurses cannot help you unless you trust them and comply with their instructions, the Three Jewels cannot help unless you place your trust in them. All desirable spiritual goals can be attained by trusting the Three Jewels, but trusting in the Three Jewels will not help you to attain harmful or worldly objectives.

> 34 When conceptual construction rises up as pollution demons and evil spirits, it is the weapon of my own evil deeds turned upon me for sinning against the gods and mantras. From now on I shall crush all conceptual construction.

This verse is about transgressing holy vows or precepts that you have taken. This very negative karma will bring you all kinds of misfortunes, such as attacks by harmful demons and evil spirits. External and internal negative experiences result from improperly performing religious practices and not keeping the vows you have made to worldly gods, or to supramundane ones such as Avalokiteśvara, Mañjuśrī, Mahākāla, or Yamāntaka. Realizing this, you should think: "From now on I will conquer my wrong thinking." Wrong thinking can refer either to conceptual thought, or to seeing things that are actually pure as impure.

> 35 When I wander far from home like a helpless person, it is the weapon of my own evil deeds turned upon me for driving spiritual teachers and others from their homes. From now on I shall not expel anyone from their home.

With no control over our lives, we may come to be exiled from our homes and to be wandering in strange places, as I have, coming all the way from Tibet to Wisconsin. Like feathers, we are carried far away by the winds of karma. What caused this was misbehavior toward our gurus or parents, such as evicting them from their homes. The motivation for such actions is our view of a real personal identity and our self-cherishing attitude. The worst results come from acting on these wrong views in relation to higher spiritual beings, but it applies to anyone, even to forcing animals from the area where they are living because they may be harming us in some way. We must reverse such attitudes and wish only peace and happiness for others, desire to have such evils done by others ripen upon ourselves, and vow never to throw people out of their homes for our own selfish purposes.

> 36 When calamities occur like frost and hail, it is the weapon of my own evil deeds turned upon me for not properly guarding my vows and moral conduct. From now on I shall keep my vows and moral conduct pure.

This verse brings up the kinds of hardship farmers experience when their crops are destroyed by natural calamities. Sometimes drought, frost, or a tornado hits an area, but it spares a particular farm, or it strikes only one place. These calamities affect everyone in an area who has the same type of karma. The cause of such catastrophes is having broken our religious vows and not keeping the precepts of pure moral conduct. Breaking the vows of monastic discipline, bodhisattva conduct, or tantra leads to rebirth in lower realms. A secondary consequence may be damage to our subsequent human environment, as described in this verse. Therefore, we should resolve to keep our vows pure from now on.

> 37 When I, a greedy person, lose my wealth, it is the weapon of my own evil deeds turned upon me for not giving charity or making offerings to the Three Jewels. From now on I will zealously make offerings and give charity.

This verse is about greedy people who are ambitious for wealth, property, high position, or other worldly success, but do not achieve their desires no matter how hard they try. The causes of this situation are miserliness, not giving charity to those in need, and not making offerings to the Three Jewels. The Three Jewels are the best field for the production of merit, just as a very rich field produces an abundance of crops. Sentient beings are also a great object for our compassion and charity; we can desire to and actually give them food, clothing, or whatever they need. Some people are so miserly that they try to hold on to their wealth even at the point of death. The future consequences of stinginess are that you will never be financially successful and that all your efforts to make money will fail. This is only a minor consequence in the human realm; the primary result of lack of charity is birth in the realm of hungry ghosts, possibly for eons. Realizing this, you should resolve, "From now on, I will strenuously endeavor to make offerings to the Three Jewels and be generous to those in need." Even if you make a great charitable contribution, the positive effect of that action can be ruined if you do it out of egocentricity, the desire for prestige, or in competition with others.

> 38 When my companions mistreat me for being ugly, it is the weapon of my own evil deeds turned upon me for venting my rage by erecting ugly images. From now on I shall erect images of the gods and be slow to anger.

If someone is born with a defective, unattractive, or deformed body, they experience great suffering when others denigrate them. Here too, you should not react in anger at being disparaged by others; instead, you should consider that your being born with this ugly physical form is a result of your past anger and hatred, having spoken harsh words, shown an ugly face, and displayed a hostile attitude toward others. Also, out of our terrible rage, we destroyed beautiful statues or temples or caused ugly things to be made. Therefore, we should resolve in the future to make beautiful images of Buddhas and other deities, statues, paintings, stupas, and so forth. By doing this with respect, you will in the future attain a very good birth with an attractive body.

There is a story in the sutras of a monk who had a very beautiful voice. His voice was so beautiful that elephants would stop outside his house just to listen to him. One time a king riding on an elephant passed this monk's house. All of a sudden the elephant stopped to listen to the monk, who was in his room chanting. The king had not wanted to stop and wondered why his elephant did so. The king then heard the monk's beautiful voice, and wanting to see the person who was chanting, he went into the house. What he saw was a monk with a very small, crooked, ugly body. He couldn't imagine how this could be the same person who had such a beautiful voice;

an ugly body and a beautiful voice seemed totally incongruous. He asked the Buddha about this, and the Buddha gave this explanation. He said that a long time ago, after the passing of the previous Buddha Kaśyapa, this monk was a worker building an enormous stupa. He was tired and always complained about the work, and he was very negative about his job. However, when the stupa was completed, he changed his mind about it. Feeling satisfaction that the work had been very well done, he bought a beautiful-sounding bell for the stupa. These actions gave rise to different results; because of his ill temper about building the stupa, he obtained a small and ugly body, but because he later rejoiced in the stupa and offered a beautiful bell to adorn it, he obtained a beautiful voice.

39 When lust and hate are stirred up no matter what I do,
it is the weapon of my own evil deeds turned upon me
for hardening my malevolent, evil mind. Obstinacy,
from now on I shall totally extirpate you!

In this connection Śāntideva said (*BCA* 4.44):

> Even if I am burned, killed, or beheaded, I will never
> bow down to the enemy, the afflictions.

Submitting to our inner enemy, the afflictions, will bring many lifetimes of pain and suffering, while tortures such as being beheaded or burned will only bring temporary pain and suffering and can even be used for our own purification and for the benefit of others. If you have the choice between temporary suffering and long-term suffering, it is always best to take the temporary. Therefore, you should try to cut out the root of your suffering, the obstinate self-cherishing attitude. Once you have eliminated this through wisdom, there will be no basis on which the afflictions can re-establish themselves.

When despite all your efforts to conquer the afflictions, your mind remains disturbed by lust and hatred, it is the result of not having applied the antidote in the past and of allowing the afflictions to stubbornly remain in your mind. Thinking that way, you should resolve that from now on this kind of obduracy should be totally uprooted from your mind.

> 40 When none of my practices reach their goal, it is the weapon of my own evil deeds turned upon me for internalizing a pernicious view. From now on, whatever I do shall be solely for the sake of others.

This verse addresses difficulties in our spiritual practices, our lack of success in realizing objectives such as meditating on bodhicitta. This is caused by a wrong or inferior view that exists deep in our minds. By inferior view we mean the self-cherishing attitude of seeking worldly pleasures, or even of working toward religious goals, but only for one's own sake rather than for the benefit of others. Ego-clinging is like a knife that cuts and destroys our practice. From now on we should do everything for the sake of others, cherishing others rather than ourselves.

> 41 When I cannot control my own mind even though I engage in religious activity, it is the weapon of my own evil deeds turned upon me for concentrating on my own aggrandizement in the present life. From now on I shall concentrate on the desire for liberation.

This verse is also about engaging in Dharma practice and other wholesome activities, but finding that our minds are still uncontrollable. Our minds aren't tamed and made more flexible by our virtuous conduct, as they should be, but remain rough and hard. The cause of this is that in past lives we concentrated on the eight worldly concerns: gain and loss, fame and disgrace, praise and blame, pleasure and pain. We sought only our own glorification in that life. We may have performed religious activities, but we did them for our own worldly selfish purposes. What we need to do from now on is to continue in our religious practice with renewed energy and direction, and to abandon worldly concerns and dedicate ourselves solely to liberating all sentient beings from cyclic existence.

> 42 When I despair as soon as I've sat down and reflected, it is the weapon of my own evil deeds turned upon me for shamelessly flitting about from one new friend of high status to another. From now on I shall be serious about my friendships with everyone.

This verse also deals with difficulties in spiritual practice; for example, you may go into retreat and sit down to practice some special meditation, but as soon as you do so, you realize that things aren't going right and you feel despair. The cause of this is that in the past we shamelessly changed our minds about teachers or other friends, abandoned relationships when we thought we found someone else more important, and spoke badly about our former associates. When we realize that our difficulty is caused by the imprint of past actions, we should resolve to be very careful in the way we interact with our teachers and associates.

> 43 When I am deceived by others' cunning, it is the weapon of my own evil deeds turned upon me for increasing my selfishness, pride, and insatiable greed. From now on I shall markedly reduce all of them.

This verse concerns people who are deceptive and secretive, who hide their bad qualities and pretend to virtues they don't have. When such a devious person, perhaps even a friend, relative, or teacher, takes advantage of you, it is the result of similar deceptions you performed in the past, having deceived others out of your pride, conceit, and insatiable greed. If you had not done that, you would not be experiencing this result; therefore, you should think: "From now on I will lessen my selfish attachments." Dissatisfaction is a great evil; it is best to be fully satisfied with whatever one has. As Nāgārjuna taught his friend King Gautamīputra in *The Letter to a Friend,* "Satisfaction is the most excellent of all riches." Even if you are a king dwelling amid gold and silver, if you are not satisfied, you are mentally poor. But if a beggar sitting on a filthy cloth, with only enough poor food to fill his stomach for a day, is satisfied, he is much wealthier than the king.

> 44 When I am sidetracked by attachment or aversion while studying or teaching, it is the weapon of my own evil deeds turned upon me for not considering my own devilish faults. From now on I shall examine these impediments and abandon them.

This verse concerns those who give Dharma teachings as well as those who listen to them. When we are teaching or studying, the teaching itself may repulse or attract us, thereby becoming a cause of the afflictions rather than a cause of emancipation. This results from not having examined in past lives the devilish faults in our minds, especially the selfish attitude and view of a real personal identity, which are the source of all the afflictions. Under the power of such afflictions, someone can teach the Dharma motivated by the eight worldly concerns, rather than by concern for others' welfare. It is also possible to listen to the teachings with the wrong attitude, such as the desire to acquire knowledge in order to sell it to others, or to gain wealth and fame for oneself. The right attitude is to see yourself as a patient needing liberation from the sickness of the three poisons, karma, the view of a real personal identity, and all the pain of cyclic existence, and thus to eagerly seek the medicine of the Dharma teaching from the guru, who is like a physician. Studying with the wrong motivation is a waste. It is by not reflecting on our selfishness and mental afflictions that they gain power over us and create negative results in the future. Therefore, you should determine that from now on, you will fully examine and abandon these mental obstacles.

> 45 When all the good I've done turns out badly, it is the weapon of my own evil deeds turned upon me for repaying kindness with ingratitude. From now on I shall very respectfully repay kindness.

When we try to help others with the kindest of intentions, we may in return be treated badly, attacked, or opposed. For example, the abbot of a monastery may admonish the monks about their behavior in order to benefit them, but some of the monks may react with anger and defensiveness and reject his counsel. Even in your personal life, in dealing with friends, employees, or family, your altruistically motivated actions can elicit a negative response. Such a response can cause you to feel angry and self-righteously indignant, thinking, "I have helped these people over such a long time, and this is how they show their gratitude!" You may want to entirely stop assisting them. This hostile reaction is caused by your self-cherishing attitude and view of a real personal identity, which destroy any beneficial effect of your actions. Rather than yield to this evil tendency with blame and anger, we should understand the cause, which is that we did not welcome the help or advice of others in the past; we ungratefully repaid others' wonderful kindness with anger and malice. Therefore, we should not blame the ungrateful person; we should have sympathy for the person, recognizing the negative karma he or she is creating. Instead, we should blame our prior ungrateful behavior, joyfully accept the consequences, and resolve from now on to respectfully and gratefully accept kind help and advice. We need to apply this attitude universally to all sentient beings who, as our mothers and fathers, have done us great kindness in the past.

> 46 In short, when calamities befall me, it is the weapon of my own evil deeds turned upon me, like a smith killed by his own sword. From now on I shall be heedful of my own sinful actions.

In this life, unexpected disasters may befall us, and our most cherished hopes may come to nothing. This is like a blacksmith who may be killed by the swords and other weapons he has made. We too create weapons that turn on us by performing negative actions that have undesirable results. Therefore, we have no reason to blame anyone else since we have injured ourselves by the weapon of our own actions. Thus, we should resolve to conscientiously avoid any unwholesome actions.

> 47 When I experience suffering in the wretched states of existence, it is the weapon of my own evil deeds turned upon me, like a fletcher killed by his own arrow. From now on I shall be heedful of my own sinful actions.

This verse is similar to the previous one. The harsh and lengthy sufferings of the lower realms of birth are caused by the weapon of our bad actions returning to us. The example given is of a fletcher, an arrow maker. There is a story about a fletcher who made sharp arrows with poisonous points so as to kill the enemy more effectively. He was ordered to the battlefield by the ruler and was then struck and killed by a poisoned arrow that he had made himself.

As Śāntideva said (*BCA* 5.7c–8b)

> Who created the burning iron pavement of Hell? Where do the Sirens come from? The sage taught that all these arise from the sinful mind.

Since all suffering is created by nothing other than our own actions, we should avoid all unwholesome actions in the future.

> 48 When the sufferings of the householder befall me, it is the weapon of my own evil deeds turned upon me, like parents killed by their cherished son. From now on it is right for me to leave worldly life forever.

"Householder" usually refers to a layman devoted to worldly activities who has a family, raises children, and has a secular job. Sometimes it can even apply to ordained monks or nuns, that is, those who have the same mentality as a householder, getting caught up in business deals, politics, and day-to-day worldliness. There are many undesirable things that can happen to householders, even those who have tried to do a good job caring for family and children. Sometimes, due to their own inner afflictions, children become very angry over some trivial conflict and completely forget their parents' care and nurturing, turn against them, and even kill them. We all have read about these kinds of cases in the newspapers: children killing parents, friends killing friends, neighbors killing neighbors. All these actions come from the view of a real personal identity and the self-cherishing attitude. If you experience such evil occurrences, realize that they were brought about by having acted in a similar manner out of powerful hatred and ingratitude in past lives. This verse, like the previous ones, points to the inner enemy as the cause of our pain. Having reflected on this, we should wish strongly to get out of this painful worldly life to lead a life of spiritual practice that can be of great benefit to ourselves and others.

> 49 Since that's the way it is, I seize the enemy! I seize the thief who ambushed and deceived me, the hypocrite who deceived me disguised as myself. Aha! It is ego-clinging, without a doubt.

This concludes the section of verses presenting a detailed description of the painful effects of the view of a real personal identity and self-cherishing attitude. This verse points to a clear realization of the real problem, and shows how to destroy the inner enemies with the help of the tutelary deity Yamāntaka. The previous verses are not exaggerations; they really show how the inner enemies are the root cause of everything undesirable in cyclic existence. In the past you did not recognize them; you obeyed those terrible thieves who hid out and robbed you of your wealth of wholesome qualities that bring peace and happiness. They are much worse than ordinary thieves who just take property or money; they have cleverly deceived us by masquerading as ourselves so that we don't even recognize them as enemies. Our selfishness makes us the center of the world and it seems natural and beneficial to us. Now, through study, reflection, and meditation we have finally unmasked the enemies who have imprisoned us in painful cyclic existence for such a long time. At this time, you utter an exclamation of recognition, *e ma* in Tibetan, like "Aha," meaning something like, "Now I know the real enemies that must be destroyed."

> 50 Now, O Yamāntaka, raise the weapon of action and spin it furiously over your head three times. Spread far apart your feet, which are the two truths, open wide your eyes of method and wisdom, and bare your fangs of the four powers and pierce the enemy!

Now you have recognized the true enemy. Among the many wrathful protective deities is Yamāntaka, whose wrath is directed against the ignorant attitudes of egocentricity, selfishness, and grasping at true, independent, existence. All these destroy our chance to gain enlightenment. The symbolic meaning of Yamāntaka is the direct realization of selflessness—that there is no permanent self or soul and that real personal identity and the object of self-cherishing do not truly exist. This is the ultimate truth, the realization of emptiness that is truly the destroyer of our real enemies.

Yamāntaka stands with his two feet apart, symbolizing the two truths, the right foot the conventional truth and the left the ultimate. His two eyes symbolize the two types of bodhicitta, the conventional bodhicitta of the loving, kind attitude of wishing to achieve buddhahood for the benefit of all sentient beings, and the ultimate bodhicitta of the realization of emptiness. These two are also called method and wisdom; together they form the beginning of the bodhisattva path. Yamāntaka bares his four fangs, which symbolize the four powers to purify negativities; these are the powers of reliance, regret, repentance, and purification. In this verse we call upon Yamāntaka to destroy our inner enemies.

You should think, "O mighty Lord Yamāntaka, please help me. You are the lord over death and the perfect wisdom that can eliminate my inner enemies. You are the knower of the two truths, the destroyer of ignorance. Please attack my view of a real personal identity and self-cherishing attitude: Kill them, destroy them, stamp them out. Help me get rid of the two enemies that have been plaguing me since time began. Please replace these two demons with the two bodhicittas."

> 51 O King of Spells who torments the enemy, summon that vow-breaker who is destroying me and others, that savage called "Ego-Clinging, the Enchanter," who, brandishing the weapon of action, runs uncontrollably through the jungle of cyclic existence.

> 52 Call him, call him, wrathful Yamāntaka! Beat him, beat him, pierce the heart of the enemy, Ego! Roar and thunder on the head of the destroyer, false construction! Mortally strike at the heart of the butcher, the enemy, Ego!

Verses 51 and 52 are similar to the preceding one in that they request Yamāntaka to strike at the heart of our inner enemies, at the view of a real personal identity and the self-cherishing attitude. Śāntideva said (*BCA* 8.155):

> O Mind, for countless eons you have wished to accomplish your own purpose, yet despite great hardships, you have gained only misery.

Acting only for our own selfish purposes over countless eons has brought us nothing except misery and suffering. Isn't it about time to break this cycle and start working for other sentient beings and our liberation? If we had started doing this in the past, we wouldn't be in cyclic existence today.

> 53 Hūṃ! Hūṃ! O great tutelary deity, produce your miraculous apparitions! Dza! Dza! Bind the enemy tightly! Phaṭ!

> Phaṭ! I beseech you to release me from all fetters! Shig!
> Shig! I beseech you to cut the knot of clinging!

Here we are calling Yamāntaka with the syllable "Hūṃ!" the seed syllable of perfect wisdom. We ask him to rise up and activate his special powers, which are the two types of bodhicitta. "Dza! Dza!" means bring the enemies, tie them up, and do not release them. "Phaṭ! Phaṭ!" and "Shig! Shig!" mean destroy them, annihilate them, and free us from the enemies of self-cherishing and the view of a real personal identity. When Yamāntaka cuts through the knot of the self-cherishing attitude, we will be rid of the enemy.

> 54 Approach, great tutelary deity Yamāntaka. I beseech you at this very moment to rip to shreds this leather sack of actions and the five poisonous afflictions that mire me in the mud of worldly action.

Here we are making an additional request of Lord Yamāntaka. We ask him to cut from our backs the sack of negative karma and poisonous afflictions caused by our two inner enemies.

> 55 Although it has brought me suffering in the three wretched states of existence, not knowing enough to fear it, I rush to its cause. Roar and thunder on the head of the destroyer, false construction! Mortally strike at the heart of the butcher, the enemy, Ego!

We have performed many improper actions of body, speech, and mind in the past under the influence of our self-cherishing attitude. Therefore, we have been born countless times in the three lower realms of terrible pain and suffering, but we stupidly haven't recognized why this has happened. In our present life, we are still chasing after our own selfish purposes, harming others, and cherishing only ourselves. We should really stop and think and ask ourselves: "Who is doing this to me? Who is making me act like this?" If we reflect, we will see that it is our self-cherishing attitude that brings us such suffering.

> 56 Although my desire for comfort is great, I don't accumulate its causes. Although my tolerance for suffering is small, my desire and greed are great. Roar and thunder on the head of the destroyer, false construction! Mortally strike at the heart of the butcher, the enemy, Ego!

All of us want to accomplish things quickly and with little effort, whether in religious, business, or personal endeavors. We do not want to undergo any hardship and we expect to achieve our objectives effortlessly. When we do not get what we want, it is because our self-cherishing attitude kept us from doing what was needed to achieve it.

> 57 Although that which I desire is near at hand, my effort to achieve it is small. Although my projects are many, none of them are completed. Roar and thunder on the head of the destroyer, false construction! Mortally strike at the heart of the butcher, the enemy, Ego!

This verse is similar to the last one. We desire to have continual happiness, peace, pleasure, and wealth. All the good things we have in this life come from our past actions. If we didn't earn the necessary merit in our past lives, we won't obtain anything positive in this life. Yet we are ruthless in pursuit of the good life, not recognizing that it can only be obtained by attending to its proper causes.

> 58 Although I have many new friendships, my modesty and friendships are of short duration. Although I freeload off of others, I eagerly pursue those who pilfer. Roar and thunder on the head of the destroyer, false construction! Mortally strike at the heart of the butcher, the enemy, Ego!

This verse deals with relationships. In Tibet, traveling entertainers announce their entrance into a town with drums. The townspeople, who are attracted by the drum rolls, rush over to them without even knowing what is going on. Similarly, we always run around attracted by wealth, comfort, good food, and fine clothing. If we can't acquire these things legitimately, we try to obtain them by some underhanded means.

> 59 Although I am skilled at flattery and asking for things indirectly, my despair is great. Although I assiduously amass things, miserliness binds me. Roar and thunder on the head of the destroyer, false construction! Mortally strike at the heart of the butcher, the enemy, Ego!

How you obtain the things you need is very important, and using the improper means to do so will result in bad consequences for you. When you have something and try to hoard it, you will be the loser later on. You should share what you have with those who have less; stinginess is the cause of future poverty.

> 60 Although whatever I have done has been insignificant, I am swollen with pride. Although I have no reputation, my hunger for it is great. Roar and thunder on the head of the destroyer, false construction! Mortally strike at the heart of the butcher, the enemy, Ego!

This verse points out to us our wrong views. Even though we haven't shown the least bit of kindness for others, we keep reminding them of all we have done. If we do good for others, it should be done discreetly, without the recipient knowing. Boasting and bragging are negative traits arising from our self-cherishing mind.

> 61 Although my preceptors are many, my ability to keep my vows is small. Although my disciples are many, I give little time to help and look after them. Roar and thunder on the head of the destroyer, false construction! Mortally strike at the heart of the butcher, the enemy, Ego!

It is possible to have too many spiritual teachers. If you ignore or misinterpret their teachings, you will create strong negative results. It would be better to have strong faith and a good relationship with fewer teachers; that will be much more beneficial.

> 62 Although my promises are many, my practical assistance is minimal. Although my fame is great, if it were examined,

> the gods and demons would put me to shame. Roar and thunder on the head of the destroyer, false construction! Mortally strike at the heart of the butcher, the enemy, Ego!

Taking religious vows incurs many obligations, such as not harming others and acting toward them in accordance with the teachings. If we take such vows and fail to fulfill our promises, we create very negative consequences for ourselves. It is highly shameful if a famous spiritual teacher inwardly does not live up to what he preaches. The bad consequences of such hypocrisy are the results of self-cherishing.

> 63 Although my learning is scant, my penchant for empty verbiage is great. Although the extent of my religious instruction is slight, I pretend to understand everything. Roar and thunder on the head of the destroyer, false construction! Mortally strike at the heart of the butcher, the enemy, Ego!

The main purpose of religious practice is to control and purify the mind, to understand its true nature by the realization of emptiness. Some people without much study or knowledge erroneously think that they know a lot; some people study haphazardly without subduing their minds; some sit with a blank mind or chase stray thoughts like a crazy monkey. Students without the motivation to really learn may get a vague impression of the sutras without true understanding. This type of approach is an obstacle to the learning and understanding that are necessary for the achievement of spiritual goals. If such a person tries to impress people with his or her knowledge of the teachings, he or she will likely misinform them. Such actions originate from self-cherishing and are very negative in their consequences.

> 64 Although my companions and underlings are numerous, not one is dependable. Although I have many masters, not one is a reliable protector. Roar and thunder on the head of the destroyer, false construction! Mortally strike at the heart of the butcher, the enemy, Ego!

This verse deals with great leaders or teachers surrounded by many followers.

You should take care of the people who depend on you. If your subordinates do not respect or follow you, it is the result of your past disrespect and disobedience to your teachers. Such bad actions are caused by self-cherishing, which should be destroyed.

> 65 Although I have high status, my merit is less than an evil spirit's. Although I am a great religious teacher, my passions are grosser than a demon's. Roar and thunder on the head of the destroyer, false construction! Mortally strike at the heart of the butcher, the enemy, Ego!

This verse is also about great teachers and leaders. Without proper education and the cultivation of virtuous qualities, they cannot lead others properly and will mislead them under the influence of their evil inner demons.

There once was a very great and famous Tibetan lama who held the position of the Ganden Tripa, the head of Ganden monastery. He said that if he had not studied the Dharma from the time he was very young, and if he had not experienced so many hardships, he would not have been able to teach so well. It was because of his intense studies and difficult circumstances that he became a great teacher. To be a good teacher you must spend a great deal of time in preparation. You cannot be a proper teacher if you continue to rely on the inner demons of the view of a real personal identity and the self-cherishing attitude.

> 66 Although my view is lofty, my behavior is worse than a dog's. Although my good qualities are many, their basis is carried off by the wind. Roar and thunder on the head of the destroyer, false construction! Mortally strike at the heart of the butcher, the enemy, Ego!

This verse is about someone who behaves very badly but professes to have special knowledge or vows. When one receives certain high tantric teachings but has a bad attitude and behaves worse than an animal, one is creating very negative consequences for oneself under the influence of one's inner demons. This person will not achieve any spiritual growth and is throwing away the good foundation that he or she had received in the teachings. Proper tantric teaching should be preceded by an understanding of the common path based on the sutras; only after you have comprehended that path can you go on to the tantric teachings. To practice the tantra without this basic understanding is like trying to ride a wild elephant.

> 67 All desires enter into me and I blame all my quarrels on others for no reason. Roar and thunder on the head of the destroyer, false construction! Mortally strike at the heart of the butcher, the enemy, Ego!

This verse, like previous ones, talks about a person full of selfish desires who blames others for all his or her quarrels. Naturally, we should place others' needs above our own; we should take the responsibility for quarrels that have come about due to our past negative actions.

> 68 Although I have put on the saffron robe, I appeal to evil spirits for protection. Although I have taken religious vows, my behavior is demonic. Roar and thunder on the head of the destroyer, false construction! Mortally strike at the heart of the butcher, the enemy, Ego!

This verse concerns ordained monks or nuns. They may have changed their way of dress and shaved their head, and so have the external appearance of a monk or nun, but they have not changed internally. Instead of depending on the Three Jewels, they rely on their inner demons. Such people have put their trust in the wrong place and this will only bring them pain and suffering.

> 69 Although the gods give me happiness, I worship evil spirits. Although the Dharma guides me, I deceive the Three Jewels. Roar and thunder on the head of the destroyer, false construction! Mortally strike at the heart of the butcher, the enemy, Ego!

Real pleasure and happiness come from the buddhas; a person who knows this but still makes offerings to evil spirits is under the power of his or her two inner demons. The Three Jewels—the Buddha, Dharma, and Sangha—are the only protection we can truly rely upon.

> 70 Although I have always resorted to secluded places, I am carried away by distraction. Although I request instruction in the holy Dharma and the religious sciences, I cherish divination and shamanism. Roar and thunder on the head of the destroyer, false construction! Mortally strike at the heart of the butcher, the enemy, Ego!

This verse concerns religious practices. If you are in a religious retreat, you should work on your spiritual practice and not be distracted by worldly thoughts and activities. A person who is distracted is deceiving himself or herself and others. This too is due to the influence of self-cherishing and will create negative consequences.

> 71 Forsaking the moral path to liberation, I cling to my home. Pouring my happiness into the water, I run after suffering. Roar and thunder on the head of the destroyer, false construction! Mortally strike at the heart of the butcher, the enemy, Ego!

Pure moral conduct is the cause of achieving all spiritual goals, from higher births to enlightenment. When you discard moral conduct and become a worldly householder, you are throwing away your opportunity to achieve true happiness. People under the influence of self-cherishing, who say they are not able to maintain their spiritual vows, are exchanging these vows for future suffering and problems.

> 72 Turning away from the gateway to liberation, I wander in remote places. Despite acquiring the precious jewel of a human body, I wind up in hell. Roar and thunder on the head of the destroyer, false construction! Mortally strike at the heart of the butcher, the enemy, Ego!

> 73 Putting aside the particulars of spiritual development, I engage in business. Leaving my guru's school, I idle about the town. Roar and thunder on the head of the destroyer, false construction! Mortally strike at the heart of the butcher, the enemy, Ego!

Verses 72 and 73 deal with people who give up their Dharma study and practice to search for worldly pleasures, money, or possessions. Such persons will only wind up suffering in hell as a result of their self-cherishing behavior. Śāntideva said that you should love and cherish all sentient beings more than you love and cherish yourself. You should meditate on the benefits of cherishing others instead of yourself, and you should remove any self-cherishing thoughts from your mind. You should meditate on helping other sentient beings to have a better life, for them to be happier and more peaceful. This is the way bodhisattvas must think; thinking in any other way will only cause us more pain and suffering.

> 74 Abandoning my own livelihood, I plunder others' property. Forsaking my parents' food, I rob others of sustenance. Roar and thunder on the head of the destroyer, false construction! Mortally strike at the heart of the butcher, the enemy, Ego!

This verse is about someone who gives up his or her own livelihood and possessions and then tries to take things from others; using deceit to acquire things is the same as stealing. Sometimes people who live in a religious community may conceal what they have and deceptively try to acquire more from others. This is extremely negative and very dangerous conduct. Instead of acting like this out of self-cherishing, we should work for the welfare of others.

> 75 Aha! Although my endurance for meditation is small, my precognition is sharp. Though I have not realized even the beginning of the path, I run around to no purpose. Roar and thunder on the head of the destroyer, false construction! Mortally strike at the heart of the butcher, the enemy, Ego!

This verse addresses those people who wish to gain high supernatural powers, such as seeing the future or reading others' minds; these powers are the result of certain kinds of yogic practices. But practicing yoga to obtain these powers without the necessary basic religious training and understanding is merely the work of the inner demons. To acquire such powers in order to boast about them is to cheat both yourself and others. You need to start at the beginning of the path.

> 76 When someone gives me useful advice, my hostile mind takes that person for an enemy. When someone deceives me, I repay that heartless one with kindness. Roar and thunder on the head of the destroyer, false construction! Mortally strike at the heart of the butcher, the enemy, Ego!

Often when our kind friends, relatives, or teachers give us some honest advice in a caring and loving way, we react negatively; we disagree with them and become hurt and angry. In contrast, when someone who is not a friend flatters us with false praise, we may like this person and consider him or her to be a friend. Under the influence of self-cherishing, we react negatively to our friends' kind counsel, and positively to our enemies' lies; we do not properly discriminate in our responses. Because this will cause us suffering in the future, such behavior should be eliminated.

> 77 I tell my intimate friends' secrets to their enemies. I shamelessly take advantage of my acquaintances. Roar and thunder on the head of the destroyer, false construction! Mortally strike at the heart of the butcher, the enemy, Ego!

When we do not honor the confidences that our friends have entrusted to us, we are under the influence of our self-cherishing attitude. It is very bad to hurt our trusted friends; to do so not only hurts them but also ourselves through the future consequences of such actions.

> 78 My frustration is intense and my thoughts are coarser than everyone else's. I am hard to get along with and I continually provoke others' bad character. Roar and thunder on the head of the destroyer, false construction! Mortally strike at the heart of the butcher, the enemy, Ego!

This verse deals with people who have a bad attitude; they are always suspicious, mistrustful, and skeptical. Because of their suspicions they are always bad tempered and behave so obnoxiously that no one wants to be around them. Such persons are controlled by their self-cherishing mind and will commit bad actions with negative consequences for themselves.

> 79 When someone seeks my assistance, I ignore him and secretly cause him harm. When someone agrees with me, I won't concur, but seek quarrels even at a distance. Roar and thunder on the head of the destroyer, false construction! Mortally strike at the heart of the butcher, the enemy, Ego!

This also is about the person with a bad personality. Such people never oblige those who request assistance; instead they try to cause harm or find fault with the other person. Such activities will only bring harm in the future.

> 80 I do not appreciate advice and I am always difficult to be with. Many things offend me and my clinging is always strong. Roar and thunder on the head of the destroyer, false construction! Mortally strike at the heart of the butcher, the enemy, Ego!

Like the preceding verses, this one is about character flaws. It speaks about the kind of person who doesn't pay attention to what other people say. Such people are easily hurt, hold grudges, and in general are difficult to be around because of their bad attitude. Under the control of their self-cherishing, such people create painful future consequences for themselves.

> 81 I exalt myself above the high and low and consider holy people my enemies. Because my lust is great, I energetically pursue young people. Roar and thunder on the head of the destroyer, false construction! Mortally strike at the heart of the butcher, the enemy, Ego!

This is about someone who is not very intelligent but who is nevertheless conceited. This person is jealous of those with more ability and finds fault with them. Such a person treats virtuous people like enemies, and under the sway of personal desires, runs after attractive young people. Instead of acting this way, we should admire great Dharma practitioners and rejoice in their teachings; even if we can't match their achievements, we should take pleasure in them.

There is a story about a king who invited the Buddha and his followers to dinner. When the Buddha arrived, a beggar was sitting at the gate of the palace. When this beggar saw Buddha approaching, he realized that he had nothing to offer him—he had only his begging bowl. The beggar admiringly reflected on the king's good fortune in inviting the Buddha. When the dinner was over and the Buddha was about to leave the palace, he dedicated the merit that resulted from his visit. In his dedication, he referred to the merits of the beggar and not to those of the king. When he was asked why he did this, he answered that the king had not acquired any merit because he was proud of serving dinner to the Buddha and did so for his own fame. While the king's thoughts were on the worldly goals of fame and honor, the beggar's thoughts were for others, since he rejoiced at the king's good fortune; therefore, the beggar received the merit for the dinner. This illustrates the benefit of always rejoicing at others' good qualities.

> 82 Because my friendships are of short duration, I cast aside former acquaintances. Because my new friends are many, I lay before them empty promises of enjoyment. Roar and thunder on the head of the destroyer, false construction! Mortally strike at the heart of the butcher, the enemy, Ego!

Again this is about an aspect of bad personality; here the verse speaks about not treating friends well and jumping from one relationship to the next without forming any real close friendships. Once people find out about such a person, they don't want to have anything more to do with him or her.

> 83 Having no precognition, I eagerly resort to lying and deprecation. Having no compassion, I snatch away the confidence from others' hearts. Roar and thunder on the head of the destroyer, false construction! Mortally strike at the heart of the butcher, the enemy, Ego!

This verse is about the kind of person who tries to impress people by falsely claiming to have supernatural powers. When this deception is discovered, others will treat him very badly. Such a person has little compassion for those close to him. This lack of sincerity, love, and compassion causes such a person great pain and suffering; he or she experiences misfortune and tries to blame others, striking out at those nearby.

> 84 Having studied little, I wildly guess about everything. Since my religious education is slight, I have wrong views about everything. Roar and thunder on the head of the destroyer, false construction! Mortally strike at the heart of the butcher, the enemy, Ego!

This verse, like some previous ones, addresses poorly educated people who have little self-confidence and therefore doubt others' knowledge. If people like this had studied the Dharma and acquired knowledge, they would be more open and respectful of others and could rid themselves of their inner enemies. Without education, such people are controlled by their self-cherishing attitudes and will continue to commit negative actions.

> 85 Habituated to attachment and aversion, I revile everyone opposed to me. Habituated to envy, I slander and deprecate others. Roar and thunder on the head of the destroyer, false construction! Mortally strike at the heart of the butcher, the enemy, Ego!

This is about the person who is habitually angry, always looking down on others and finding fault with what they do and say. He or she is resentful and disrespectful of other people. Even the Buddha acted in this way at times in some rebirths before he achieved buddhahood. We can reverse these kinds of negative actions and change the way we think and act.

> 86 Never studying, I despise the vast teaching. Never relying on a guru, I revile religious instruction. Roar and thunder on the head of the destroyer, false construction! Mortally strike at the heart of the butcher, the enemy, Ego!

This verse is very similar to previous ones. Its target is the person without much knowledge or motivation for learning who is very narrow minded.

When such a person hears the great Buddhist teaching, he or she doesn't accept it and becomes very hostile to it. This negative person, who does not rely on a religious teacher or on the teachings is controlled by self-cherishing and creates very unfavorable karma.

> 87 Instead of explaining the scriptures, I falsely set up my own system. Not having mastered pure vision, I curse and yell. Roar and thunder on the head of the destroyer, false construction! Mortally strike at the heart of the butcher, the enemy, Ego!

According to the scriptures, the spiritual path was laid out by those who traveled on it and achieved enlightenment. This verse is about someone who ignores the tradition and invents a system of his or her own based on mistaken ideas derived from hearing about strange experiences and unusual phenomena. Such a person deceives others by telling them that he or she knows the path. Because of this person's lack of knowledge, he or she remains confused and argumentative.

> 88 Without condemning sacrilegious activities, I launch numerous criticisms against all the Buddha's words. Roar and thunder on the head of the destroyer, false construction! Mortally strike at the heart of the butcher, the enemy, Ego!

> 89 Having no shame about things I should be ashamed of, I am perversely ashamed of the Dharma, which is not something shameful. Roar and thunder on the head of the destroyer, false construction! Mortally strike at the heart of the butcher, the enemy, Ego!

Verses 88 and 89 also address the person who deprecates religious teachers and the teachings. These people do not know the difference between right and wrong; they do shameful things and without any understanding always criticize Buddhist teachings. They don't realize that by acting in this way they are creating negative karma and future suffering for themselves.

> 90 No matter what I do, it is never done right; everything I do is inappropriate. Roar and thunder on the head of the destroyer, false conception! Mortally strike at the heart of the butcher, the enemy, Ego!

This verse is about bad behavior in general, doing everything incorrectly all the time. The root cause of all our suffering in cyclic existence is egocentrism, a self-centered way of thinking that grasps "I" or "me" as something absolute. This way of thinking traps sentient beings in cyclic existence; in order to escape it, we must free ourselves of the view of a real personal identity.

The sharp wheel-weapon turns back upon us. In all our lives we have been under the power of the view of a real personal identity and the self-cherishing attitude. These two are like evil kings dwelling within our minds and causing us much misery. We should think: "Because of the power of these two evil forces, I and all other beings are suffering; therefore, I must separate myself from them. I must work for the benefit of other sentient beings and not think of myself. I must joyfully accept any hardships or undesirable things that happen to me while working for the welfare of all sentient beings. No matter what misfortune befalls me, I will happily take it upon myself and make it into something of benefit to others." Like a bodhisattva, you should think: "I am glad that these negative things are happening to me; I am glad that I am receiving the consequences of my bad actions so that the effects of these bad actions will be eliminated."

The previous verses give many examples of the evils created by our inner demons. Now, keeping these things in mind, we again call upon Yamāntaka.

> 91 Aha! You whose strength is that of the ultimate body of the Sugata who conquers the demon of the egotistic view, you wielder of the staff, the weapon of the wisdom of selflessness, turn it over your head three times, without hesitation!

Here we are calling upon Yamāntaka to conquer the demon of the egotistic view, which is the same as the view of a real personal identity accompanied by the self-cherishing attitude. How does he destroy them? It is through the power of the Sugata, which means the Well-Gone-One, the

Buddha, who has perfect realization of the truth and has removed all obscurations and suffering at the root. The Sugata is a being who has achieved or gone to perfect cessation. The real essence of Buddha is the ultimate body, the conventional Buddha is the blissful realization, which takes various forms, such as the enjoyment body or the manifestation body, in order to assist sentient beings. Here the reference is probably to a manifestation body, the reality of the perfect wisdom of Mañjuśrī in the form of a wrathful deity such as Yamāntaka. The manifestation body doesn't conquer the demons directly; the real destroyer is the wisdom of the ultimate body, which has the power to remove all evils. Symbolically, Yamāntaka is shown carrying the staff of the wisdom of selflessness or emptiness, which is represented as having a handle made of human bone with a skull on top, symbolizing impermanence. The wisdom that is represented by the staff is a special tantric form of gnosis, combining bliss with the realization of emptiness that is common to both sutra and tantra. Requesting Yamāntaka to turn the staff over his head three times may refer to the three objects that are destroyed by this wisdom: egocentricity, the self-cherishing attitude, and the impure mental and physical conditions that they create.

> 92 I pray you, kill the enemy with your fierce wrath! I pray you, subdue my evil thinking with your great wisdom! I pray you, protect me from my evil actions with your great compassion! I pray you, destroy this Ego once and for all!

Yamāntaka is very fierce; he has weapons in his hands, four bared fangs, and his body is poised to attack and kill the enemy. Here we are requesting him to conquer with his great wisdom our wrong conceptual thoughts stemming from the view of a real personal identity and self-cherishing. We are asking him to protect us with his great compassion from our bad karma, which brings us such harsh suffering. In that way, he is being asked to completely destroy ego-clinging, the great enemy of the world.

> 93 However much suffering those in cyclic existence may endure, I pray you, heap it surely upon ego-clinging! However many of the five poisonous afflictions anyone may experience, I pray you, heap them surely upon this ego-clinging, which richly deserves them!

Now you should think that all the sufferings of sentient beings in the six realms of cyclic existence should be piled on ego-clinging. This is connected to the meditation of *tonglen,* giving and taking. In this practice you wish strongly, without any fear or hesitation, that all the sufferings of sentient beings be brought deep into your heart, upon your self-centered or self-cherishing attitude. You meditate white light rays going out on the breath from one nostril and extending to all suffering everywhere. All the suffering is then collected by these rays and brought back in the form of black light rays that enter through the other nostril and go into your heart area; there they ripen on the self-cherishing attitude and destroy it. It is like destroying an enemy by piling up weapons, poisons, diseases, and thunderous fire. In another lojong practice you meditate on how wonderful it would be to take upon yourself all the unbearable sufferings afflicting all sentient beings, who are like your mother. The causes of their suffering are the five poisons of ignorance, desire, hatred, envy, and miserliness. Since these five poisons continually create problems for our mother sentient beings, we should pile them up upon ourselves.

> 94 Although through reasoning I have identified without a doubt all the roots of evil, if you judge that I am still abetting them, I pray you to destroy the holder himself!

Through studying the Buddhist teachings we come to recognize without any uncertainty that the root of all evil is the view of a real personal identity and self-cherishing. But even though you've done that, you may still side with the enemy and try to argue in its favor; if that is so, then you should also destroy the physical holder of these views. From a tantric point of view, it is considered preferable to destroy the physical body of an evil spirit or demon that contains such nonvirtuous thoughts in order to bring it to a better life. This can only be done by a high tantric practitioner who has great compassion and wisdom. For such a person, such an action will not have negative consequences; even negative actions like killing, stealing, and sexual misconduct can be as beneficial as medicine.

> 95 Now, drive all blame onto one thing! I shall cultivate gratitude toward all beings, take into my mind what others abhor, and turn over the roots of my virtue to all beings.

This expresses what we have to do from here on. We usually blame countless external causes, but now we should place the blame only on the view of a real personal identity and the self-cherishing attitude. Nobody and nothing else should be blamed. We should think that all the merit that has enabled us to have a fortunate human life at this time came from sentient beings who were the objects of our virtuous conduct. Therefore, we should meditate on the great kindness of sentient beings. Also, we should wish to take all the misfortunes of others into our minds so that we can experience them, and we should desire that others, and not ourselves, receive all our merits and virtues that are the cause of peace and happiness. This, again, is the meditation of giving and taking.

> 96 Just as the pattern of colors in a peacock's feather is due
> to poison, may the afflictions be transformed into the aids
> to enlightenment by my taking on the physical, verbal, and
> mental deeds of other living beings, past, present, and
> future.

This continues the discussion of giving and taking. You should take upon yourself all the bad actions and their consequences that were or will be performed by sentient beings through the three doors of body, speech, and mind in the past, present, and future. This is like the peacock who digests poisonous plants and so produces his beautifully colored feathers. Taking all undesirable things upon yourself does not hinder your spiritual development; it actually furthers the rapid attainment of enlightenment for the sake of others. This is what is meant by changing unfavorable conditions into the means to achieve the Buddhist path. We should pray for this to come about.

> 97 I give the roots of my virtue to living beings so they may be
> cured, as a poisoned crow is healed by medicine. I dedicate
> my life to the liberation of all beings so they may quickly
> achieve the buddhahood of the Sugata!

Just as a crow can recover from poisoning by the administration of medicine, living beings can be freed from their afflictions and suffering by receiving the benefit of our virtuous activities that we dedicate to them. They thus can be saved, not from ordinary physical death, but from the spiritual death of losing their chance for emancipation. Through this type of powerful prayer, our minds generate a highly meritorious attitude. We should hold firmly this most essential aspiration in life, which is wishing that all beings be liberated and attain perfect buddhahood; there is no better or higher type of prayer than this. If you go to temples or other religious sites, don't pray for long life, wealth, or other things for yourself; your main prayer should be to benefit sentient beings.

> 98 Until I and those who have been my parents have attained
> enlightenment in the Highest Realm, may we support each
> other with a single thought, even when wandering about in
> the six states of existence owing to our actions.

This is a prayer that through doing this type of practice, I and all sentient beings who have been my parents will in the future attain "The Highest Realm," which is a special kind of pure land. After obtaining enlightenment in this pure land, you can produce the body of a perfect buddha, with its thirty-two major and eighty minor marks. The body of the buddhas in this pure land is the enjoyment body. However, because this body is not visible to ordinary sentient beings, the buddhas assume many different manifestations as humans, animals, wrathful beings, peaceful beings, and so on.

Buddhas can manifest in any form because all forms may be useful in cyclic existence. "The Highest Realm" can refer to a particular place, that is, to the pure land, or to the highest attainment, which is the position of buddhahood itself. But, until that is obtained, we pray that sentient beings who are wandering helplessly about in the realms of cyclic existence due to the influence of their karma be freed from hatred toward each other and that they cherish each other with kindness and compassion as if they were of one mind and one heart. In that way, all of us will be able to accomplish the great way of bodhisattva conduct.

> 99 When I enter the three wretched states of existence for
> the sake of even one living being, may I save him or her
> from the suffering of that wretched destiny without
> compromising a great being's way of life.

This verse especially encourages us to engage in bodhisattva conduct. You have to enter into the three lower realms, even for the sake of one sentient being, and suffer for a long time without losing the attitude and the conduct proper to a great bodhisattva. We pray to free living beings from the sufferings of bad migrations. Here not only are we taking responsibility for all sentient beings, but in addition we are willing to sacrifice ourselves in order to liberate even one. This represents the perfection of the bodhisattva's qualities of patience and diligence. In connection with this, Śāntideva said that even if bodhisattvas have to remain in the Avici hell for eons for the sake of a single sentient being, their compassion will not be shaken, they will not be sorrowful, and they will joyfully work toward supreme enlightenment. That kind of courage is the perfection of religion. Śāntideva also said that the joy that comes from making others happy is the best kind of happiness: isn't that enough? What need is there for the joy of personal emancipation? Those who have this type of dedication willingly take birth into the lower realms to help liberate the beings there from their suffering; they have the courageous attitude that they can accomplish this by themselves, without any help.

> 100 At that very instant, the guards of hell will realize that I am
> a guru, and their weapons will turn into a rain of flowers.
> May peace flourish unharmed!

This is similar to some of the prayers found in the dedication chapter of Śāntideva's *Bodhicaryāvatāra* (*BCA* 10.41–46). This kind of aspiration can be utilized to help us generate bodhicitta.

> 101 Even those in wretched states of existence shall obtain
> superknowledge and mantras, assume the bodies of gods
> and men, and generate bodhicitta. In return for my
> kindness, may they repay me with Dharma practice!
> Taking me as their guru, may they properly attend me!

Through the power of a bodhisattva's dedication of his or her great merit even the beings in hell and the other lower realms of birth will obtain virtuous qualities such as supernatural knowledge and be born immediately in the higher realms as gods and humans. This mainly refers to a good human life with all the necessary conditions for practicing the religious path, especially the highest path of the Mahayana, the practice of the six perfections. Thus, bodhisattvas repay the kindness of sentient beings who were their parents by leading them to the rapid attainment of enlightenment. By showing the spiritual path to sentient beings, you become like a guide, teacher, or guru; through guru devotion, by the proper teacher-disciple relationship, they will attain the stages of the path.

> 102 Then, may all the beings in higher realms also deeply
> meditate on selflessness, just as I do, cultivating the
> nonconceptual meditative absorption on the identity
> of existence and peace. May they recognize this identity!

Until this verse, the text has been concerned with the conventional bodhicitta practice, that is, exchanging self and other, and giving and taking. This verse begins the section on ultimate bodhicitta, the meditation on emptiness. After meditating on compassionately helping sentient beings, you pray that the beings born in the three higher realms—humans, demigods and gods, who are similar to you—will meditate properly on selflessness. You pray that they will not discriminate, in an ultimate sense, between cyclic existence and nirvana. They should enter the meditative equipoise that recognizes that although cyclic existence and nirvana are different conventionally, they are identical insofar as the ultimate nature of both is emptiness of inherent existence.

> 103 Having done so I will crush the enemy. Having done so
> I will crush conceptual construction. After cultivating
> selflessness through nonconceptual wisdom, how can
> I not obtain the causes and effects of the form body?

There are two main enemies or targets of mind training. One is the view of a real personal identity, which holds that an inherently existing self is present somewhere within our psychophysical aggregates. That view is extirpated by the realization of emptiness, by ultimate bodhicitta. Alongside the view of a real personal identity there is always the other enemy, a selfish, self-cherishing attitude that views oneself as the best person, worthy of all good things, and consigns all bad things to others. This attitude is conquered by cherishing others and seeing the many negative consequences of cherishing oneself, in other words, by conventional bodhicitta. At this point in the teaching, we are learning about ultimate bodhicitta.

The verse says that if you meditate as previously described, then you will conquer the inner enemies of the view of a real personal identity and the self-cherishing attitude. The second line specifically refers to destroying the view of a real personal identity. You will also become completely accustomed to the wisdom that realizes the union of emptiness and bliss; through that you will obtain the perfect form body of a buddha and its causes. The sage Dharmakīrti says that if all the causes of something are present, the result will be produced whether you desire it or not. The causes of buddhahood are the two types of bodhicitta. Thinking that cherishing others is the root of all good qualities and self-cherishing is the cause of all suffering, you slowly begin to develop the exchange of self and other, and giving and taking, that is, training in conventional bodhicitta. This is what is referred to as "method." However, a bird can only soar high into the sky using two wings, one strong wing is not enough. Similarly, to fly to the highest level of perfect enlightenment, you must have the two wings of method and wisdom working together. Wisdom or method individually cannot accomplish the goal. Now we are looking at the component of wisdom: first, understanding the object of wisdom and then how to put it into practice. From here on, the text discusses the way to practice ultimate bodhicitta.

> 104 Now hear this! Everything is dependently co-arisen.
> Being dependently co-arisen, they are not independent.
> Changing this way and that, they are false appearances
> and illusions; they are images that appear like a whirling
> firebrand.

This verse starts with a vocative, *"kaye,"* calling the disciples or practitioners to listen. "Everything" refers in particular to the view of a real personal identity and self-cherishing attitude, which are produced by dependent co-arising. This means that they do not exist by themselves; they exist only in dependence on their parts, upon causes and conditions. Things only exist through the aggregation of their causes. Dependent co-arising, in Sanskrit *pratītyasamutpāda,* is the king of logical reasons for proving that things are empty of existing in the way that they appear. Things seem to exist independently, solidly or substantially; in reality, everything is existent only in a relative, dependent, and conventional manner. Emptiness can be misunderstood as nihilistically asserting that nothing exists, that everything is only imagination. Instead of that, we should understand that things do exist in a relative way, dependent on causes and conditions, but that they do not exist independently or ultimately. There are many similes for this, as we shall see. For example, we might say that a temple is nice; but what do we mean when we say "temple"? There is no independent entity "temple," because it depends on its many parts: the ceiling, walls, floors, pillars, windows, and so on. We have an image in our minds corresponding to our temple, and we may think that it is better or more beautiful than other temples. We think about it as an entity, but when we search what is behind the name, we see that the temple is based on a combination of many things. The name produces a rough conceptual thought that sees the temple as a substantial entity and leads us to grasp the temple as a real, independent thing, rather than as a label nominally imputed on its parts. If you search thoroughly, no substance can be found.

Things can change back and forth; something impure can become pure, the imperfect can be perfected, that which is born will cease. The sky can be filled with clouds and later be clear. Thus, everything is purely relative and changeable. Things appear real, but on examination they are not real; they are like an elephant produced through a magical illusion. They are like a torch that is quickly whirled around, producing an image of a ring of fire. The rapid movement confuses the eye so that we perceive a whole image. Of course there is no real ring of fire there; the appearance depends on the nature of fire, the movement, and the eye seeing it. The existence of the ring of fire is like that of an image in a clear mirror.

> 105 Like the plantain tree, life has no inner core. Like a bubble, a lifetime has no inner core. Like a mist, it dissipates upon close examination. Like a mirage, it is beautiful from afar. Like a reflection in a mirror, it seems as if it were really true. Like clouds and fog, it seems as if it were really stable.

Similarly, the essence of life or the person is said to have no substantial inner core, like a tree trunk growing in water that is hollow inside and easily breakable although it looks solid. It is as fragile as a bubble that appears only for a minute. Similarly, it is like mist, which appears solid and heavy from a distance, but when you get close to it, you cannot see or touch anything substantial. It is like a mirage of water in a desert, produced by heat and wind and the eye's misperception; it seems beautiful from a distance but is only an illusion. Things appear to be real, like a face reflected in a mirror; it seems like they will remain forever—like the big cumulus clouds high up in the sky in Tibet at the end of the rainy season, which seem solid, like white mountains.

> 106 This butcher, the enemy Ego, is just the same. It seems as if it really exists, but it has never really existed. It seems as if it is really true, but it has never been really true anywhere. It seems as if it is vividly appearing, but it is beyond the realm of affirmation or denial.

Our inner enemies of the view of a real personal identity and self-cherishing, which are like butchers who are servants of the devil, seem like they've always existed in our mind and are permanent. But when you examine them, as in the similes above, you will find nothing that inherently exists in the past, present, or future. Things seem as if they are really true, but they never ultimately exist in that way anywhere, at any time. Things appear to the mind as if standing by themselves, but they are beyond both the false imputation of true existence on something that doesn't exist in that way, and the false imputation of absolute nonexistence on something that exists relatively. The middle between these two extremes is the Mādhyamika.

> 107 And as for the wheel of actions, it is just the same: though it lacks an inherent nature, yet it appears, like the reflection of the moon in water. Actions and their consequences are a variegated multitude of falsehoods. Even though they are just appearances, I urge you to embrace virtue and avoid sin.

Since everything is free of the two extremes of falsely imputing true existence and total nonexistence, the wheel of actions is like that too. The wheel of actions refers to the process of cyclic existence: the creation of karma by the inner afflictions, the production of births by karma, going around the wheel of births from beginningless time. If things do not exist truly, what is solid in this wheel of actions? It is also empty of inherent existence; it is purely relative and dependent. Therefore, this wheel of cyclic existence can change or entirely vanish. If it were inherently existent, it could not be changed at all and you could never be freed from cyclic existence. The good news is that it is empty, relative, phenomenal, and conditional.

Up to here, Dharmarakṣita has tried to show that everything is empty of inherent existence using different logical reasons and analogies. Whatever exists is empty of ultimate existence. But if everything is empty, what is left? Why are we seeking nirvana? How does cause and effect work? Here he shows how things exist in a conventional way, such as good and bad, samsara and nirvana. In the Prajñāpāramitā sutras, the Buddha taught that there is no samsara, no nirvana, no form, sound, smell, path, or goal; this is all from the point of view of emptiness. The four noble truths, cause and effect, and other teachings are taught from the perspective of the conventional point of view. Things do exist, although not in the manner that they appear to: even a magical elephant or a reflection in a mirror has some type of existence. They exist because the necessary causes and conditions for their appearance are present. They are like a dream in that they exist in an erroneous way because they are not what they seem. Yet they are not totally nonexistent, like a rabbit's horns.

It is like the reflection of the moon on a cloudless night in a clear, still body of water. That image of the moon in water may appear exactly like the moon in the sky, but the moon in the water is just a reflection; it exists as a reflection and a dependently arisen phenomenon, although not as the real moon, which it appears to be. In the same way, actions and their results, such as happiness and suffering in different births, are like a multicolored spectacle; they exist conventionally like the reflection of the moon in water, but not inherently. On that relative level, it should be accepted that there are virtuous and nonvirtuous acts, and that there is a goal to be achieved. We have to practice virtue and eliminate the defilements; it's very wrong to think that "everything is empty, so I don't have to do anything." You have to practice bearing in mind that virtues and sins, samsara and nirvana exist relatively but not in an absolute manner. For example, regarding the practice of charity, the *Madhyamakāvatāra* says: "The act of giving, what is given, and the recipient should be clearly understood as empty; that is the supermundane practice of giving. Being attached to them as real is just the worldly practice of charity." This is how Dharmarakṣita is telling us to practice.

> 108 When in a dream a peat fire blazes, we are terrified by the heat, although it is without substance. In the same way, although the hell realms and such are without substance, we fear the smelter's fire and other tortures. As that is so, we should forsake evil actions.

This verse also shows us an example of how things exist relatively. When we have a nightmare, such as dreaming we are being burned by a big fire, we can wake up in fright. Even though that fire does not truly exist as it appears to in the dream, it will produce fear as the result. In the same way, the tortures of the hot and cold hells experienced by the hell-denizens as a result of their previous actions do not inherently exist, yet the experience of pain, suffering, and terror resulting from these tortures does exist. Therefore, we should abandon those evil actions that result in our experiencing such hellish misery.

> 109 In a feverish delirium we may feel as if we are wandering around suffocating in a deep cave, even though there is no darkness at all. In the same way, even though ignorance and the like are without substance, we should get rid of our delusions through the three wisdoms.

Sometimes, an ill person can be delirious and hallucinate that he or she is going into a deep, dark place. You can have this experience even though the deep cave does not exist in reality. In the same way, ignorance, which consists of the view of a real personal identity and the self-cherishing attitude, produces many kinds of afflictions that lead to actions and their results. Because these afflictions, actions, and misery lack an inherent nature and exist in a merely conventional manner, almost like illusions, they can be removed. Their antidote is the three types of wisdom: the wisdom that comes from study, the wisdom that comes from examining what you have studied, and finally, the wisdom that comes from meditation. Through meditation the understanding of emptiness will become clearer and clearer, until finally you will obtain a direct realization of emptiness. This direct realization is the main weapon that destroys from the root all confusion about reality.

110 When a musician plays a melody on a lute, the sound lacks inherent nature, if we analyze it. But when the sweet sounds emerge, their unanalyzed aggregate eases the anguish in people's hearts.

111 When we analyze all causes and effects, they lack inherent nature as either identical or different. Yet phenomena vividly appear to arise and perish, and we experience pleasure and suffering as if they really existed. Even though they are just appearances, I urge you to embrace virtue and avoid sin.

The example here is a musician who sings and plays a stringed instrument like a guitar. If you do not analyze it, the music seems inherently beautiful. When you do analyze these sounds, you can break them down into the individual notes that have come together in a certain combination to produce pleasing sounds. When you break it down into all its parts, you cannot find any inherently beautiful music. However, if you do not analyze these sounds, the beautiful music, which arises in dependence on the strings, the musician, the notes, and so on, brings enjoyment that clears away people's mental anguish. This is similar to actions and their results, which are empty of inherent nature when they are analyzed from the ultimate point of view. You cannot find a stable basis upon which real phenomena can be identified. For example, we can look at the self, which is based on an aggregate of many parts of body and mind, to see whether it is the same as or different from the aggregates. When you investigate, you won't find any inherent nature of a self either the same as or different from the aggregates. Similarly, various kinds of pleasant and unpleasant things clearly appear to arise and be destroyed based on their causes and conditions, even though they have no absolute nature; we experience them in a conventional manner. Therefore, Dharmarakṣita advises us to take up virtuous actions and to forsake unwholesome actions even though they do not inherently exist.

112 When drops of water fill a jar, the first drop does not fill it, nor the last, nor each drop individually. Yet the dependently arisen aggregate fills the jar.

> 113 Similarly, when someone experiences their reward of
> pleasure or pain, it is due neither to the first moment
> of the cause, nor to the last moment, and so on. Yet the
> dependently arisen aggregate makes us experience pleasure
> or pain. Even though they are just appearances, I urge
> you to embrace virtue and avoid sin.

Like the two preceding verses, this verse gives an example of conventional cause and effect. When drops of water drip into a jar it will finally be filled. It is not filled by the first drop or by the last; it is filled by the combination of all the drops together. Similarly, when people experience happiness or suffering in cyclic existence, it is due to various causes. Things do not arise causelessly; if they did, anything could arise at any time. Causes are not permanent, because if they were always present, then the result would always be produced; it is the variety of changing causes that produces the many kinds of different results. Each cause is itself made up of many individual moments, all of which together produce the result. Therefore the aggregate of nonvirtuous causes produces the experience of suffering, and the aggregate of virtuous causes creates the experience of happiness. Since we wish to be happy and to avoid suffering, we should adopt wholesome behavior and forsake actions that are unwholesome.

> 114 Aha! The appearance that delights our mind, though independent when unanalyzed, definitely lacks an inner core.
> However, the fact that phenomena appear as if they exist
> is profound and difficult for the dull-witted to understand.

If phenomena are not analyzed from the ultimate point of view, but are just labeled, for example "tree" or "table" or "person," they seem to independently and truly exist. Such appearances are delightful to us. Actually, when they are examined, you will see that they have no inner essence, that no objective existence is discoverable. Things are not able to bear analysis, as was said earlier about the mirage, cloud, or mist—from afar you see something solid, but when you try to catch it, it disappears. Yet, things do appear to exist objectively. This reality is very profound and thus it is difficult for less intelligent beings to comprehend it. The philosophical systems that are inferior to the Mādhyamika discuss emptiness, but their understanding is much more rudimentary.

> 115 Now, when you are absorbed in meditative equipoise on this, what is there really to a mere appearance? How can either existence or nonexistence exist? How can anyone anywhere assert "it is" or "it is not"?

When you put the realization of emptiness into meditative practice in one-pointed meditative absorption, the negation of inherent existence will appear clearly and there will be no appearance of conventional phenomena. Everything will have the "one taste" of emptiness and the variety of conventional phenomena will not appear. At that time, nonexistence itself will be seen not to exist inherently, and the mind will dissolve in its own emptiness like water dissolved in water; both absolute existence and absolute nonexistence will totally disappear. There is no valid thesis that things exist or things do not exist; these will all vanish. From the ultimate point of view, in both sutra and tantra, there are statements that everything is the same, that there is no difference between good and evil, or between samsara and nirvana. Such statements are true only in light of the realization of emptiness; from the conventional, commonsense point of view, these statements are reckless and crazy. When a bodhisattva is absorbed in meditation, which directly cognizes emptiness, there are no appearances; but when he or she rises from that meditation, the senses are open again, and form, color, and other phenomena appear. Bodhisattvas do not misunderstand them, but they still see them falsely as dualistic; dualistic perception is only eliminated when buddhahood is attained. It is like magicians who know that the illusions they have created are false: although they still see them, they are not deceived into believing in their reality, as the audience may be. At the time of enlightenment, nothing is perceived incorrectly; the obstacles to knowledge are completely removed. Emptiness is present in the mind of a buddha all the time, and at the same time conventional phenomena and cause and effect are seen. Only buddhas can combine the meditative realization of emptiness with postmeditative activity.

> 116 Subject and object lack ultimate reality. If your mind remains in its innate nature, uncontrived and shining, free

from all discrimination and conceptual proliferation, you will become a great being.

Neither subject nor object has ultimate reality. Even the concept of emptiness is itself empty, so we speak of the emptiness of emptiness. In this sense, there is nothing inherently to be practiced or discarded, and reality is free from conceptual elaboration. Everything, including the mind, is empty of inherent existence from the very beginning; this is the natural state of things. Meditating on this reality, you will gain powerful wisdom that will remove the ignorance you have been creating for so long. Then, you will become a great being, a noble person who directly realizes emptiness.

117 Thus, by practicing the conventional and ultimate bodhicitta, and thereby uninterruptedly carrying the two accumulations through to completion, may I perfectly realize the two aims.

In the preceding section, we discussed the ultimate truth, the ultimate bodhicitta, the direct realization of the emptiness of inherent existence. Before that, we discussed the conventional bodhicitta, the bodhisattva's compassion for suffering sentient beings. These are the two wings taking us quickly to enlightenment and making it possible for us to benefit sentient beings, who are like our mothers. Dharmarakṣita has explained both of them. This last verse, verse 117, is in the form of a prayer. You pray that by the practice of the conventional and ultimate bodhicitta you will complete the two accumulations of merit and wisdom. When these are complete, then you will obtain perfect buddhahood. In your prayer, you say that your purpose is to achieve the two goals, that of others and of yourself. This is similar to the dedication of Nāgārjuna: "By this virtue, may all sentient beings complete the accumulation of merit and wisdom. Through these accumulations may beings obtain the two holy bodies." The two holy or perfect bodies are the form body and the ultimate body. The form body is the perfect body of the Buddha, with all the major and minor marks, along with the perfect environment of the pure land. The ultimate body refers to a mind with perfect wisdom and compassion in which all suffering and obstacles have been eliminated. With this prayer, the work is concluded.

PART TWO

THE POISON-DESTROYING PEACOCK MIND TRAINING

བློ་སྦྱོང་རྨ་བྱ་དུག་འཇོམས།

Attributed to Dharmarakṣita

བློ་སྦྱོང་རྨ་བྱ་དུག་འཇོམས།

༄༅།། བཙན་དུག་ནགས་སུ་རྨ་བྱ་རྒྱུ་བ་ཞེས་བྱ་བ།

རྗེ་བཙུན་གཤིན་རྗེའི་གཤེད་ལ་ཕྱག་འཚལ་ལོ།

1
རྒྱལ་བུ་ཐམས་ཅད་སྒྲོལ་དུ་གྱུར་པ་ན།
བུ་དང་བུ་མོ་རྒྱལ་སྲིད་སྦྱིན་པ་ལྟར།
ཤིན་ཏུ་འཕྲེང་བའི་ནོར་དང་འཁོར་ལ་སོགས།
འཕངས་པ་མེད་པར་ཡོངས་སུ་བཏང་བར་བྱ།།

2
རྒྱལ་བུ་སྙིང་སྟོབས་ཆེན་པོར་གྱུར་པ་ན།
སྟག་མོ་རང་གི་ཤ་ཡིས་གསོས་པ་ལྟར།
ཤིན་ཏུ་གཅེས་པའི་སྒྱུ་ལུས་ཕུང་པོ་འདི།
ཤ་ཟའི་ཚོགས་ལ་དགའ་བས་སྦྱིན་པར་བྱ།།

3
རྒྱལ་པོ་བྱམས་པའི་སྟོབས་སུ་གྱུར་པ་ན།
གནོད་སྦྱིན་རང་གི་ཁྲག་གིས་གསོས་པ་ལྟར།
བཅད་པར་དཀའ་བའི་སྙིང་ཁྲག་དྲོན་མོ་འདི།།
ཁྲག་འཐུང་དག་ལ་བརྩེ་བས་སྦྱིན་པར་བྱ།།

The Poison-Destroying Peacock Mind Training

[The Peacocks' Roaming Through the Jungle of Virulent Poison]

I bow down to Lord Yamāntaka.

1

Just as he gave away his children and his realm when he was Prince Viśvāntara, so you too should give away without reservation the wealth, companions, and so forth that you hold so dear.

2

Just as he nourished the tigress with his own flesh when he was Prince Mahāmaitrībala, so you too should joyfully give your dearly cherished heap of an illusory body to the mob of flesh-eating demons.

3

Just as he nourished the harmful demons with his own blood when he was King Maitrībala, so you too should lovingly give warm blood from your heart, which is so difficult to cut, to the blood-drinking demons.

4
ཚོང་དཔོན་ཁྲེའུ་ཆུ་འབེབས་གྱུར་པ་ན།
བདེ་གཤེགས་མཚན་བརྗོད་ཉ་རྣམས་དྲངས་པ་ལྟར།
ཆོས་ཀྱིས་འཕོངས་པའི་སྐྱེ་བོ་ཐམས་ཅད་ལ།
དམ་པའི་ཆོས་ཀྱི་སྦྱིན་པ་བཏང་བར་ཤོག།

5
རྒྱལ་བུ་དགེ་དོན་ཆེན་པོར་གྱུར་པ་ན།
སྡིག་དོན་ལོག་སྒྲུབ་ཐུགས་རྗེས་བཟོད་པ་ལྟར།
འཁོར་གྱི་ལོག་སྒྲུབ་གཤིས་ངན་འཁྲུགས་པ་ལ།
སྙིང་རྗེ་ཆེན་པོས་ལྷག་པར་བརྩེ་བར་ཤོག།

6
བྱང་ཆུབ་སེམས་དཔའ་སྤྲེའུར་གྱུར་པ་ན།
སྡིག་ཅན་ཁྲོན་པའི་གནས་ནས་དྲངས་པ་ལྟར།
ངན་པ་དག་ལ་ཕན་འདོགས་མི་ཤོད་ཀྱང་།
བཟང་ལན་མི་འདོད་ཐུགས་རྗེས་དྲང་པར་ཤོག།

7
ཀྱེ་ཧུད་ཕ་མར་མ་གྱུར་སུ་ཡང་མེད།
འཁོར་བའི་ནགས་ན་བདེ་བ་སྐད་ཅིག་མེད།
ངན་པའི་ཚོགས་ལ་ངན་ལན་བོང་ར་འདྲ།

4

Just as he saved the fish by reciting the name of the Tathāgata when he was the chief merchant's son Jalavāhana, so you too should give the gift of the holy Dharma to all beings who lack it.

5

Just as he compassionately endured Prince Pāpārtha's ingratitude when he was Prince Mahākalyānārtha, so you too should have great compassion toward your companions' ingratitude when it is stirred up by their evil nature.

6

Just as he pulled the sinner out of the well when he was the monkey bodhisattva, so you too should guide evil people compassionately without expecting good in return, even to one's detriment.

7

Alas! There is no one who has not been my parent. There is not one instant of happiness in this jungle of cyclic existence. Returning evil to the crowd of evildoers is like [adding manure to] a donkey's stall.

8
ད་ནི་ཐུབ་ཆེན་དཔའ་བོའི་རྣམ་ཐར་འདི།
གུས་པས་བླངས་ནས་གཉེན་པོ་མི་བསྐྱེད་ན།
དཔའ་བོ་འཇུག་པའི་ལག་ལེན་ཡོང་མི་སྲིད།
དེ་ཕྱིར་སྲོག་ལ་བསྐོས་ལ་དཀའ་སྤྱད་བསྟེན།།

9
བདེ་བར་གཤེགས་པ་འདས་ཚུལ་བསྟན་རྗེས་སུ།
དེ་ཡི་རྗེས་སུ་སློབ་པར་འདོད་པ་རྣམས།
འདི་འདྲའི་ལག་ལེན་རྒྱུད་ལ་མ་བསྟེན་ན།
སྐྱེ་བོ་རྣམས་ཀྱི་བདེ་སྐྱིད་ཟད་དོགས་ཡོད།།

10
དེ་ཕྱིར་དཔའ་བོ་རྣམས་ཀྱི་སྐྱིད་ཆོས་འདི།
ཅི་ལ་ཐུག་ཀྱང་དཀའ་སྤྱད་སྲོག་ལ་བསྐོས།
འདི་ནི་དཔའ་བོ་འཇུག་པའི་ལག་ལེན་ཏེ།
ལེའུ་དང་པོ་དུག་གི་བཅུད་ལེན་ཡིན།།

བཙན་དུག་ནགས་སུ་རྨ་བྱ་རྒྱུ་བ་ཞེས་བྱ་བ།

རྗེ་བཙུན་གཤིན་རྗེའི་གཤེད་ལ་ཕྱག་འཚལ་ལོ།།

8

If you have accepted this spiritual biography of the great sage-hero with respect, but have not generated the antidote, the actual heroic practice will be impossible. Thus, keep to the practice of austerities even at the risk of your own life.

9

If those who desire to imitate the Sugata after he has appeared to pass away do not keep this practice in their minds, there is a risk that the happiness of living beings will disappear.

10

Therefore, this is the heroes' happy way of life: to endure hardship come what may, even at the risk of your own life. This is the heroes' actual practice: part one of *The Elixir Made from Poison.*

The Peacocks' Roaming Through the Jungle of Virulent Poison

I bow down to Lord Yamāntaka.

11
ཆོས་འདི་གསན་དང་དཔའ་བོ་དོན་གཉེར་ཀུན།
འཁོར་བའི་ནགས་ན་རྨ་བྱ་མཛེས་པོ་དང་།
ཉོན་མོངས་དུག་ལྗ་ལྗོན་པའི་ཤིང་དུང་དུ།
དུག་གིས་སྨིན་པའི་སྨན་ལ་དགར་མི་ཆོར།།

12
འདོད་ཆགས་ལས་ཀྱི་དུག་མཚོ་འཁོལ་མ་ལ།
འདོད་ཆགས་ལྷ་བུར་གཞན་དང་མ་བསྟུན་ན།
འདོད་ཆགས་ཅན་གྱིས་ལོག་སྒྲུབ་བྱས་དོགས་ཡོད།
འདོད་ཆགས་ལྷ་བུས་དུག་འདི་གཞོམ་པར་བྱ།།

13
ཞེ་སྡང་དུག་གི་མེ་ཏོག་འབར་བ་ལ།
གཤིན་རྗེའི་གཤེད་ལྟར་ཁྲོ་རྒྱལ་མ་བསྟན་ན།
ཞེ་སྡང་ཅན་གྱིས་བར་ཆད་བྱས་དོགས་ཡོད།
ཞེ་སྡང་ལྷ་བུས་དགྲ་བགེགས་བསྒྲལ་བར་བྱ།།

14
གཏི་མུག་དུག་གི་འདམ་རྫབ་སྦྱར་བ་ལ།
མི་རོ་ལྷ་བུར་བཟོད་སྲན་མ་བསྐྱེད་ན།
གཞིས་ངན་རྣམས་ཀྱིས་སྡིག་བསགས་བྱས་དོགས་ཡོད།
གཏི་མུག་ལྷ་བུས་མཉམ་ཉིད་བསྒོམ་པར་བྱ།།

11

Listen to this teaching! In the jungle of cyclic existence no one with heroic ambitions should take pleasure in the beautiful peacock or the poison-ripened healing herb growing in the shade of the tree of the five poisonous afflictions.

12

If you do not feign lust and behave as others do, there is the danger that the lustful may act ungratefully when the poisonous lake of lustful action boils. With simulated lust you should destroy this poison.

13

If you do not display an angry manner like Yamāntaka's, there is the danger that angry persons may create obstacles when the flowers of the poison of hatred come into bloom. With simulated anger you should kill the demonic enemies of the Dharma.

14

If you do not generate corpse-like forbearance, there is the danger that the evil-natured may commit sin when the mire of the poison of ignorance congeals. With pretended ignorance you should cultivate equanimity.

15

ཕྲག་དོག་དུག་གི་ལྗོན་ཤིང་རྒྱས་པ་ལ།
ང་ཁྲོད་ལྟ་བུར་ཕྱི་ནང་མ་ཕྱེ་ན།
མུ་སྟེགས་སོགས་ཀྱིས་བསྟན་པ་ཞིགས་ཉེན་ཡོད།
དེ་ཕྱིར་ཕྲག་དོག་ལྟ་བུས་དམ་ཆོས་སྐྱོང་།།

16

ང་རྒྱལ་དུག་གི་ལྗོན་ཤིང་འབར་བ་ལ།
ང་རྒྱལ་ལྟ་བུར་ཕོ་ཚུགས་མ་བཟུང་ན།
བདུད་ཀྱི་ཚོགས་ཀྱིས་མགོ་སྐོར་བྱས་ཉེན་ཡོད།
དེ་ཕྱིར་ཐུབ་བསྟན་བཟུངས་ལ་ཕས་རྒོལ་གཞོམ།།

17

དེ་ལྟར་དུག་གི་དཔུང་ཚོགས་མ་ལུས་པ།
བདེན་མེད་སྣང་སྟོང་སྒྱུ་མ་ལྟ་བུའི་ཉམས།
ང་བདག་འཆིང་བ་གཅིག་ཏུ་ཚུར་སྒོམ་ལ།
རྨ་བྱ་ལྟ་བུར་ཟས་སུ་ཟ་བར་བྱ།།

18

གཞན་གྱི་བློ་ལ་སྣ་ཚོགས་ཀུན་སྟོན་ཀྱང་།
ཕུགས་སུ་གཉེན་པོའི་བཙན་ཚུགས་མ་ཤོར་བར།
དགེ་སྡིག་དག་གི་བླང་དོར་སྒྲིག་ལ་བསྒོམས།
སྡུག་བསྔལ་གྱུར་ཀྱང་བྱང་ཆུབ་དང་དུ་བླངས།།

15

If you do not distinguish between inside and outside as you would "I" and "you," there is the danger that nonbelievers and others may destroy the teaching when the tree of the poison of envy is flourishing. Therefore, with simulated envy you should protect the holy Dharma.

16

If you do not assume the virile posture that resembles pride, there is the danger that the hosts of demons may deceive you when the tree of the poison of pride comes into bloom. Therefore, with simulated pride you should uphold the Sage's teaching and crush its opponents.

17

Thus, the entire mass of poisons should be experienced as if it were an illusion, untrue, something that appears but is empty. Tie up the poisons into the single bond of "I" and "mine," and, like a peacock, take it as nourishment.

18

Although you may present yourself in various ways to others, deep inside, without losing the powerful strength of the antidote, you should take up virtue and reject sin even at the risk of your own life. Although you may suffer, eagerly pursue enlightenment.

19

འདི་ལྟར་ཤེས་བྱ་ཀུན་ལ་མཁས་ན་ཡང་།
རང་གི་བདེ་སྐྱིད་ཁྱད་དུ་མ་བསད་ན།
སྲེད་པའི་དབང་གིས་ཆགས་སྡང་ཞུགས་ཉེན་ཡོད།
དེ་ཕྱིར་རང་འདོད་ཁྱི་རྐུན་བཞིན་དུ་བརྡུང་།།

20

མཁས་པ་རྣམས་ཀྱི་དྲུང་དུ་བསྟེན་གྱུར་ཞིང་།
གཞུང་ལུགས་རྣམས་ལ་བློ་གྲོས་མ་སྦྱངས་ན།
མཁས་པ་རྣམས་ལ་སྒྲོ་སྐུར་བྱས་དོགས་ཡོད།
དེ་ཕྱིར་ཤེས་བྱ་ཀུན་ལ་གོམས་པར་བྱ།།

21

ཉིན་དང་མཚན་དུ་སྡུག་བསྔལ་གྱུར་ན་ཡང་།
འཁོར་བ་སྤྱི་ཡི་ཉེས་དམིགས་མ་བསམས་ན།
ད་དུང་སྡུག་བསྔལ་རྒྱུ་ལ་འཇུག་དོགས་ཡོད།
དེ་ཕྱིར་ལས་ཀྱི་ཉེས་དམིགས་སྙིང་ལ་གཟེར།།

22

དེ་ལྟར་ཡིན་མོད་མི་འདོད་སྡུག་བསྔལ་རྣམས།
བདག་འཛིན་འཇོམས་པའི་གཉེན་པོར་བསྟེན་པར་བྱ།
བདུད་དམག་བྱེ་བ་དུང་ཕྱུར་དགྲར་ལངས་ཀྱང་།
ངའོ་སྙམ་པའི་འཇིགས་སྐྲག་སྐྱང་བར་བྱ།།

19

Even if you are the master of all knowledge such as this, if you do not condemn happiness for yourself there is the danger that the power of craving may enmesh you in lust and hatred. Therefore, you should beat down selfishness, like a thieving dog!

20

Though you may devote yourself to serving the learned, if you do not sharpen your understanding of the doctrinal systems there is the danger that you will overestimate or underestimate these scholars. Therefore, you should become proficient in all knowledge.

21

Even if you suffer day and night, if you don't think about the shortcomings of all cyclic existence, there is yet the danger that you may become embroiled in the causes of suffering. Thus, nail the punishments for actions onto your heart.

22

That being the case, you should rely upon dreadful suffering as the antidote that conquers ego-clinging. Even if myriad demon armies were to rise up as your enemy, you should throw off the terror that comes from thinking "I."

23
གཞན་དོན་བྱས་པས་ངན་འགྲོར་ཤོར་སྲིད་ཀྱང་།
འགྱོད་པ་མེད་པས་ཉམས་དགར་བསྟེན་པར་བྱ།
དབུགས་ལེན་གཤེད་མས་ལུས་ལ་ཁྲབ་གྱུར་ཀྱང་།
བདག་ལ་ཕན་པའི་རིམ་གྲོ་བསྟེན་མི་བྱ།།

24
སེམས་ཅན་ཡོངས་ཀྱི་ལས་ངན་འཁུར་དགོས་ཀྱང་།
ཁུར་འོས་འཁུར་བས་སྡུག་ཡུས་ཆུང་བར་བྱ།
འགོ་བའི་ནད་ཀྱིས་ལུས་ལ་བཏབ་གྱུར་ཀྱང་།
རང་གི་ཉོངས་པས་ཟློག་པའི་ཐབས་མི་བྱ།།

25
འདི་ལྟར་མི་འདོད་ཐོག་ཏུ་མ་བབས་ན།
འདོད་པའི་ཐོག་ཏུ་ནམ་ཡང་འཇུག་མི་སྲིད།
མཁས་པས་དཔྱད་ན་མི་འདོད་མ་ལུས་པ།
འདོད་དགུའི་འབྱུང་གནས་ཡིན་པས་དང་དུ་བླངས།།

26
འདི་ལྟར་ལོག་སྒྲུབ་དང་དུ་ལེན་པ་ཡི།
སེམས་དཔའ་རྣམས་ཀྱི་གོ་ཆ་མ་གྱོན་ན།
འཁོར་བ་པ་ལ་བདེ་བ་ཡོང་མི་སྲིད།
དེ་ཕྱིར་མི་འདོད་དང་དུ་བླང་པར་བྱ།།

23

Although you may fall into wretched states of existence by working for others' benefit, serve them gladly, without regret. Although the butcher who takes away your breath may snatch your body, do not rely on religious rituals to help yourself.

24

Although you must bear the bad actions of all sentient beings, the pride you take in your sufferings will diminish by bearing that which should be borne. Although infectious diseases may afflict your body, do not employ measures to fight them off, as they are a result of your own faults.

25

Thus, we will never be able to get what we desire unless that which is undesirable befalls us. When the wise examine that, they willingly embrace everything undesirable as the source of everything desirable.

26

If we don't put on the armor of the bodhisattvas who willingly embrace others' ingratitude, happiness will never come to those in cyclic existence. Therefore, willingly accept all that is undesirable.

27
འདི་ནི་ཐུབ་པ་ཆེན་པོའི་རྣམ་ཐར་ལས།
དམ་པ་རྣམས་ཀྱིས་བསླབ་པར་བྱ་བའི་ཆོས།
དཔའ་བོ་རྣམས་ཀྱི་འཇུག་པར་བྱ་བ་སྟེ།
ལེའུ་གཉིས་པ་དག་གི་བཅུད་ལེན་ཡིན།།

བཙན་དུག་ནགས་སུ་རྨ་བྱ་རྒྱུ་བ་ཞེས་བྱ་བ།

རྗེ་བཙུན་གཤིན་རྗེའི་གཤེད་ལ་ཕྱག་འཚལ་ལོ།

28
བློ་ལྡན་གང་གིས་ཉིན་མཚན་དུས་དྲུག་ཏུ།
འཁོར་བ་སྐྱི་དང་སྒྲོས་ཀྱི་སྐྱོན་རྣམས་ལ།
བརྟགས་ཤིང་དཔྱད་པས་ཤིན་ཏུ་སྐྲག་གྱུར་ནས།
སོ་སོར་ཐར་པའི་སྡོམ་པ་བླངས་ཏེ་བསྲུངས།།

29
རང་ཉིད་ཐར་པའི་སྡོམ་པ་བརྟན་པ་ན།
རང་ཉིད་ཇི་སྲིད་བྱང་ཆུབ་མ་ཐོབ་པར།
འགྲོ་བ་འདི་དག་ཕ་དང་མར་བཅད་དེ།
དེ་དག་དོན་དུ་སྨོན་འཇུག་སེམས་བསྐྱེད་དེ།།

27

This is the Dharma according to the great sage's spiritual biography;

it should be studied by the holy ones. It is the heroes' actual practice:

part two of *The Elixir Made from Poison.*

The Peacocks' Roaming Through the Jungle of Virulent Poison

I bow down to Lord Yamāntaka.

28

The intelligent person who analyzes and examines the general

and specific faults of cyclic existence during the six periods of day

and night will be terrified and thus take and guard the vow

of personal emancipation.

29

Once the commitment to your own emancipation is firm and

you have recognized that all living beings have been your parents,

you should for their sake generate the attitudes of aspiration

and engagement until you attain enlightenment.

30
བྱམས་བརྩེའི་སེམས་ཀྱིས་སྨོན་འཇུག་བརྟན་པ་ན།
རང་ཉིད་འཁོར་བའི་ནགས་སུ་སྡུག་བསྔལ་ཀྱང་།
ཅི་ཡང་མི་སེམས་སྡུག་བསྔལ་གཞན་དོན་དུ།
སྲོག་དང་བསྡོས་ནས་དཀའ་སྤྱད་བསྟེན་པར་བྱ།།

31
དེ་ཚེ་མ་རུངས་སྐྱེ་བོ་མཐའ་ཡས་དང་།
ལོག་སྒྲུབ་མཐའ་ལས་འདས་པ་སྐྱོང་བ་ན།
རྨི་ལམ་སྒྱུ་མ་ལྟ་བུར་སྤྲོས་དང་བྲལ།
རང་བཞིན་བརྟགས་ལ་ཆོས་ཀྱི་དབྱིངས་སུ་བསམ།།

32
དེ་ལྟར་བདེན་མེད་སྣང་མེད་མཚོན་གྱུར་ཚེ།
ལྷག་པར་སྤོབས་པ་བསྐྱེད་དེ་འཇིགས་སྐྲག་ལ།
ཅི་ཡང་མི་སེམས་གང་དུའང་མི་རྟོག་པར།
གཞན་དོན་འབབ་ཞིག་ལྷུན་གྱིས་སྒྲུབ་པར་བྱ།།

33
འདི་འདྲའི་ཉམས་ལེན་ཁུར་དུ་འཁུར་བ་ན།
ནག་པོའི་ཕྱོགས་ཀྱིས་ཆེས་ཆེར་མ་བཟོད་ནས།
བར་དུ་གཅོད་པའི་སྤྲིན་ཕུང་འཁྲིགས་པ་ན།
རྣམ་དག་མཁའ་ལ་སྔགས་ཀྱི་རླུང་གིས་གཏོར།།

30
When aspiration and engagement are firmly established with an attitude of loving-kindness, you will think nothing of your own suffering in the jungle of cyclic existence. Even at the risk of your own life, keep to the practice of austerities and endure suffering for others' sake.

31
When you experience vast numbers of malevolent persons and their infinite ingratitude, you should examine their true nature, which is free from discursive proliferation like a dream or an illusion, and contemplate the ultimate reality.

32
Thus, when true nonexistence and apparent nonexistence become directly present, you will become extremely courageous and never again entertain terrifying thoughts. Without conceptualizing, you will effortlessly achieve others' welfare.

33
When you shoulder the burden of this kind of practice, the dark quarter may find it increasingly hard to tolerate you. Should clouds of hindrances mass together, the wind of mantra will scatter them throughout the clear sky.

34
དྲག་པོའི་སྔགས་ཀྱི་ཧཱུྃ་སྒྲ་སྒྲོགས་པ་ན།
ཁྲོ་བོ་དྲག་པོའི་ང་རྒྱལ་སྐྱེ་སྲིད་པས།
ཕུང་པོ་སྒྱུ་མའི་གྲོང་ཁྱེར་ལྷ་བུ་ལ།
སྒྲ་ནི་སྤྲུལ་པའི་གླུ་དབྱངས་ལྷ་བུར་ཞེས།།

35
གང་ཡང་རང་སེམས་སྣ་ཚོགས་སྤྲུལ་པ་ལས།
ངོས་བཟུང་མེད་དེ་སྤྲུལ་པའི་ཡིད་ཞེས་བཞིན།
ཡེ་ནས་ཡོད་མ་སྨྱོང་བས་རང་སར་གློད།
ཆོས་ཀྱི་དབྱིངས་གཟིགས་བདེན་པར་གྲོལ་བར་བྱ།།

36
གང་ཡང་ཅི་ལྟར་དགྲ་དང་འདྲེར་ལངས་ཀྱང་།
གང་དུའང་མི་སེམས་ཅིར་ཡང་མི་རྟོག་པར།
རང་གཞན་ཆགས་སྡང་རྟོག་པའི་འོག་ཏུ་ཐི།
དྲན་སྣང་ཁྲོ་བོ་གཤིན་རྗེ་གཤེད་དུ་བལྟ།།

37
དེ་ཚེ་ཕ་མ་འགྲོ་བ་མ་ལུས་པ།
ཡིན་ངེས་སྙམ་དུ་ཐེ་ཚོམ་མེད་པར་བསྐྱུ།
ཉེ་རིང་མེད་པར་ཐུགས་རྗེའི་དཀྱིལ་དུ་སྦྲ།
ཕྱོགས་རིས་མེད་པར་བདེན་པ་གཉིས་ཀྱིས་བསྐྱང་།།

34

Because the arrogance of the Wrathful Terrible One may be produced when you call out the "huṃ" of his mantra, you should know that the aggregates are like an illusory city and sound is like a phantom's song.

35

Recognize the varied contents of your own mind as nothing other than phantoms. Like the mind of a phantom, your own mind has never existed at all, so leave it to itself. When you see ultimate reality, you will be truly free.

36

Some may arise as enemies and demons, but regard them not at all. Trample on attachment to self and aversion to others without conceiving of them in any way. View memory and perception like the wrathful Yamāntaka.

37

Once you are convinced that all living beings have been your parents, gather them together without hesitation. Free from bias, give them refuge in your compassion and impartially protect them with the two truths.

38

དེ་ལྟར་གོམས་ན་ཐུབ་པའི་རྣམ་ཐར་ཡིན།

འདི་ལྟར་བསྒྲིས་ན་དཀོན་མཆོག་འཛུམ་པ་འཆོར།

འདི་འདྲའི་མི་ལ་ཆོས་སྐྱོང་ངང་གིས་འཁོར།

མཁྱེན་པར་མཛད་ཅིག་ཐུབ་པའི་སྲས་པོ་རྣམས།།

39

བདག་གིས་ཁྲེལ་མེད་ཆོས་ལ་ཐོ་ལེས་གདབ།

བག་མེད་ཆོས་ལ་བསམས་ཏེ་སྐྲུག་བྲོ་བལྟ།

འདི་ཡང་དཔའ་བོ་འཇུག་པའི་ལག་ལེན་ཏེ།

ལེའུ་གསུམ་པ་དུག་གི་བཅུད་ལེན་ཡིན།།

བཙན་དུག་ནགས་སུ་རྨ་བྱ་རྒྱུ་བ་ཞེས་བྱ་བ།

རྗེ་བཙུན་གཤིན་རྗེའི་གཤེད་ལ་ཕྱག་འཚལ་ལོ།

40

ཉེ་བར་འཁོར་ལྟར་བཙུན་པ་མཐར་ཐུག་ཅིང་།

རྟ་ཐལ་བཞིན་དུ་བག་ཡོད་མཛེས་གྱུར་ཀྱང་།

བྱང་ཆུབ་ལམ་ལ་ཕ་མ་མ་འདྲེན་ན།

རང་བདེའི་ཐར་པ་རྟོག་པས་སྡེ་རྒྱུ་ཡིན།།

38

To train in this way is to follow the Sage's spiritual biography. If you act accordingly, the Jewels will burst into smiles and the Dharma protectors will naturally surround you. Know this well, children of the Sage.

39

I spit on the shameless way of life! Having considered the heedless life, I view it with disgust. This is the heroes' actual practice: part three of *The Elixir Made from Poison.*

The Peacocks' Roaming Through the Jungle of Virulent Poison

I bow down to Lord Yamāntaka.

40

Though you may be as perfect a monk as Upāli and as conscientious and handsome as Aśvajit, if you don't lead your parents along the path to enlightenment, you should trample underfoot the liberation of personal bliss.

41
རིག་པའི་གནས་ལ་མཁས་པའི་མཐུ་ཐོབ་ཅིང་།
སྙན་པའི་གྲགས་པས་བླུན་པོ་ཀུན་དགའ་ཡང་།
བསྟན་པའི་ཁུར་ཆེན་སྤྱི་བོར་མི་ལེན་ན།
སྨྱོན་པའི་བྲོ་རྡུང་བཞིན་དུ་དོར་བྱ་ཡིན།།

42
བླ་མ་ལྷ་བུར་ཀུན་གྱིས་བཀུར་ན་ཡང་།
བསྟན་པ་སྤྱི་ཡི་ཁུར་ཆེན་མི་འཁུར་ཞིང་།
རང་གི་འདོད་པ་དང་དུ་ལེན་བྱེད་ན།
འཕགས་པ་རྣམས་ཀྱིས་ཐོ་ལེས་གདབ་བྱ་ཡིན།།

43
བཟང་པོ་ལྷ་བུར་ཀུན་གྱིས་ཟློམ་ན་ཡང་།
ལོག་ལྟའི་ནགས་སུ་བདག་ལྟ་འཁྲུགས་པ་ཡིས།
སྟག་མོ་བུ་ཟན་བཞིན་དུ་འཇིགས་པ་སྟེ།
བཀའ་སྲོད་སྲུང་མ་རྣམས་ཀྱིས་བསྒྲལ་བྱ་ཡིན།།

44
ངུར་སྨྲིག་གོས་ཅན་ཞི་དུལ་མཛེས་གྱུར་ཀྱང་།
བྱི་ལ་བཞིན་དུ་བསམ་པ་མ་རུངས་པའི།
དམ་པའི་གཟུགས་ཅན་གསོ་རུ་མེད་པ་དེ།
མ་མོ་རྣམས་ཀྱི་ཁ་རུ་གདབ་བྱ་ཡིན།།

41

Though you may achieve great expertise in the sciences and delight in your reputation like a government official, if you don't take upon your head the great burden of the teaching, your reputation should be dismissed, like a madman's dance.

42

Though everyone may honor you like a guru, if you do not bear the great burden of the whole teaching but eagerly pursue your own desires, the noble ones should spit on you.

43

Though everyone may claim you are a good person, you are as terrible as a tigress who eats her young because your egotistic view grew in the jungle of wrong views; the attendant protectors should destroy you.

44

Though you may wear the saffron robe and be of congenial temperament, there is no cure for a cat-like, vicious-minded impersonator of a holy person; you should be thrust into the mouth of the she-demons.

45
ཁྲི་ཁྲག་དགུ་ཡི་གཙོ་བོར་འདུག་གྱུར་ཀྱང་།
ཁྱབ་འཇུག་བཞིན་དུ་རང་རྒྱུད་མ་ཐུལ་བའི།
ཆགས་སྡང་འོད་ཟེར་ཕྱོགས་བཅུར་འཕྲོ་བ་དེ།
གཤིན་རྗེ་གཤེད་ཀྱི་ཞལ་དུ་གདབ་བྱ་ཡིན།།

46
འཛུམ་ཞིང་དེས་པས་ཐམས་ཅད་སྐྱོང་ན་ཡང་།
བདག་གི་རྗེས་སློབ་ཟག་པ་འཕེལ་བྱེད་པ།
མི་དད་ཅན་གྱི་གཙོ་བོར་གྲགས་པ་དེ།
གནས་ལུགས་སྟོམ་པའི་ཚང་དུ་སྤང་བྱ་ཡིན།།

47
ཁྱིམ་ནས་བྱུང་ཞིང་བསྟན་པའི་སྒོར་ཞུགས་ཀྱང་།
ཁྱིམ་པ་བཞིན་དུ་བྱ་བ་མཐའ་ཡས་ཞིང་།
བླང་དོར་ཐམས་ཅད་ཁྱེད་དུ་གསོད་པ་དེ།
དྲང་སྲོང་རྣམས་ཀྱི་དམོད་པས་བསྒྲལ་བྱ་ཡིན།།

48
ངུར་སྨྲིག་གྱོན་ནས་ཚུལ་ཁྲིམས་མི་བསྲུང་ཞིང་།
འདོད་པའི་ལས་ལ་སྣང་བ་འབྲུམས་གྱུར་ནས།
དམ་པ་རྣམས་ལ་སྒྲོ་སྐུར་འདེབས་པ་དེ།
མཁའ་འགྲོ་རྣམས་ཀྱིས་ཕ་རོལ་བསྒྲལ་བྱ་ཡིན།།

45

Though you may be the lord of tens of thousands,

the light rays of your unruly mind's lust and hate pervade

the ten directions, like Vishnu; you should be thrust into

the mouth of Yamāntaka.

46

Although you may govern all with smiles and affability, you

are reknowned as the chief of the faithless, causing your followers'

defilements to increase; you should be thrust out of the den

of the genuine vow.

47

Though you have left home and passed through the door of the

teaching, like a householder you still busy yourself with myriad

activities and disparage all proper religious behavior; you should be

destroyed by the sages' curses.

48

Though you wear the saffron robe, you do not guard your morals.

Letting your fantasies run to lustful acts, you overestimate or

deprecate the holy ones; you should be utterly destroyed by

the ḍākinīs.

49
རྙེད་པའི་ཆེད་དུ་དམ་པའི་གཟུགས་བཟུང་ནས།
ཁྱི་ཕག་བཞིན་དུ་འདོད་ཡོན་སྤྱོད་བྱེད་ཅིང་།
སྔགས་སུ་ཁས་བླངས་ཐམས་ཅད་བསླུ་བ་དེ།
རྡོ་རྗེ་འཛིན་པས་ཐབ་ཏུ་གཞུག་བྱ་ཡིན།།

50
ཐེག་ཆེན་སྐད་དུ་ལས་འབྲས་ཁྱད་གསོད་ཅིང་།
སྟོང་པའི་གྲད་ཀྱིས་འཁོར་ཚོགས་བསླུ་བ་ཡི།
འགོང་པོ་བཞིན་དུ་སྐྱུ་རུ་རྫུ་བ་དེ།
དམ་ཚིག་ཅན་གྱི་སྔགས་ཀྱིས་བསྒྲལ་བྱ་ཡིན།།

51
བསྟན་པ་སྤྱི་ལ་ཡོང་ཡེ་མི་ཕན་པའི།
སྔགས་དང་མན་ངག་ཟབ་མོར་རློམ་པ་དང་།
རྟོག་པས་སྦྱར་བའི་ཚིགས་བཅད་ངན་པ་རྣམས།
དམ་པ་རྣམས་ཀྱིས་དམངས་སུ་གདབ་བྱ་ཡིན།།

52
དེ་ལྟར་བསྟན་པ་སྤྱི་ལ་གནོད་བྱེད་ན།
རེ་ཞིག་གང་གིས་གང་ལ་ཕན་གྱུར་ཀྱང་།
ཚད་ནད་ཅན་ལ་འབྲས་ཆང་བླུད་པ་ལྟར།
ཕན་བྱ་ངན་པ་ཆུ་ལ་སྐྱུར་བྱ་ཡིན།།

49

Assuming the guise of a holy person in order to gain wealth,
you pursue objects of sensual pleasure like a dog or a pig, claiming
your actions as tantric and deceiving everyone; you should be thrust
into the fire altar by the vajra-holders.

50

You, the demonic impostor who, in the name of the Mahayana,
disparages moral causality and deceives your followers
with empty boasts, should be destroyed by the spells of the vow-keepers.

51

Your claims about mantra and the profound oral instruction are
of no benefit to the teaching at all, and your wretched verses are
written out of your imagination. Thus, the holy ones should degrade
you to the lowest class.

52

Even though you might help someone temporarily with something,
like giving rice beer to a person with fever, if you should harm the
teaching, you are a person of such pernicious usefulness that you
should be thrown into the river.

53
ཐོས་པ་ཆུང་ངུའི་སྒྲུབ་ཐོབ་ངན་པ་དག།
ཐུན་མོང་ཐོབ་ནས་མཆོག་ཏུ་ང་རྒྱལ་ཏེ།
ལམ་རིམ་མེད་པས་བླུན་པོ་ཁྲིད་པ་རྣམས།
མཁས་པ་རྣམས་ཀྱིས་ཁྲི་དམའ་དབབ་བྱ་ཡིན།།

54
སངས་རྒྱས་བསྟན་ལ་དགྲ་བོ་ལངས་པ་ན།
སོ་སོར་ཐར་ལ་བཟང་པོར་སྙོམ་སྒྱུར་ནས།
ལེགས་པར་ཞད་པའི་འབུལ་མཆོག་མི་བྱེད་པར།
བསྟན་པ་འཇིག་ལ་དམ་པ་མཚར་རེ་ཆེ།།

55
འདི་ལྟར་སོ་སོར་ཐར་པ་ཕར་ཞོག་གིས།
རང་ཉིད་ངན་འགྲོ་ཆེན་པོར་འགྲོ་དོགས་པས།
བསྟན་པ་ཞིག་པའི་དགྲ་བགེགས་མི་སྒྲོལ་དེ།
དམ་ཉམས་དགྲ་བགེགས་ཕ་རོལ་བསྒྲལ་བྱ་ཡིན།།

56
ཉོན་མོངས་ལས་ཀྱིས་བདས་པའི་གཏི་མུག་ཅན།
བསྟན་དང་སེམས་ཅན་སྤྱི་ལ་མི་སེམས་པར།
རང་ལ་གནོད་པ་བྱས་པའི་དགྲ་བོ་ལ།
ཁྲོས་ནས་སྔགས་ཀྱིས་ཕ་རོལ་སྒྲོལ་བ་དེ།
ཚུལ་ཁྲིམས་འཆལ་ལམ་མ་འཆལ་མཚར་རེ་ཆེ།།

53

Base adepts with little education proudly consider themselves superior when they obtain the ordinary supernatural powers. Because they are not on any stage of the path, the wise should humiliate such deluded fools like dogs.

54

When enemies rise up against the Buddha's teachings, it would be absurd if your pride in the excellence of the monastic vows stopped you from performing the authorized rituals for returning your vows and made you keep them in the face of the teaching's destruction.

55

You may fear that if you put aside your monastic vows you may be born into an extremely wretched state of existence. However, anyone who does not destroy the demonic enemies of religion, those who are demolishing the teaching, is breaking their vows. The demonic enemies of religion must be utterly destroyed.

56

Ignorant people, driven by their afflictions and actions and without any regard for the teaching or for living beings will, out of anger, utterly destroy with magic spells the enemy who has injured them. To ask whether or not such people have broken their vows is ridiculous.

57
གང་ཡང་རྒྱལ་བ་རྣམས་ཀྱིས་ཁྲེལ་བ་ཡི།
རང་དོན་ལ་ནི་རྣམ་པ་ཀུན་མི་བསྟེན།
ཕྱོགས་བཅུའི་རྒྱལ་བ་རྣམས་ཀྱིས་བསྔགས་གྱུར་ན།
ཇི་ལྟར་གྱུར་ལ་དེ་ལྟར་སྒྲུབ་པར་རིགས།།

58
མཁྱེན་པར་མཛོད་ཅིག་བློ་དང་ལྡན་པ་རྣམས།
ལག་ལེན་ཐམས་ཅད་ཐོག་མཐའ་དག་ནས་བྱ།
ཆོས་དང་འགལ་བ་སྤྱོག་དང་བསྒོམས་ལ་སྤང་།
སྐྱེ་ལ་མི་གནོད་རང་ལ་ཅི་ཕན་བྱ།།

59
ལྷུན་པོས་རིམ་གྱིས་མཐོང་བར་མ་གྱུར་ཀྱང་།
མཁས་པ་རྣམས་ལ་ལྷོང་གི་སོ་སོར་གསལ།
འདི་ཡང་དཔའ་བོ་འཇུག་པར་བྱ་བ་སྟེ།
ལེའུ་བཞི་པ་དུག་གི་བཅུད་ལེན་ཡིན།།

བཙན་དུག་ནགས་སུ་རྨ་བྱ་རྒྱུ་བ་ཞེས་བྱ་བ།

རྗེ་བཙུན་གཤིན་རྗེའི་གཤེད་ལ་ཕྱག་འཚལ་ལོ།།

57

Do not engage in any self-interested action that the victors have scorned. Come what may, it is proper to carry out whatever has been praised by the victors of the ten directions.

58

People of intelligence, know that all practices should be performed punctiliously. Whatever is opposed to the teaching should be rejected, even at the risk of your life. Injure no one and benefit yourself.

59

While fools do not come to understand things even by degrees, they are clear and vivid to the wise. This is the heroes' actual practice: part four of *The Elixir Made from Poison.*

The Peacocks' Roaming Through the Jungle of Virulent Poison

I bow down to Lord Yamāntaka.

60
གང་ལ་བསམ་པ་ངན་ཞིང་སྡང་ཞུགས་པའི།
ནག་པོའི་ཚོགས་རྣམས་མ་ལུས་དྲུང་འདིར་ཤོག།
ཤ་ཟ་ཁྲག་འཐུང་བྲེ་བ་དུང་ཕྱུར་རྣམས།
ལུས་ཅན་བདག་གི་དྲུང་དུ་དེ་རིང་ཤོག།

61
ལྷ་དང་ཀླུ་དང་གནོད་སྦྱིན་ཚོགས་རྣམས་དང་།
དྲི་ཟ་ལྷ་མ་ཡིན་དང་ལྟོ་འཕྱེའི་ཚོགས།
མཁའ་ལ་རྒྱུ་བའི་ཡི་དགས་མཐའ་ཡས་དང་།
ལན་ཆགས་འབྱུང་པོའི་ཚོགས་རྣམས་དྲུང་འདིར་ཤོག

62
ལྷན་ཅིག་སྐྱེས་པའི་ལྷ་དང་དྲང་སྲོང་དང་།
བགེགས་དང་ལོག་འདྲེན་གདོན་ཆེན་བཅོ་བརྒྱད་དང་།
མ་མོ་རྣམས་དང་ལས་མགོན་ཐམས་ཅད་དང་།
སྐྱབས་གསུམ་འཕགས་པའི་ཚོགས་རྣམས་གནས་འདིར་འབོད།།

63
དེ་ལྟར་མ་ཚང་མེད་པར་འཁོར་འདས་རྣམས།
དབང་པོ་ཉིད་དུ་དྲུང་འདིར་འབོད་པ་ལ།
ཐེ་ཚོམ་མེད་པར་བདག་གིས་དམ་བཅས་པའི།
རླབས་པོ་ཆེ་ཡི་གཏམ་འདི་ཆཤད་ཀྱིས་ཉོན།།

60

May all the malicious and hostile hordes of evil ones, wherever they may be, come here to me! May all the trillions of flesh-eaters and blood-drinkers come here to me, a being of flesh and blood, today!

61

May all the troops of gods, serpent deities, harmful spirits, heavenly musicians, titans, snake spirits, the numberless hungry ghosts who roam the sky, and the armies of retributive spirits come here to me!

62

May the co-natal deities, the sages, the Bringer of Obstacles and Evils, the eighteen great demons, all the protective goddesses and assistant protectors, the Triple Refuge, and the troops of noble ones assemble in this place!

63

Thus, all who belong to cyclic existence or who are beyond it, after gathering in front of me as witnesses, should listen without hesitation as I deliver the great discourse that I have vowed to present.

64
སྔོན་ཆད་རྒྱུ་རྐྱེན་སྐལ་བ་བཟང་པོ་ཡིས།
དེང་སང་འབྱོར་བ་བཅུ་ལྡན་ལུས་འདི་ཐོབ།
ཡ་མཚན་སྐྱེས་པས་ཉིན་མཚན་རངས་གྱུར་ནས།
ད་ནི་ཕན་བདེའི་དཔལ་ལ་ཅིས་མི་སྤྱོད།།

65
སྨོན་ལམ་དག་པས་ཁྱིམ་ནས་རབ་ཏུ་བྱོན།
རང་འདོད་སྤངས་ནས་སྨོན་འཇུག་གོས་སུ་གྱོན།
སེམས་མཆོག་སྐྱེད་ནས་གཞན་དོན་ཁུར་དུ་འཁུར།
ལམ་ལ་ཞུགས་ནས་བདེ་མཆོག་ཟས་སུ་ཟོས།།

66
ཡང་འདི་གསོན་དང་ཐམས་ཅད་འདུས་པའི་འཁོར།
ནག་པོའི་ཕྱོགས་ཀྱི་གདུག་རྩུབ་འདི་འདྲ་ཞིང་།
སྐལ་མེད་རྣམས་ཀྱི་བསོད་ནམས་འདི་འདྲ་བས།
ཁོ་བོ་བདེ་བ་ཅན་དུ་སྨོན་མི་གྱུར།།

67
ཚོགས་མ་བསགས་པའི་འབྱུང་པོ་མཐའ་ཡས་ཤིང་།
ངན་སོང་རྣམས་ཀྱི་སྡུག་བསྔལ་དོས་དྲག་པས།
སྡིག་སྤྱོད་རྣམས་ཀྱི་སྤྱོད་པ་འདི་འདྲ་ན།
ཞི་བདེའི་གནས་སུ་ཁོ་བོ་དགར་མ་ཚོར།།

64

Through the good fortune of previous causes and conditions I have obtained this body that has the ten advantages. I rejoice day and night over this wonderful birth, so how could I not make use of this treasure of benefit and happiness right now?

65

Enter the homeless life with a pure prayer. Renounce your selfish desires and put on the garment of aspiration and engagement. Acquire the supreme thought and take up the burden of others' welfare. Enter upon the path and take supreme bliss as your nourishment.

66

All the congregation that is assembled here, listen further! Since the savagery of the dark quarter is such, and the merit of the unfortunate is so, I shall not aspire to paradise.

67

There are infinite beings who have not accumulated the collections, and the suffering of those in the wretched states of existence is a heavy burden. When such is the career of sinners, I would not feel happy in a peaceful place.

68
བྱིས་པ་རྣམས་ཀྱི་གཉེན་པོ་བསྒྱུར་སླ་ཞིང་།
བདུད་སྡེ་རྣམས་ཀྱི་བསམ་སྦྱོར་འདི་འདྲ་ན།
མི་རྟག་ཚེ་ལ་སྡོད་པའི་སྐབས་མེད་པས།
དབེན་པའི་གནས་སུ་འདུག་ལ་དཀར་མ་ཆོར།།

69
བསྟན་པ་འདི་ལ་སྣང་བའི་དགྲ་མང་ཞིང་།
བཙན་སར་ཕྱིན་པའི་གྲུབ་ཐོབ་འདི་འདྲ་ལ།
སྙིགས་མའི་དུས་འདིར་སྣང་ཚུལ་ལུགས་ངན་པས།
ཁོ་བོ་མཁའ་སྤྱོད་གནས་སུ་དཀར་མ་ཆོར།།

70
ད་ནི་འཇིག་རྟེན་ཁམས་རྣམས་ཐམས་ཅད་ཀྱི།
མཐུ་ཅན་ཐམས་ཅད་བདག་གི་དགྲར་ལངས་ཀྱང་།
ཁོ་བོ་བ་སྤུ་ཙམ་ཡང་མི་གཡོ་བར།
འཁོར་བའི་ནགས་འདིར་གོ་ཆ་བགོ་བར་བྱ།།

71
གང་ན་འགོ་བའི་ནད་ཀྱིས་འཐེབས་གྱུར་ཏེ།
རིམས་ནད་ཆེན་པོས་འཇིག་རྟེན་གཡོས་གྱུར་ཀྱང་།
སྨན་པ་ཉིད་དམ་ནད་པའི་གཡོག་དག་ཏུ།
དྲག་པོའི་གོ་ཆ་ཆེན་པོ་བགོ་བར་བྱ།།

68

For immature persons the antidote is easily subverted, and such is the plan of demons. Because there is no time to rest in this impermanent life, I would not feel happy dwelling in a solitary place.

69

The enemies who hate the teaching are many, and the adepts who have gone to a safe retreat are few. Because to outward appearances the situation in this degenerate age is bad, I cannot feel happy in heaven.

70

Now, even if all the mighty ones in all the worldly realms were to rise up as my enemies, I shall, without the stirring of so much as a hair, put on my armor in this jungle of cyclic existence.

71

Wherever infectious diseases may strike, or great plagues disrupt the world, I shall put on the great mighty armor in order to serve as a doctor or nurse.

72
མ་ནུས་སེམས་ཅན་དྲིན་གྱིས་བསྐྱངས་པའི་ཚེ།
ལོག་སྒྲུབ་ཆེན་པོས་སྡུག་སུན་ཕྱུང་བ་ན།
ལྷག་པར་དེ་ལ་ཕན་ཞིང་བརྩེ་བ་ཡི།
དཔའ་བོ་རྣམས་ཀྱི་གོ་ཆ་བགོ་བར་བྱ།།

73
གང་ན་སྟག་མོ་མི་ཟན་འཇིགས་པ་རྣམས།
མི་ཡི་སྲོག་ལ་འཇབ་ཅིང་རྒྱུག་པ་ན།
སེམས་ཅན་དོན་དུ་ཐེ་ཚོམ་མི་ཟ་བར།
ཕྱོགས་དེར་བགྲོད་པའི་གོ་ཆ་བགོ་བརབྱ།།

74
འཇིག་རྟེན་དག་ན་ཞེན་ཏུ་མི་འདོད་པའི།
ལྷས་ངན་སྣ་ཚོགས་དམག་ཏུ་འཐིབས་པ་རྣམས།
དགྲ་བདག་གཞིས་ངན་རང་ཉིད་གཞོམ་པའི་ཕྱིར།
གཡང་དུ་ལེན་པའི་གོ་ཆ་བགོ་བར་བྱ།།

75
འཇིག་རྟེན་དག་ན་ཞེན་ཏུ་མི་མཁོ་བའི།
ལས་དང་ཉོན་མོངས་སྒྱུ་མ་འཁྲུགས་པ་རྣམས།
བདག་ཏུ་འཛིན་པའི་སྲོག་དང་བྲལ་བའི་ཕྱིར།
དང་དུ་ལེན་པའི་གོ་ཆ་བགོ་བར་བྱ།།

72
When I have been kindly taking care of helpless persons and
they savagely reject me with gross ingratitude,
I shall put on the armor of the heroes who greatly help and
love those people.

73
Wherever terrifying man-eating tigresses lie in wait and hunt
human lives, I will put on my armor without hesitation and
go there for the good of sentient beings.

74
When all sorts of ill omens portending calamity cover
the worlds in darkness, I shall put on the armor that welcomes
them as auspicious signs of the conquest of the evil-natured
enemy, ego, itself.

75
When the illusions of undesirable actions and afflictions are stirred
up in the worlds, I shall put on the armor of willing acceptance
in order to put an end to the life of ego-clinging.

76
ཕཊ་ཡ་ཧོ་ཡ་འཆི་བདག་ཧླ་ར་ཡ།
སྐྲིད་འདོད་འགོང་པོའི་སྲོག་ལ་ཛྭ་ལ་རཾ།
སྣོམ་ལས་ལེ་ལོའི་མགོ་ལ་ཆེམས་སེ་ཆེམས།
འཁོར་བའི་འབྲེལ་ཐག་ཐད་ཐད་ཆོད་པར་མཛོད།།

77
བདག་ཅག་འཁོར་བ་འདི་རུ་སྡུག་བསྔལ་བས།
འདི་ཡི་ལན་རྩ་རྫོ་རུས་གཏུགས་པ་ན།
རྣམ་རྟོག་སྙིང་གི་གཞལ་ཡས་ཡ་གི་ན།།
ངའོ་ཞེས་པའི་རྒྱལ་པོ་བཞུགས་པ་མཐོང་།།

78
དེ་ལ་ལེ་ལན་བདས་ཤིང་འཐབ་པ་ན།
ཅི་ཟེར་བདག་ནི་ཐོག་མེད་དུས་ནས་ཞུགས།
ཕྱི་ནང་བར་གསུམ་ཡོངས་ལ་བདག་གིས་ཁྱབ།
བདེན་བརྫུན་ཚོགས་དུག་གཙོ་བོ་ཡོངས་ལ་དྲིས།།

79
བདག་ཉིད་བདག་གི་དགྲ་ཡིན་སུ་ལ་འཐབ།
བདག་ཉིད་མགོན་ཡིན་ཐམས་ཅད་སུ་ལ་སྐྱོབ།
བྱ་དང་མི་བྱ་ཡོངས་ལ་དཔང་པོ་རང་།
རང་གིས་རང་ཉིད་ཐུལ་ན་གྲོལ་བར་འགྱུར།།

76

Destroy! Hurrah! Kill the Lord of Death! Burn up the life of the demon hedonism! Thunder down on the head of lazy indifference! Completely sever the ties that bind you to cyclic existence!

77

If we energetically seek the ultimate cause of our suffering here in cyclic existence, look up there in the palace of conceptual mind where King Ego dwells.

78

When you have rebuked and fought him, what does he say? "I have existed from beginningless time; I pervade the inside, the outside, and the in-between. Ask the chief of the six senses whether this is true or false.

79

"Since your ego is your enemy, against whom shall you fight? Since your ego itself is the protector, whom shall you protect? It is the very witness of all that you have done and left undone. When you have tamed your ego, you shall be liberated.

80
གཞན་གྱིས་གཞན་ཞིག་འདུལ་ན་འཐབ་རྩོད་ཡིན།
འཐབ་ཅིང་རྩོད་པའི་དུང་ན་སྡིག་ཅན་མཆར།
ངེས་ཏེ་ཆགས་སྡང་ཅན་ལ་གྲོལ་སྐབས་མེད།
དེས་ན་རྟོགས་པ་མེད་པའི་རྣལ་འབྱོར་བདེ།།

81
ཨ་ལ་དེ་སྐད་བྱ་བ་ཅི་ལ་ཟེར།
ཡོད་པར་འཛིན་པའི་སྒྲོག་ལ་སླ་ར་ཡ།
མེད་པར་འཛིན་པའི་སྒྲོག་ལ་ཛྭ་ལ་རཾ།
བདག་འཛིན་འགོང་པོ་ཡིན་ནོ་གཙོ་བོ་ཆོམས།།

82
གཙོ་བོ་ཡིད་ཀྱི་རྣམ་ཤེས་མ་ཐུལ་ན།
བདག་འཛིན་རྒྱལ་པོས་འགབ་ལ་འཁྲིད་ཉེན་ཡོད།
གཙོ་བོ་ཡིད་ཀྱི་རྣམ་ཤེས་ཐུལ་བ་ན།
མིག་སོགས་གཙོ་བོ་གཞན་ཡང་བརླག་པར་འགྱུར།།

83
དེས་ན་ཡིད་ཀྱི་རྣམ་ཤེས་འདི་ཐུལ་དང་།
གཟུགས་སྒྲ་དྲི་རོ་ལ་སོགས་ཡོད་མ་མཆིས།།
བདག་དང་བདག་གིར་འཛིན་པ་ཡོད་མི་འགྱུར།
རྣམ་རྟོག་རྒྱལ་པོ་ཁྲིན་དང་བྲལ་བར་མཆིས།།

80

"When someone is tamed by another, there will be a struggle; in such a struggle the number of sinners will be immense. It is certain that there is no chance of liberation for those who lust and hate. Therefore, nonconceptual yoga is bliss."

81

Ah! What can you say to that speech? Kill the life of clinging to existence! Burn up the life of clinging to nonexistence! Crush the chief, the demon ego-clinging!

82

When the chief, mental consciousness, is not tamed, there is the danger that King Ego-Clinging may lead it astray. When the chief, mental consciousness, is tamed, vision and so forth will be destroyed along with the chief.

83

Therefore, you should tame mental consciousness, and form, sound, smell, taste, and the rest will cease to be. "I" and "mine" will cease to be, and King Conceptualization will then lack a basis.

84
དེ་ལྟར་རྒྱལ་པོ་དེ་ལ་སླུས་པ་ན།
རྣམ་རྟོག་རང་གྲོལ་ཆོས་ཀྱི་དབྱིངས་སུ་གོ།
ཚོགས་དྲུག་མི་བདེན་སྒྱུ་མའི་གླང་པོ་འདྲ།
གཟུང་འཛིན་མི་བདེན་སྤྲུལ་པའི་འཕྲིན་ལས་འདྲ།།

85
དེ་ལྟར་ལགས་པས་རྣམ་རྟོག་དྭང་ནས་ཕྱུང་།
གཟུང་འཛིན་མེད་པས་བདག་ལྟ་དབྱིངས་སུ་བསྒྱུར།
ང་ཁྱོད་མེད་པས་ཆགས་སྡང་གཉུག་མར་ཞོག།།

86
རི་བོང་རྭ་ལྟར་རྟོ་རྟུལ་མི་མངའ་བའི།
དབང་པོ་རབ་འབྲིང་འཆིང་བའི་སྒྲོག་དང་བྲལ།
མོ་གཤམ་བུ་ལྟར་སྤང་བླང་མི་མངའ་བའི།
འཁོར་འདས་ཐམས་ཅད་མཉམ་པ་ཉིད་དུ་དྲིལ།།

87
རུས་སྦལ་སྤུ་ལྟར་རིང་ཐུང་མི་མངའ་བའི།
སྐྱེ་འཇིག་ཐམས་ཅད་དབུ་མ་ཆེན་པོར་གློད།
བྲག་ཆ་ལྟ་བུར་ཡེ་ནས་སྟོང་པ་ཡི།
ཐ་སྙད་ཆོས་རྣམས་དོན་དམ་གཅིག་ཏུ་དྲིལ།།

84
When you have spoken to the king in this way, you will know that conceptual construction is inherently free and is the ultimate reality. The six senses are false, like a magical elephant. Subject and object are false, like a phantom's deeds.

85
Such being the case, extirpate conceptual construction! Since there is neither subject nor object, transform the egotistic view into space! Since there is neither "I" nor "you," transfer attachment and aversion to the innate.

86
Remove the shackles of high and mediocre intellect, which, like rabbit horns, are neither sharp nor dull. Unite into equality everything worldly and transcendental, which, like a barren woman's child, is neither clever nor foolish.

87
Release into the great middle all arising and perishing, which, like the hair of a tortoise, is neither short nor long. Unite into a single ultimate all conventional phenomena, which, like an echo, have been forever empty.

88

ཨ་ཨ་སྐྱེ་མེད་ནམ་མཁའ་ལྟ་བུའི་ངང་།
ཨི་ཨི་འཇིགས་མེད་སྤྲོས་དང་བྲལ་བའི་སྐུ།
ཨོཾ་ཨོཾ་རྣམ་དག་ཆོས་སྐུར་ངོ་འཕྲོད་ནས།
ཀཱ་རུ་ཎི་ཀའི་ཐུག
ས་རྗེས་འཛིན་པར་ཤོག།

འདི་ལྟར་བཙན་དུག་ནགས་སུ་རྨ་བྱ་རྒྱུ་བ་ཞེས་བྱ་བ།

ཞེས་བྱ་རབ་འབྱམས་ལ་བློ་གྲོས་ཀྱི་མིག་བྱང་ནས་ལས་རྒྱུ་འབྲས་ལ་བསླུ་བ་མེད་པའི་མཐུ་སྟོབས་ཐོབ་ཅིང་། ལྟ་བ་གཉིས་སུ་མེད་པའི་དོན་ལ་ཐེ་ཚོམ་མེད་པར་གྱུར་པ། རི་ནག་པོའི་ཁོང་ན་གནས་པའི་རྣལ་འབྱོར་པ་དྷ་རྨ་ར་ཀྵི་ཏ་ཞེས་བྱ་བ་བདག་གིས་སེམས་ཅན་ལ་དམིགས་པ་མེད་པའི་སྙིང་རྗེ་ཆེན་པོས་ཀུན་ནས་བླངས་ནས་སྦྱར་བ་དགེ་ལེགས་སུ་གྱུར་ཅིག། སརྦ་ཤུབྷཾ།།

88

Ah, ah, the nature of non-arising is like space. Ee, ee, the body of nonperishing is free from discursive elaboration. Oṃ, oṃ, having recognized it as the ultimate body, may the compassion of the Compassionate One sustain us.

The Peacocks' Roaming Through the Jungle of Virulent Poison

Colophon

Having purified the eye of my intelligence in the wide range of knowledge, and having acquired the power of not being deceived as to moral cause and effect, and having no doubt about the meaning of the nondual view, I, Dharmarakṣita the yogi, dwelling in Black Mountain Cave, composed this motivated by objectless great compassion for living beings. May it be auspicious! May it be auspicious for all *(sarvaśubhaṃ)!*

Commentary on Dharmarakṣita's *The Poison-Destroying Peacock Mind Training*

Geshe Lhundub Sopa

THE TITLE OF THIS WORK is *The Poison-Destroying Peacock.* Its alternate title is *The Peacocks' Roaming Through the Jungle of Virulent Poison;* this alludes to the comparison between the peacock and the bodhisattva, about which I will have more to say later. The alternate title is followed by the salutation:

I bow down to Lord Yamāntaka.

Yamāntaka is the wrathful manifestation of Mañjuśrī, the deity of perfect wisdom. Among the many depictions of Yamāntaka is one that represents him as particularly ferocious—with a bull's head, thirty-two arms, sixteen legs, horns, surrounded by flames, and carrying various types of weapons in his hands. All of these are symbols of special tantric inner qualities, like wisdom, compassion, and certain kinds of love and power. One cannot really show these inner qualities, but one can represent them symbolically, for example, with weapons and fire and the actions of cutting and destroying that they perform. In a similar way our inner mental weapons of wisdom, compassion, and love are the antidotes to our afflictions.

Our minds are subject to many delusions and afflicted mental states, especially the three poisons of ignorance, desire, and hatred, which in turn give rise to many other types of poison. You can think of it as a poison tree—with ignorance, desire, and hatred as its trunk, and jealousy, stinginess, and the other emotional afflictions as its poisonous branches, subbranches, flowers, leaves, and fruits, which branch out and blossom forth, completely filling our minds. This is what is referred to in the Abhidharma as the 84,000 afflictions. All of us already possess them in their entirety: We live with them, get up in the morning with them, and go to sleep with them. Some of them are strong, some are in the background, some are dormant, some have awakened, but all of them are present in our minds. That is why we have no peace or happiness and are always frustrated, worried, and anxious. The afflictions impel us to physical actions, such as fighting with others, showing others an unpleasant expression, lying, and using sharp words. Until these poisons are completely eliminated from our minds, we will have no real peace and will be unable to attain perfection. When we remove these negative mental states from our minds, we must replace them with positive ones. Instead of attachment, hatred, and jealousy, we should have wisdom, compassion, love, and all the other noble mental states that go along with them. When you possess such mental states, you will be called a buddha, a perfectly enlightened person, and will be free from all problems, misery, and suffering along with the negative or impure karma that causes them. It is the three poisons and the other mental afflictions that are the source of bad karma, and when they are removed, there will be no negative actions and their consequences.

When you remove the poisons, you will at the same time gain hundreds of special qualities. It is sometimes said that the buddhas have four powers and eight types of fearlessness, compassion, love, and bodhicitta. Each of these special qualities can be divided more specifically, for example, into the sixteen or twenty kinds of realization of emptiness, just as the three poisons branch out into the 84,000 afflictions. Just as the poisons are manifested by physical and verbal misdeeds and the sufferings that are their consequences, the good qualities also have their external manifestations; the weapons and other attributes of Yamāntaka are symbolic of the physical and mental qualities that are manifested when one attains buddhahood.

Why is a form of the deity Mañjuśrī invoked in this text? It's because all of our problems, selfishness, lack of compassion, love and patience, all of these arise from our view of a real personal identity and the self-cherishing attitude that accompanies it. What is the opponent of this ignorance that falsely holds things to inherently exist? What is the real antidote? It is wisdom, the highest wisdom, which perceives the lack of an inherent self, that is, the realization of emptiness. By developing this type of wisdom through meditation, ignorance can be destroyed, thus cutting out all the roots of cyclic existence and its faults. Such wisdom, manifesting in the form of a deity or buddha, is called Mañjuśrī, who has both a peaceful and a wrathful form. The peaceful Mañjuśrī usually takes the form of a bodhisattva holding a flaming sword symbolizing wisdom, because a sword can cut and flames can burn. The sword of wisdom cuts and burns our ignorance and the sufferings that result from it.

One of the beginning practices of mind training is prostration, or bowing down. Generally, at the beginning of Indian texts there is a salutation to a deity for whom the author has a special kind of faith. Sometimes, we bow down to all the bodhisattvas, the buddhas of the ten directions, or to Mañjuśrī. Here, we bow down to Yamāntaka because he is the special deity of this text.

The Poison-Destroying Peacock is made up of five sections or chapters, the first of which is concerned with the Buddha's former lives, when he was a bodhisattva. In my explanation of this text, I use as a guide the topical outline written by the famous Mongolian scholar Losang Tamdrin (bLo bzang rta mgrin, 1867–1937). In the sutra system many eons are required for religious practice to accumulate the merit necessary to attain buddhahood. The *jātakas* are a collection of many stories about how in his former lives the Buddha gave away his body, wealth, and even his family to others, and how he performed many other noble deeds out of altruism and loving-kindness. He made even those who tried to harm him the focus of his help, to free them from suffering. In this manner, the first part of the text shows how we can emulate the life of Buddha Śākyamuni. Śāntideva said (*BCA* 2.57):

> There is an omniscient physician capable of removing all pains.
> Isn't it the height of stupidity not to comply with his advice?

When you want to completely cure a particular disease that is causing you distress, you seek out a medical specialist. But, finding the right doctor is not enough; no matter how good the doctor is, you'll have to follow his or her orders. You might not like certain things that the doctor prescribes, for example, to not eat or drink some things or to not do certain things that you enjoy. It will be a hardship, but the doctor's orders are most important—if you want to be cured, you must rely on them. If you find a wonderful doctor but reject all of his or her advice, it won't help; the effectiveness of the doctor's treatment depends on the patient's compliance. If you are compliant with the regimen, however, there is an excellent chance that you will recover fully from your illness. Even if what the doctor orders is very disagreeable, you should take his or her instructions joyfully or patiently. For example, you may have to have part of a limb amputated or something equally unpleasant, but you must accept it, because that procedure will cure your illness, and you should focus on that result.

In the same way, spiritually we are seeking permanent emancipation, peace, and the happiness of relief from the disease of misery that characterizes all cyclic existence. Seeking complete, permanent spiritual freedom from suffering means wanting to be free from the misery of cyclic existence for more than just a short time, for more than a day, a few years, or even this lifetime. Complete freedom from suffering and its causes is nirvana or emancipation; to sever suffering and its causes from the root results in permanent cessation. You can have temporary relief from suffering, but that is not what the Buddha meant when referring to the noble truth of cessation. The noble truth of cessation refers to using the noble truths of suffering and the cause of suffering as the objects of cessation. Liberation is their permanent cessation; when you are liberated in this sense, you will have peace and happiness and will never fall back into the suffering of cyclic existence. This is a spiritual or religious goal, not just for yourself, but for the benefit of all beings. If you free yourself but fail to liberate others, you will not be able to feel the great joy of emancipation, because you will still see the continuous suffering of others, of sentient beings who have, from the beginningless cycle of births and deaths, been your own dear mothers and fathers. Therefore, permanent freedom from misery and suffering for both yourself and others is the spiritual goal. To phrase it in a positive way, the goal is highest peace and happiness, and perfect mental, physical, and environmental qualities.

According to Buddhist teachings, this goal is not mere imagination or empty words; it is actually achievable. This goal is contained in the four noble truths taught by the Buddha. The truth of suffering describes what actually exists. The truth of cause presents the actual causes of suffering. These causes are not permanent and absolute, and thus they are eradicable; they can be completely extinguished. This is what we mean by permanent cessation as the main goal or objective. The way to obtain this cessation is the path, which is like a spiritual treatment prescribed by the perfect, omniscient Buddha. The Buddha is the real spiritual doctor and all his teachings are treatments. The Buddha himself underwent such treatment for many eons and then finally achieved the perfect goal—peace, happiness, complete omniscience, and realization. Of course it is difficult to take up this practice, but it is worthwhile because doing so will lead to your own objective and goal. Everybody wants happiness; this is a goal shared by everyone. But it can be obtained only by taking up the spiritual regimen of the Buddha's teaching.

To what extent should treatment be applied? In medical treatment there are three levels: for life-threatening illnesses, for less severe illnesses, and for the subtle basis of disease. Similarly, Buddha's teaching has various levels because we can't get rid of all the misery and problems of cyclic existence at once or with just one method. There is no single powerful medicine that can remove all suffering; as I often say, there is no spiritual panacea. Therefore, for each of the 84,000 delusions that cause suffering, there is a distinct antidote to be applied; this is the beginning of practice.

The Poison-Destroying Peacock, a great teaching about the bodhisattva way of thought and practice, presents, like other mind-training texts, ways of becoming aware of your thoughts, changing them, and reinforcing those changes. The first section offers examples for us to emulate from the Buddha's previous lives. The Buddha did not attain enlightenment by a sudden leap; according to the Mahayana scriptures, he practiced for many lifetimes over three countless eons. These accounts of his previous lifetimes were taught by the Buddha himself, not by anyone else. Since he was omniscient, he could answer many questions about the past and the future. When certain unusual events occurred during the Buddha's lifetime, some of the disciples wondered about their causes; because of his omniscience, the Buddha could explain their origins. These jātaka stories may seem fantastic to us, but our minds have no limitations, and when we develop them, many seemingly impossible things can be easily accomplished.

1 Just as he gave away his children and his realm when he
was Prince Viśvāntara, so you too should give away
without reservation the wealth, companions, and so forth
that you hold so dear.

This first verse introduces the famous story about the Buddha when he was the bodhisattva Prince Saving-All, in Sanskrit, Prince Viśvāntara (Pāli: *Vessantara*). Many eons ago the Buddha was a prince who was naturally extremely compassionate, loving, peaceful, and kind. Of course, he had previously trained his mind over the course of many lives, which accounts for this temperament. When he saw people living in poverty and want, he felt great compassion and love; he desired to rescue them and share his wealth with them.

The main activities of a bodhisattva are the six perfections (Skt: *pāramitā*). First, there is the perfection of giving, then the perfections of moral conduct, patience, and so on. The bodhisattva trains in these six perfections in many lives, first mentally and then by actually carrying them out. Because of his prior training and activity, the prince did not hesitate to give away all his possessions; he even gave away his own wife and children. Whenever he traveled, he distributed gifts to all who were needy. As a prince, and as expected of royalty in those days, he traveled with a large retinue and on a huge white elephant adorned with decorations. In one kingdom he visited, the king coveted his elephant and sent some poor Brahmins to beg for it, since he knew the prince was generous. They went to him and asked for it, saying "We want your white elephant." The prince was overjoyed; it was as if he had a thirst to give things to those who asked.

Of course, he was highly intelligent and realized that the Brahmins should have asked for food, clothes, or other basic necessities, but instead they asked for the elephant, of which they had no need. But he gave them the elephant anyway and then proceeded on foot. His ministers, military officers, and people were opposed to his giving away his elephant and went to his father and said it was fine for him to give money and other things away, but improper for him to give away the elephant. If he continued to act like this, they feared that all the royal possessions would gradually be given away. But the king couldn't refuse his son outright, because of his great love for him, and he wasn't able to convince him to stop giving away his possessions. The prince continued to give things away and opposition mounted among the people. They were afraid that he would give away their possessions as well, causing the country and its people to become poor. They thought that the young prince was a spiritual being, not fit to be in the position of king, and they suggested that he be sent to a hermitage. They reasoned that the king could hold on to the country's property, and the prince would be able to practice religion in a jungle hermitage; finally, the king agreed to this.

The prince left for the hermitage with his wife and two children—a young daughter and son. On the way he met an old beggar whose wife served as his bearer. As she was getting too old to carry things, the beggar asked for the prince's two children as servants. Although he loved them greatly, he gave them to the beggar; his wife knew nothing of this, having gone off for a while. When she returned and saw that the children were missing, she feared that they had been killed by beasts or taken away by thieves. The prince explained to her that he had given them to the beggar and she was somewhat relieved to know that they were still alive. Although she was sad, she understood his heroic mental attitude and didn't blame him.

Because of the prince's heroic act, the earth shook and the god Indra came down to investigate in the guise of a poor Brahman. He said to the prince that he needed a wife and asked the prince to give him his. The prince gave his wife to him without hesitation. Later, Indra appeared in his true shining heavenly body, praised the prince, restored his wife and children to him, and gave him back his wealth and kingdom in even greater abundance than before. This then is the famous story of the first verse.

> 2 Just as he nourished the tigress with his own flesh when he was Prince Mahāmaitrībala, so you too should joyfully give your dearly cherished heap of an illusory body to the mob of flesh-eating demons.

This story about the Buddha's previous birth as Prince Mahāmaitrībala is also well known in Tibet and other Buddhist countries; it is usually referred to as the story of the Buddha's sacrifice of himself to the hungry tigress. In a great kingdom in India there was a king who had three children; the youngest was called Mahāmaitrībala, who was exceptionally loving and compassionate. His very name means "He whose strength is great loving-kindness." In this story, the king and his three sons went to a wild area outside the city on an outing, the sons continuing further for a walk deep into the jungle. There the youngest, Mahāmaitrībala, saw a very hungry and emaciated tigress with her five cubs; in fact, she was so hungry that she was about to eat one of her own young. Mahāmaitrībala asked his older brothers, "Is there anybody who can feed this tigress with his own flesh and blood?" The older princes said, "Nobody can do that." He told his brothers that he had something to do in the forest, that they should start back and he'd follow them. When they were gone, he went to the tigress with the intention of giving his body to her, but her jaws were tightly closed and she could not eat. So he got a sharp stick and cut his body to draw blood, and she drank it. After drinking his blood, she became stronger and was able to slowly eat his flesh until his body was completely devoured.

In thinking about the body, there is the expression "the essenceless body of the stains of the five poisons." This phrase means that we should think that our body is without essence; unless we utilize it for a special religious purpose, it has no real meaning. It is impermanent, changing all the time; even if you don't want it to change and want to stay youthful forever, it won't do so. It changes moment by moment, in the time it takes to snap your fingers. Also, if you investigate the nature of the body, you will find that it is impure and dirty; there is nothing that is really attractive about it. In this story the prince says: "At this time, my body can be of great benefit to beings who are about to die; so now I have the opportunity to donate it, to practice the virtue of giving, to benefit both myself and the recipient." Thinking in such a way, Prince Mahāmaitribala gave his body to the tigress and died. As a result he was born as a god in the highest heaven.

This verse tells us that a bodhisattva, just like the Buddha, should be able to give away his or her cherished illusory body, that he or she should joyfully give that body to carnivorous beasts. When you reach a certain bodhisattva level, such things can be practiced. At that time, there is no holding back and you will experience great joy and power from your generosity. When you practice giving and sharing with others for a long time, out of total compassion and love, you will be able to experience this joy easily. As Śāntideva said (*BCA* 5.87):

> In the absence of the pure thought of compassion do not give away your body. [But when the pure thought of compassion is present] you should give it away no matter what occurs, in this life and others, as the cause for realizing the great aim.

This means that until you reach the bodhisattva level where you have totally spontaneous love and compassion, you should not give away your body. When you hear the story of the prince giving his body to the tigress, it does not mean you should go out and look for a tigress to feed your body to. In your present state of mind, fearful and attached to your body, you would still lack real compassion and be motivated by thinking that this would help you to be reborn in heaven. Such things are not to be done. As Śāntideva said (*BCA* 7.25):

> The Guide teaches us to give vegetables and so on at first.
> After becoming accustomed to this, later on, by degrees,
> we can even give up our own flesh.

When a bodhisattva fully develops the mental practice of universal love and compassion, then he or she begins to act with charity. The perfection of giving doesn't mean actually giving away your body and everything you possess, or feeding everyone in the world until you have fed all of them—this is impossible. The perfection of giving means giving up your attachment to your body, life, and possessions and completely devoting yourself to others whenever they are in need. You will think, "This is not mine anymore; it belongs to sentient beings." And you will be ready at any time, without the slightest hesitation, to give away whatever is useful or beneficial to others. As Śāntideva says, you can start by giving small things, like vegetables, and gradually reach higher and higher, until finally you are ready to give your own flesh and blood. When you have skillful method and wisdom, you will know when and how you should give to others. Giving everything is easy for a bodhisattva who has exchanged self with other. For us, even hearing about this can be disagreeable because we are so attached even to trivial things.

> 3 Just as he nourished the harmful demons with his own blood when he was King Maitrībala, so you too should lovingly give warm blood from your heart, which is so difficult to cut, to the blood-drinking demons.

This verse continues the theme of the preceding ones. Here, the king's name means "He whose strength is loving-kindness." In ancient times, long before his enlightenment, the Buddha was a mighty king who loved others greatly. Once, blood-drinking demons came to the kingdom and saw a shepherd playing and singing joyfully in a wild place; they were surprised that he could remain in such a dangerous place without fear. The demons questioned him about this, and in response, he told them that he could stay there peacefully because the kingdom was protected by a great, loving king. The demons wished to see the king for themselves, so they went to his palace and begged, and the king gave them many good things: clothes, jewelry, and so forth. But they were not satisfied; they said they didn't need such things, that they wanted warm flesh and blood, especially his blood. The king then gave the demons his blood without fear or hesitation. They were so surprised that they couldn't drink it, and they apologized to him. Then, the king gave them a great religious teaching that resulted in their future births as humans who practiced religion.

The point of this verse is that when people act badly, a bodhisattva's response is to help them, unlike ordinary people who would retaliate against them. Bodhisattvas seek to benefit evildoers, not only in the present, but also with the intention of helping them toward their future goal of peace and freedom from suffering. Bodhisattvas vow that in the future, when they attain perfect enlightenment, their first task will be to lead present evildoers to emancipation.

When the Buddha was enlightened in Bodh Gaya, he gave his first sermon on the four noble truths to his five disciples, who immediately achieved arhatship, or the path of seeing. The Buddha later told Ānanda that those five monks had earlier been the five blood-drinking demons.

> 4 Just as he saved the fish by reciting the name of the Tathāgata when he was the chief merchant's son Jalavāhana, so you too should give the gift of the holy Dharma to all beings who lack it.

The previous verses talked about the giving of material things and one's body and life; this verse is about the gift of the Dharma. There are three kinds of giving: giving material things; giving protection, for example, from drowning or fire or punishment; and giving the gift of the Dharma. The last type means giving instruction or teaching without holding back in a stingy way, giving the best explanations of the Buddha's teachings that you are able to make. The story in this verse is about another of the Buddha's past lives, when he was the chief merchant's son Jalavāhana. The name Jalavāhana means "water-carrier." In this story the bodhisattva Jalavāhana saved many fish from dying in a lake that was drying out. He brought water from a great distance to replenish the lake and save the lives of the fish, and he also recited the name of the Tathāgata and other sacred words and gave religious instructions to the fish, which eventually resulted in their liberation. We need to teach the Dharma to those who are deprived of it; this is an important part of practicing the Dharma; it is a type of charity.

> 5 Just as he compassionately endured Prince Pāpārtha's ingratitude when he was Prince Mahākalyānārtha, so you too should have great compassion toward your companions' ingratitude when it is stirred up by their evil nature.

The subject of this verse is compassion. Sometimes, no matter how well we treat others, their response is negative or ungrateful. Whether you behave pleasantly or in a hateful, hostile manner toward bodhisattvas, their response is always gentle, peaceful, loving and kind. Because a bodhisattva makes no mental distinction between friendly and unfriendly people, he or she has equanimity toward all sentient beings. This means that the bodhisattva does not discriminate between someone he or she likes and wants to help and someone he or she dislikes and wants to harm. If you make such distinctions, it means you don't have an attitude of complete equality. Equanimity means to have equal love and compassion toward everyone, not, by the way, that you should hate them equally!

Śākyamuni Buddha had a cousin, Devadatta, who had no respect for the Buddha and was always competing with him and trying to harm him. This story concerns their relationship in one of the Buddha's past lives a very long time ago, when the Buddha was Prince Mahākalyānārtha, or "He whose aim is great virtue." At that time he had a brother, Prince Pāpārtha, "He whose aim is sin." No matter how kindly Prince Mahākalyānārtha acted toward his brother, Prince Pāpārtha responded only with evil. In spite of this, Prince Mahākalyānārtha was compassionate and patient with him. It was this Prince Pāpārtha who was born in a later life as Śākyamuni's cousin, Devadatta. This verse recommends that we treat our friends and associates in the same way, responding only with kindness and compassion even if they ungratefully try to harm us because they are under the power of hatred and desire.

> 6 Just as he pulled the sinner out of the well when he was the monkey bodhisattva, so you too should guide evil

> people compassionately without expecting good in return,
> even to one's detriment.

This verse is the last one concerned with the jātaka stories; it also relates how the bodhisattvas are able to bear ingratitude and practice giving without any expectation of reward. Whenever ordinary people do something for others, they expect something in return; even if they do a small thing, they expect a big reward, and they may refrain from doing good if they don't see any potential return. However, when the bodhisattvas practice charity, it is purely to benefit others, with no expectation of anything in return.

Bodhisattvas sometimes manifest in animal or other forms in order to save others, as in this story about the time that the Buddha was born as a bodhisattva in the form of a monkey living in the jungle. At that time, the monkey bodhisattva rescued a man who had fallen into a well. They were both exhausted by the rescue and decided to rest in shifts to watch out for each other. That night, while the monkey was sleeping, the man thought, "I am so weak. How will I ever be able to get out of this jungle? I need to eat some meat to get enough strength, so I'll have to kill the monkey and eat his flesh." Then the man picked up a large rock and threw it at the monkey bodhisattva. It didn't kill him, it only hit him and woke him up. Not suspecting that the man had wished to injure him, the monkey asked him what had happened. The man couldn't speak or move but sat shamefaced and weeping. The bodhisattva realized what had happened and felt great compassion for the man because he would suffer in the future owing to such an evil action. He was much more concerned for the man than for himself. Despite what the man had done, the monkey bodhisattva gave him advice, fed him, and led him out of the deep jungle. When they were about to take their leave, the monkey bodhisattva sincerely advised the man: "You are a human being, far superior to me, a mere monkey. A human being can accomplish great virtue. From now on, you should avoid evil and practice only virtue."

The man went home, and received karmic retribution right away. In most cases, karma bears fruit in future lives, not in the life in which it has been created. But when an action is very powerful, its effect can be experienced in that very life. In this case, the man contracted leprosy upon leaving the jungle; his body was racked with pain, smelled bad, and looked extremely repulsive. People thought he looked like a demon; they avoided him and threw stones to drive him away. This was the result of his evil behavior toward the monkey bodhisattva; nevertheless, the bodhisattva had treated him with great compassion, and that is the main point of the verse.

> 7 Alas! There is no one who has not been my parent. There is not one instant of happiness in this jungle of cyclic existence. Returning evil to the crowd of evildoers is like [adding manure to] a donkey's stall.

This verse introduces the second main topic of this section, the reason why we should follow the bodhisattva path. First, we have to understand that cyclic existence is full of hardship. This verse begins with a statement about the nature of cyclic existence. We contemplate the fact that all beings are related, because everyone has been our parent many times. Then, we consider that there is not even an instant of real happiness in cyclic existence for these beings because they suffer birth, aging, sickness, and death. There are so many evildoers in cyclic existence because sentient beings, who are motivated by their egotism, harm each other directly or indirectly, and evil leads to more evil. The last line means that to return evil for evil is like filling a donkey's stall with manure and other filth; that is, to respond with more evil to the evil done to you is like adding more manure to an already filthy place like a donkey's stall, thereby perpetuating the cycle.

> 8 If you have accepted this spiritual biography of the great sage-hero with respect, but have not generated the antidote, the actual heroic practice will be impossible. Thus, keep to the practice of austerities even at the risk of your own life.

After you have heard the heroic life stories of the great sage, as in the previous verses, you have to continually strive to develop a strong antidote to wrong attitudes in order to overcome difficulties in performing these practices. You have to think that you are the only one who can do these difficult actions for others, and vow that you will take on any hardship for the benefit of other beings even at the sacrifice of your own life. You have to think: "I must practice bodhisattva deeds, otherwise the great heroic practice will disappear."

9 If those who desire to imitate the Sugata after he has appeared to pass away do not keep this practice in their minds, there is a risk that the happiness of living beings will disappear.

This verse says that after the Buddha, who is called the Sugata, or "well-gone-one" passes away and enters nirvana, his followers must keep this practice in their minds; otherwise sentient beings' chances for happiness may disappear. Naturally, buddhas don't have a birth and death stemming from karma as we do. However, in order to demonstrate impermanence to others, they appear as if they are ordinary beings, and they seem to die when they pass into final nirvana.

10 Therefore, this is the heroes' happy way of life: to endure hardship come what may, even at the risk of your own life. This is the heroes' actual practice: part one of *The Elixir Made from Poison.*

This verse is the conclusion of the first section. "Heroes" refers to the Mahayana practitioners who give up their own selfish aims to dedicate themselves completely to others regardless of the consequences.

The second part of the text deals with enacting a skillful method so as to transform the five poisonous afflictions into nourishment or powerful medicine. It is said that if you ingest poison directly you will get sick or die, but if the poison is mixed with some other ingredient it can become a powerful medicine. One way to transform the negative effect of poison into a positive effect is by means of mantras, and some yogins can do this. Just as the peacock transforms poisonous plants into nourishing food, the Mahayana bodhisattvas can transform the internal poisons, the five afflictions of desire, hatred, ignorance, pride, and envy into beneficial qualities by engaging in special types of actions. Within this second part of the text there are three subtopics: the actual explanation, the advice, and the conclusion. The actual explanation begins in verse 11, where the basic attitude to be taken in relation to practice is articulated.

> 11 Listen to this teaching! In the jungle of cyclic existence no one with heroic ambitions should take pleasure in the beautiful peacock or the poison-ripened healing herb growing in the shade of the tree of the five poisonous afflictions.

In the first line the attention of the Mahayana practitioner is directed to this teaching; the rest of the verse deals with the actual content of the teaching. Trees in a jungle are compared to the internal treelike growth of the five poisons. We are told not to enjoy the seeming pleasure of the poisonous trees or their flowers. Although these poisons have the potential to be used as medicine and should be used in that way, they are dangerous on their own and have the capacity to cause suffering and misery. Each of the poisons has its own special kind of danger, unless we know how to utilize each to good effect. When the afflictions arise, we must prevent their bringing about harmful effects. Sometimes, bodhisattvas utilize the poisonous afflictions without actually being under their control; they have to behave in a way that makes it appear that they were motivated by attachment, hatred, and the other poisons. Some sutras and tantras teach us to use the defilements as a path to liberate ourselves or others: bodhisattvas are able to do this by employing skillful means. In tantric teachings, attachment, such as is experienced in sexual embrace or wrathful actions, can be transformed into the path. These activities are not done out of egoism and ignorance; they are skillful techniques combined with the wisdom that comprehends the true nature of reality. Their outer appearance merely takes the form of angry, lustful, or envious behavior. The verses that follow expand on this idea, each verse dealing with a different poison; verse 12 is concerned with attachment.

> 12 If you do not feign lust and behave as others do, there is the danger that the lustful may act ungratefully when the poisonous lake of lustful action boils. With simulated lust you should destroy this poison.

Here attachment is compared to a boiling lake of poison. Everyone in the desire realm of cyclic existence is always filled with strong attachment, which is harmful and mentally disturbing. But we can use the power of attachment to treat others more lovingly and harmoniously. For example, bodhisattvas sometimes need to act toward others as if they were swayed by attachment or desire in order to reduce the obstacles to helping them. Some sutras teach that in order to conquer your inner attachment and to bring benefits to others you have to become like a warrior or like a king; kings, for example, can have many offspring who will later help other sentient beings, just as Avalokiteśvara has a thousand eyes and a thousand arms to assist those who need help. If the attachment-based behavior does not arise from ignorance, it can help other sentient beings; otherwise it can have terrible consequences. Under such circumstances, you should pretend attachment in order to conquer the poison of attachment: that is the meaning of this verse. Verse 13 deals with the poison of anger.

> 13 If you do not display an angry manner like Yamāntaka's,
> there is the danger that angry persons may create obstacles
> when the flowers of the poison of hatred come into bloom.
> With simulated anger you should kill the demonic enemies
> of the Dharma.

When we encounter situations in which people are behaving badly, should we just be patient and do nothing to prevent their bad behavior? No! As this verse says, bodhisattvas should conquer the poison of anger by displaying a wrathful manner like that of Yamāntaka. For example, when children misbehave, parents shouldn't refrain from punishing them because they love them—that's not right. Sometimes parents have to act like they are angry, even though they really aren't. You should act out of love and compassion for your children and consider what skillful method will help them to learn good behavior. Sometimes the right method will be to act in an angry way, and sometimes, to display your loving attachment to them by giving them presents or hugging them.

This is why even peaceful and compassionate deities like Avalokiteśvara and Mañjuśrī are sometimes depicted in wrathful ways. Their wrathful form is symbolic of their deep compassion, just as parents may act in an angry manner out of compassion for their children. Sometimes, unless you act as if out of anger, beings who are truly angry will create great obstacles to peace, happiness, and spiritual teaching. An example of this is found in one of the stories about the Buddha's previous lives. Traveling on a boat along with five hundred merchants in search of precious jewels, the bodhisattva knew that a vicious merchant planned to kill all the other merchants to get the treasures they had gathered. There was no way to prevent such an evil deed other than by killing the vicious merchant, and by doing so, he could save the lives of all the other merchants; therefore the bodhisattva killed him out of compassion. By deterring him from murdering the others, the bodhisattva prevented him from creating a heavy load of bad karma that would bring him eons of suffering; this also allowed the evil merchant the chance for better rebirths in the future. The bodhisattva knew he would suffer terrible consequences for killing the evil merchant, but he didn't care; he did it out of compassion for others, regardless of the consequence to himself.

Even though our religious practice has not reached the bodhisattva level, we too encounter sentient beings who are filled with the five poisons. There are two ways of reacting to them; either not to help them because of our ignorance, hatred, and self-interest, or to help them using peaceful or wrathful methods. When acting wrathfully you should not get too personally involved; you should consider your motivation, the temporary consequences, and the good results in the future. We can act conscientiously in that way toward our children, relatives, and friends. If our actions are well motivated, we can take joy in them, even though they may superficially seem harmful. We should act like good physicians who have to do many painful things to our patients, in order to cure them. A doctor must understand and be attentive to the patient's emotional reactions, and he or she must be capable of doing what is necessary for the patient's ultimate benefit.

> 14 If you do not generate corpse-like forbearance, there is the danger that the evil-natured may commit sin when the mire of the poison of ignorance congeals. With pretended ignorance you should cultivate equanimity.

Ignorance, which is like mud, is the subject of this verse. When you encounter hardships, patience will help you bear them. In order not to get angry or attached, we should practice equanimity. Ignorance, or not knowing the actual nature of phenomena, appears to resemble equanimity in that it is nondiscriminating and passive, but unlike equanimity it brings about hatred and the other afflictions. Āryadeva said that ignorance is the basis of all the other afflictions; just as the body provides a basis for all of our sense organs, so ignorance pervades all of the afflictions.

When we encounter difficulties, we should not act out of ignorance, but should try to be patient and not react immediately, making it appear that we don't understand the situation. Sometimes, the best way to deal with the bad actions of others is to pretend ignorance and not do anything. Even though you may be wise, you must appear otherwise to prevent the danger of truly ignorant persons acting badly.

> 15 If you do not distinguish between inside and outside as you would "I" and "you," there is the danger that non-believers and others may destroy the teaching when the tree of the poison of envy is flourishing. Therefore, with simulated envy you should protect the holy Dharma.

This verse is about envy, which is the wish that other people not have any of the desirable things that you don't have; it is the unhappy feeling you have when someone else has better things than you. But this kind of worldly envy can be applied to the Dharma by bodhisattvas in a positive way. They feel a kind of envy for the sake of the Dharma that makes them care for it; they worry about the Dharma, because it is the cause of peace and happiness in the world, and it is endangered if people propound the wrong teachings under its name. Śāntideva has a verse in the dedication chapter of the *Bodhicaryāvatāra* (10.56):

> May the teaching, which is the sole medicine for the suffering of beings, the source of all joy, remain in the world for a long time endowed with riches and honor.

If you should encounter some erroneous teaching that leads other beings into great suffering, such as rebirth in hell, you should not be indifferent. Rather, you should take action to combat such a harmful teaching. If you do this, you will be acting with a form of jealousy. This is not like ordinary jealousy, which is just the desire to ruin someone else's happiness, rather it is the desire to root out the wrong teaching so that the correct teaching will endure. While it appears similar to jealousy, it is actually different; it is motivated by the concern that the source of happiness will be destroyed if the correct teaching disappears.

It is important to note here that this does not mean that only Buddhist teachings are correct. What is meant by "right teaching" is any teaching that leads people to happiness and enlightenment. It doesn't matter what it is called; any teaching that has this result should be protected. Conversely, if a teaching is called "Buddhism," or "tantra," but stems from ignorance or hatred or uses black magic, then it is not a proper teaching. So, it is not really a case of insider (or Buddhist) versus outsider (or non-Buddhist) teachings, as the verse literally seems to be saying.

> 16 If you do not assume the virile posture that resembles
> pride, there is the danger that the hosts of demons may
> deceive you when the tree of the poison of pride comes
> into bloom. Therefore, with simulated pride you should
> uphold the Sage's teaching and crush its opponents.

Śāntideva mentions three kinds of correct pride: pride relating to actions, to afflictions, and to your own ability. Pride about actions is taking pride in your competence to carry out bodhisattva practices without reliance on others. Pride about the afflictions is taking pride in your ability to conquer the afflictions, knowing that they cannot defeat you: all the buddhas and bodhisattvas possess this kind of pride. Pride in your own abilities relates to your ability to do difficult things that others are unable to do; this kind of pride can enhance your sense of responsibility. We should cultivate these correct forms of pride and get rid of the pride that comes from arrogance and ignorance. When the poisonous tree of pride develops and increases, you have to take a fiercely proud stance and conquer it in a fearless manner. If you don't do this, you will be easily conquered by the afflictions and deceived by a host of evil beings. Therefore, you should uphold the Buddha's teaching when others want to destroy it. When such a situation occurs, you should stand up to the enemies of the teaching and take pride knowing that you can conquer them. When internal afflictions, the egoistic view, and selfish attitudes arise, there is pride based on attachment, hatred, and jealousy toward others—that kind of pride is the enemy. You have to be strong to subdue that kind of ignorant pride; usually it conquers us, and we are the losers.

This completes the section on the ways of conquering the five poisons and transforming them into medicinal food. Verse 17 is the summary.

> 17 Thus, the entire mass of poisons should be experienced as if it were an illusion, untrue, something that appears but is empty. Tie up the poisons into the single bond of "I" and "mine," and, like a peacock, take it as nourishment.

The limitless troops of the five poisons are defeated with a special kind of wisdom. Since ignorance is the root of these poisons, it is the wisdom that realizes the truth of the emptiness of self and phenomena that can completely remove them. The poisons do not exist absolutely or inherently; they appear in dependence on certain causes and conditions, and although they appear to exist absolutely, they are empty of such true existence. Lack of true existence does not mean that the poisons do not exist conventionally; it is just that we perceive them as absolute, even though they are actually empty of such true existence. Their nature is illusory, like a magical elephant that does not exist in the way it appears to exist. The magical elephant does exist in a conventional way, and it can be the cause of an illusory perception even though it does not exist in an independent or real way. We should have an in-depth understanding that appearance and actuality are completely different, and we should realize the true nature of whatever appears to us. Thus, just like the audience at a magic show knows that the illusory elephant is not real though it appears so, we should not assume that the phenomena we perceive are absolutely real. To see things as being beautiful or ugly is a judgment based on our own thoughts and beliefs—to accept them as truly being so is a misapprehension. Based on these misapprehensions, we perform many kinds of wrong actions. Therefore, we should understand the empty nature of the illusory appearances that present themselves to us.

"Tying them up in the single bond of 'I' and 'mine'" refers to the egoistic view: All the other afflictions and wrong actions are based on the division between "I" and "you." This is the bondage that creates all suffering. Every creature in cyclic existence is enchained by this bond, apprehending subject and object as really existent. The verse tells us to group together into one all of our wrong perceptions and to eat it as food, just as when we put all kinds of food together on our plates and we eat a delicious dinner.

By understanding the illusory nature and the emptiness of phenomena, all the afflictions can be used as nutritious food, just as a peacock eats poisonous plants. We should understand that the chains of "I" and "ego" are not inherently existent: they are produced by the egoistic view. We should completely rid ourselves of this view.

The following verses contain advice on how to practice these teachings, both in the positive sense of enhancing practice and in the negative sense of clearing away the hindrances to practice. The enhancement of practice has several parts. The first is to not place too much importance on external appearance but to emphasize the internal. While we practice the path, we should strictly follow and guard the bodhisattva vows as if protecting our own life. This is the subject of verse 18.

> 18 Although you may present yourself in various ways to others, deep inside, without losing the powerful strength of the antidote, you should take up virtue and reject sin even at the risk of your own life. Although you may suffer, eagerly pursue enlightenment.

In order to conform to the mental capacities of different people, you may appear to them in different ways. However, when you do this you should not lose the strong antidote to the afflictions deep in your own mind. A bodhisattva should not harm others out of attachment and so on, he or she should take up wholesome qualities and reject what is unwholesome.

If suffering pain or hardship is in the service of gaining enlightenment for the benefit of other sentient beings, then you must voluntarily take up that suffering. You do this in a small way when sitting in meditation on a hot day—since it is uncomfortable, sweaty, and painful to your knees to sit listening to teachings on a broiling hot day. What the verse says is that regardless of the external circumstances, you should mentally take up and firmly protect the bodhisattva vows. The second bit of advice appears in verse 19:

> 19 Even if you are the master of all knowledge such as this, if you do not condemn happiness for yourself there is the danger that the power of craving may enmesh you in lust

> and hatred. Therefore, you should beat down selfishness, like a thieving dog!

You may become a great scholar, the "head of the row" as we say in Tibet, where the position of a scholar in a row is an indication of his learning. It is not like here in the West where we sit at a round table so that everyone is equal! If you become an eminent scholar there can still be the danger of feeling a desire for the eight worldly dharmas, such as fame and wealth. You should really act in the opposite manner, because your own selfish desire is a great obstacle to bodhisattva practice, and when it arises it should be beaten like a thieving dog. You may not be familiar with this in America, but in India and Tibet, dogs run loose; they have too many puppies and run around stealing food from people. People drive away this type of thieving dog by beating them with a stick or throwing stones. Similarly, the desire for fame or praise or rejoicing in some worldly honor may devour the noble mind and steal away your bodhisattva practice; therefore you must beat it down.

> 20 Though you may devote yourself to serving the learned, if you do not sharpen your understanding of the doctrinal systems there is the danger that you will overestimate or underestimate these scholars. Therefore, you should become proficient in all knowledge.

You should study all the doctrinal systems and methods of mind training in order to properly serve eminent spiritual masters. If you don't do this, you may overestimate or underestimate the qualities of master teachers, which would merely show your own ignorance. The advice in this verse and the preceding one reflects a special kind of instruction, the necessary conditions for developing and strengthening your own practice. Verse 21 also gives us advice.

> 21 Even if you suffer day and night, if you don't think about the shortcomings of all cyclic existence, there is yet the danger that you may become embroiled in the causes of suffering. Thus, nail the punishments for actions onto your heart.

When we experience great pain and suffering, we should remember that they arise from bad actions. Suffering is the result of nonvirtuous actions; happiness is the result of virtuous actions. Why should a person suffer unless he or she has done negative or evil things? We believe that no suffering occurs without a corresponding cause, because if it were causeless, then everyone would be equal in their happiness or suffering. We see in the world that some suffer and some don't; this is the result of specific karmic causes. Therefore, you should keep in mind the faults of cyclic existence and understand that your sufferings are the result of previous actions. Once a person meditates, concentrates, and gains an understanding of this process of cause and effect he or she will no longer perform negative actions and will continue to want to eliminate them. If you don't think about these shortcomings, there will be the danger of continuing to create more pain and suffering. Therefore it is said that the faults of cyclic existence should be engraved or nailed on your heart. If you do this, even though you may have to endure suffering in the present, you will clearly understand how to avoid temptation in the future and how to correct any nonvirtuous behavior.

The verses that follow are concerned with understanding what we must do to remove hindrances.

> 22 That being the case, you should rely upon dreadful
> suffering as the antidote that conquers ego-clinging. Even
> if myriad demon armies were to rise up as your enemy, you
> should throw off the terror that comes from thinking "I."

It is said that you should voluntarily accept the experience of many undesirable sufferings as the antidote for destroying your egotistical or ego-clinging view. When you experience pain or suffering, you should understand that they were created by your own self-centered attitude. You should try to fight fiercely against the cause of these sufferings, the diabolical, self-centered, egotistical view inside yourself; that view should be the main target of your anger. The next part of the verse advises us to abandon the fear that comes from thinking "I," due to attachment to our own body and life. This is a very strong feeling that makes it difficult to endure adverse circumstances that arise. Yet, we should not be frightened even if millions of armed enemies were to rise up against us. Śāntideva wrote a similar verse, which says that there's no point in worrying if enemies arise to kill you, because you will die anyway, and these enemies don't have the ability to throw you into hell. It is only unhealthy mental states that are truly frightful, because they will throw you into hell and bring about other misery and suffering. Temporary suffering should not be feared but should be welcomed as an opportunity for the ripening of your bad karma. Sooner or later you must face suffering, so you may as well accept it, thinking, "So be it." This type of thinking is the heroic bodhisattva attitude and is difficult to practice. But, if we perform wholesome actions, this heroic attitude will grow in us bit by bit.

> 23 Although you may fall into wretched states of existence by working for others' benefit, serve them gladly, without regret. Although the butcher who takes away your breath may snatch your body, do not rely on religious rituals to help yourself.

When you undertake bodhisattva deeds for others' benefit, sometimes the karmic consequences of those actions may result in your being reborn in the hell realms or other undesirable births. Even if this happens, you should have no regret and gladly accept suffering for the sake of sentient beings. The sutras teach us that at times bodhisattvas on the lower levels of the path can fall into lower realms, but that they are quickly reborn into better births through the power of their bodhicitta, like a ball bouncing off the ground. The consequence of their actions will still occur, but the length of time it must be endured will be shortened by bodhicitta. You should have a joyful attitude about doing wholesome deeds for others' benefit. For example, there is a verse in the *Guru Pūja* that speaks of diligence. Being diligent means having a special kind of joy when working to benefit sentient beings, who have all been our mothers, even if it means suffering for a long time and traveling for eons on the ocean of cyclic existence. This kind of attitude is the perfection of diligence. You should not be sad, sorrowful, or regretful, but should joyfully enter into suffering through the power of your compassion. In the course of doing so, you may encounter someone who comes to kill you, to take your breath away just like a butcher who slaughters an animal. If this happens, you should not behave egotistically to try to protect or save yourself; you shouldn't seek to save your own life just for a selfish purpose. When hindrances arise, you should accept them fearlessly, gladly embracing suffering for the benefit of other sentient beings.

> 24 Although you must bear the bad actions of all sentient beings, the pride you take in your sufferings will diminish by bearing that which should be borne. Although infectious diseases may afflict your body, do not employ measures to fight them off, as they are a result of your own faults.

The illnesses or other obstacles that arise in the course of your work for the sake of other sentient beings should be accepted as part of your practice on the path of enlightenment; this is called taking bad conditions and "carrying them to the path." For example, when people contract an infectious disease, they usually ask themselves why they are sick, and become angry and worried. You should not try to avoid these diseases; because they are the result of your own faults, you should accept them without regret. In this world we must suffer from diseases and other undesirable circumstances: a person may stalk us, thieves may steal everything we own, and our house and everything in it may be burned down to the ground. All of these arise from our own past actions; they are particular karmic consequences that we must experience because we carry the seeds of our past actions. Such seeds must ripen sometime in this life or in future births; their potential must be expended, either through purification or experience.

Whenever an action is performed, it is like a shadow following the body; wherever you go, you must face it, but you can come to gladly accept adverse circumstances by realizing that through them you expiate past bad actions. In addition, you should generate the desire to take onto yourself others' suffering, which stems from their bad actions. We should give the merits of our good deeds to others and want to take upon ourselves the consequences of their bad actions. This is the practice of "exchange." The heroic attitude of the great bodhisattvas is like that; it is a good practice to use when you are faced with bad situations. The following verses explain why you should act in this way.

> 25 Thus, we will never be able to get what we desire unless that which is undesirable befalls us. When the wise

examine that, they willingly embrace everything undesirable as the source of everything desirable.

Actually, if you do not experience undesirable things, you will never experience what is desirable. For example, if you are sick or in poverty, you'll be motivated to change that situation and so you will work hard to achieve goals such as health or wealth. Without having experienced some adversity you wouldn't strive for anything better. When the wise examine undesirable circumstances, they view them as being the source of many good things. For example, because people are miserable they desire emancipation from suffering and develop the thought of renunciation. In Mahayana practice compassion and love arise from empathizing with others' suffering, which in turn initiates the desire to lead others to enlightenment. Therefore, suffering and misery can be utilized productively in spiritual practice. Unlike the gods, who are intoxicated with what seems to them perpetual peace and happiness, we humans experience a mixture of suffering and happiness. In this way, unlike the gods, we have the opportunity to see that adversity is always occurring. We have the intelligence to question its origin and nature, to see that it is not permanent, and to consider its antidote. So, we can utilize the sufferings of human life as a source for developing the great spiritual path. The gods, on the other hand, have no incentive to accumulate merit or to cultivate religion: once their merit is exhausted, they are born into the lower realms of existence.

26 If we don't put on the armor of the bodhisattvas who willingly embrace others' ingratitude, happiness will never come to those in cyclic existence. Therefore, willingly accept all that is undesirable.

It is right to accept others' ingratitude; if you do good for others and they repay your kindness with injury, you should be patient. If you are not able to endure such ingratitude and become angry, then it will be very difficult to accomplish the aims of others. Therefore, you should wear the armor of the great bodhisattvas who are able to withstand the negative actions of others without getting hurt. Just as in past wars soldiers wore armor to protect themselves in battle, our armor is the mental armor of patience, compassion, and bodhicitta. If people abuse you verbally or treat you badly, you should be patient and not let it harm your mental attitude. If you don't wear such mental armor, sentient beings won't have any happiness; there will be no one to help them, and they cannot help themselves. For this reason you should voluntarily accept adversity and consider it in a positive light.

> 27 This is the Dharma according to the great sage's spiritual biography; it should be studied by the holy ones. It is the heroes' actual practice: part two of *The Elixir Made from Poison.*

This verse concludes the section on the reasons to accept suffering. Such teaching is found in the spiritual biography of the great sage, Buddha Śākyamuni; this is the teaching in which it is said that heroic beings should train their minds.

The third part of the text takes up the third main topic: the actual practice of bodhisattva conduct. This is presented step by step: the lower level followed by the intermediate level. At the lower level of practice, you are primarily interested in gaining your own liberation from the misery of cyclic existence in order to obtain permanent cessation and emancipation for yourself. This is the first practice that you must master; you need to be concerned with your own liberation before you can aspire to liberate other sentient beings, all of whom have been your mothers. We may say that we desire the liberation of all sentient beings in our prayers, but often this does not really touch our hearts and minds; what we are really thinking is, "I want emancipation" and we forget all the other sentient beings. Therefore, when we start to practice, we cultivate motivation for our own renunciation and liberation. After this is strongly developed we apply the same thought process to all other sentient beings.

> 28 The intelligent person who analyzes and examines the general and specific faults of cyclic existence during the six periods of day and night will be terrified and thus take and guard the vow of personal emancipation.

An intelligent person should meditate three times during the day and three times during the night. First, you should develop fear of cyclic existence, a fear of what will happen after this life, because without that fear nobody would want to behave morally. Both day and night you should investigate and then clearly visualize in your mind the general problems of cyclic existence—its miserable nature, as well as its specific faults, such as the potential for lower births involving various types of suffering. As a result of such meditation you will develop a strong fear of the miseries of cyclic existence. Then you will realize that you have to perform wholesome actions with your body, speech, and mind in order to protect yourself from misery in future lives. You may decide to take the Prātimokṣa vow, or vow of personal emancipation, which refers to the eight types of moral commitment made by lay people, monks, and nuns. These are commitments to forsake nonvirtuous mental, verbal, and physical activity, such as killing, stealing, and lying; once you take the vow, you should maintain it for life. The vow is a strong protection against negative influences and it safeguards your moral conduct. To generate the fear of negative consequences in future rebirths is difficult; it is not like being afraid of someone who has beaten or attacked you. But without this fear there is no religious practice; you would be working only for happiness in this life, which is not much different from an animal's way of life. This type of meditation is very different from the unproductive type of contemplation that consists of sitting with a blank mind without thinking or reflection. You must determine whether there are future lives and how they are related to your actions. This analytical reasoning is very important; based on it, you will develop the necessary strong fear of future suffering. This deep, precise analysis should be practiced along with calm abiding.

The intermediate level of practice is connected with the desire for liberation from cyclic existence; this is the practice of the so-called Hinayana, or inferior vehicle. It is called the inferior vehicle because it carries a small load, compared to the "great vehicle," the Mahayana. In the Hinayana, your spiritual responsibility is for your own freedom from cyclic existence, whereas the Mahayana practitioner takes spiritual responsibility to liberate all sentient beings. The specific practices of the two vehicles do not matter—it is the type of spiritual responsibility that determines the vehicle. Practicing seriously for your own objective is called Hinayana regardless of the nature of the practice, even if you are reciting tantric mantras or doing a Vajrasattva practice. If a practice is done out of fear of your own transgressions, for your own purposes, then it is a Hinayana practice even though it may resemble the Mahayana. If later on your attitude and actions are truly heartfelt for the benefit of all sentient beings, then whatever practice you are doing is called Mahayana. To take responsibility not only for yourself but for all sentient beings is a monumental objective. The following verses are based on the Mahayana practices of love, compassion, and bodhicitta and the actions motivated by these attitudes. Therefore, they are concerned with the "stages of the path of the great being." Verse 29 is concerned with the limitless, oceanlike bodhisattva activities. The basis for this is the generation of bodhicitta.

> 29 Once the commitment to your own emancipation is firm
> and you have recognized that all living beings have been
> your parents, you should for their sake generate the attitudes of aspiration and engagement until you attain
> enlightenment.

When your vows of moral conduct and your desire to achieve your own emancipation are solid, then the next step is the practice of the Mahayana bodhisattva path. To begin that you must understand your proper relationship with sentient beings, all of whom have been your parents. Parents are the most important people for us in cyclic existence: they nourish and protect us; they have the most compassion for us; they are our first friends. Once you have determined that all sentient beings have been your parents and have acted with parental kindness toward you, you should reflect on how they have been continually suffering in cyclic existence from beginningless time to the present. You should think about how they have suffered birth, aging, sickness, and death in higher and lower births, and you should meditate in this way until their suffering finally becomes unbearable to you, like a mother seeing her dearest child trapped in a fire. Then you should generate the attitudes of aspiration and engagement for their sake.

The wish to do something to help the sentient beings who have been your parents leads you to the desire to guide them to a place of permanent cessation from suffering, the state of highest perfect enlightenment. The desire to free all sentient beings from misery is called compassion; the desire for all sentient beings to have permanent happiness is called universal love. When and how can you provide for the welfare of sentient beings? You cannot do it properly unless you achieve full enlightenment or buddhahood yourself. Seeing that your own enlightenment is necessary for you to be able to solve all the problems of sentient beings, you will want to accomplish it quickly for their sake. When such a strong desire arises day and night, it is called *bodhicitta,* meaning a mind *(citta)* that seeks enlightenment or buddhahood *(bodhi).*

In order to quickly obtain enlightenment you have to get rid of all the obstacles to enlightenment and accumulate merit and wisdom, which should be dedicated for the sake of sentient beings. There are two aspects to bodhicitta: the aspiration and the actual practice. To really practice is called "engagement"; this means that you are engaging in all the activities necessary to benefit sentient beings. You take a vow to engage in all these activities; that is called the bodhisattva vow. When you have generated the aspiration to bodhicitta and taken the bodhisattva vow, that is "engagement bodhicitta." Śāntideva said (*BCA* 1.16):

> Just as one knows the difference between a person desiring to go and one who is going, just so should the wise person understand the difference between the two [types of bodhicitta].

The analogy is to someone who wants take a trip, for example to New York City. Before going, you determine why you are going and how you will get there; when you have definitely decided to go, this is similar to generating the attitude of aspiration. The aspiration, in this case to attain enlightenment for the sake of sentient beings, is not enough—you have to take the first steps on your journey. Your aspiration must be coupled with action for you to actually get there; that is why this is called the "attitude of engagement." Engagement bodhicitta occurs when a person first takes the bodhisattva vow and practices the six perfections.

When you train for a long time and finally spontaneously wish day and night to obtain enlightenment purely for the benefit of sentient beings, then, as said, you have entered the gateway of the Mahayana path. At this point you need to practice the limitless activities necessary to progress along this path. The Buddha skillfully summarized these activities into the six perfections. Each of the perfections has many special characteristics and qualities; they are all necessary to attain your objective.

The afflictions of attachment, hatred, jealousy, and so on are always waiting for the opportunity to arise and pervade our minds, just as a poison introduced through a wound will travel through the bloodstream. We carry the seeds of the afflictions all the time, and when certain conditions are met, they will ripen into mental negativities. Any situation in cyclic existence has the potential to produce attachment, hatred, or jealousy; therefore, you should always practice their antidotes to prevent them from arising and taking over your mind.

One of the Kadampa geshes said: "I remain all the time at the door of the afflictions." This means that you should act like a guard at a door; you sit in front of the door with a gun or a knife, not allowing dangerous people in, in order to protect the person inside. The great meditator is saying that he is sitting there with the antidote, a special kind of caution and mindfulness, an awareness of what is or what will be produced in the mind; this has the ability to block harmful mental activity.

> 30 When aspiration and engagement are firmly established
> with an attitude of loving-kindness, you will think nothing
> of your own suffering in the jungle of cyclic existence.
> Even at the risk of your own life, keep to the practice
> of austerities and endure suffering for others' sake.

When both aspirational and engagement bodhicitta have arisen and are firmly established with an attitude of loving-kindness toward sentient beings, then you should engage in the actual bodhisattva activities, dedicating your efforts wholly to others. Performing these actions, or even just being in cyclic existence for the sake of others, will involve hardships and difficulties. But you should not be concerned about all these difficulties, nor should you have any regrets about your own suffering, since a bodhisattva completely devotes his or her body and mind to others. When bodhisattvas experience suffering for others' benefit they have no negative thoughts or feelings of selfishness or sorrow but simply accept it. If you have the attitude that "my main interest is the peace and happiness of others," then you will have no hesitation in joyfully accepting suffering for others' benefit, even if you should lose your life, limbs, friends, or wealth, as we discussed earlier in connection with the jātaka stories.

The following verses are from the perspective of wisdom, or right view.

When you practice as a bodhisattva, it is necessary to unite method and wisdom in order to achieve your goal. We have already discussed method. From the perspective of wisdom, bodhisattvas understand the true nature of all activities, their objects, and the person who performs them, which is emptiness. They understand that everything appears dependent on causes and conditions, but that the way they appear is not real or true, and that in reality they are empty. Let's take some common examples of things that do not exist in the way they appear to. There is the reflection of the moon in the water; although the real moon is in the sky, its reflection appears real, but it is merely a reflection, not a real moon. It is the same way with a reflection in the mirror. Therefore, we say that things are empty of existing in the way they appear. We can apply the analogies of reflections and such to things that we commonly think of as real, such as the elements, the ego, others, friends, relations, enemies, thoughts, or to anything, in fact. Although they appear through causes and conditions, we think they are objectively, absolutely real—and that is the problem.

You have to keep in mind that everything has an illusory nature. Thus, you should practice meditation, which is free from discursive proliferation. Our minds are full of conceptual constructions such as good, bad, substance, attribute, ugly, beautiful—that is, discursive proliferation. "Being free from proliferation" means that in an absolute sense these constructions are all equal and empty. The type of meditation that is free of proliferation refers to what happens during the meditation session itself as distinguished from the postmeditation period. Verse 31 actually discusses this.

> 31 When you experience vast numbers of malevolent
> persons and their infinite ingratitude, you should
> examine their true nature, which is free from discursive
> proliferation like a dream or an illusion, and contemplate
> the ultimate reality.

In the world there are an infinite number of beings who seem to be doing all kinds of evil and improper things such as killing, stealing, or cheating. Even if you earnestly try to help such people, they will treat you badly in return. When you view people as being inherently and objectively real, as they appear, problems will arise in the form, for instance, of anger or attachment. What should you do when you experience ungrateful treatment from others? You should examine their true nature, as the verse says: Do they truly exist as they appear or are they in reality something else? In that examination, as in analytical meditation, we see that all these things are like a dream. When you dream, you sometimes have a sweet dream, sometimes a frightful dream, but none of the dream objects are real although they seem to be. Sometimes when you are sleeping, you may think that a dream is real, and you may become frightened and wake up or cry out. While there are causes and conditions for the appearance of dream objects, they are not real in the way they appear to be. In the same way, everything you experience is like a dream, like a magical illusion and free of proliferation. When things are examined in this manner, finally the realm of ultimate reality or emptiness (Skt. *dharmadhātu*) will appear in meditation.

The next verse shows what happens when you arise from this nonelaborative meditation, when your senses are open and phenomena again appear.

> 32 Thus, when true nonexistence and apparent nonexistence become directly present, you will become extremely courageous and never again entertain terrifying thoughts. Without conceptualizing, you will effortlessly achieve others' welfare.

What will happen when you have a direct perception that things do not truly exist in the way they appear to and that their appearance is empty? You will generate a special kind of higher courage that knows there is nothing to be afraid of, because sleeping or waking, whatever fearful people, demons, or frightening things appear, all of them are empty. Consequently you won't have any thoughts about the things that appear, such as "This is ugly, this is beautiful, this is good, this is bad"—you will not conceptualize at all about these appearances. You will act spontaneously for others' benefit without any fear, because you will know that there is nothing to be feared in an absolute sense.

> 33 When you shoulder the burden of this kind of practice, the dark quarter may find it increasingly hard to tolerate you. Should clouds of hindrances mass together, the wind of mantra will scatter them throughout the clear sky.

Bodhisattvas always encounter hindrances to their beneficial activities. Sometimes, when you practice compassion and emptiness for the benefit of others, obstructing demons appear. Evil spirits and demons do exist conventionally. These evil beings may want to harm you and others for their own purposes out of their selfishness or egoistic view. They are called "dark" to symbolize their evil attitude and obstruction to virtue.

These evil beings can be cleared away temporarily by tantric practitioners using certain kinds of mantras and other tantric techniques. When they appear, like a cloud of hindrances, you should use mantras to scatter them, like the wind blows away clouds. The analogy is to the sky: Although it has a clear and empty nature, it can be disturbed when there are the causes and conditions for clouds and storms to appear. The wind can clear away clouds; once they are scattered, the sky is clear again. In a similar way, when so many mental hindrances and obstacles to spiritual practice arise, they should be cleared away by the wind of mantra. Then the mind's true nature, which is empty like the sky, will reappear. Mantras have a power that is like the power of wind. Sometimes mantras are used for a negative purpose, to put a spell on someone, for example. But if you have universal love and compassion along with the realization of the nature of things as empty, you can use your realization and some special mantras to get rid of obstructions. You may say, "May this truth make these things disappear," or something of that nature. The text may refer to an actual mantra, or perhaps to the powerful wisdom that realizes emptiness and scatters the obstacles.

Verse 34 explains that it is most important that you should not use a mantra under the influence of the afflictions. If you engage in these practices out of anger, to retaliate against the demons because they are hurting you or those dear to you, then hatred, attachment, and ignorance will come into your mind and will render the ritual useless.

> 34 Because the arrogance of the Wrathful Terrible One may
> be produced when you call out the "huṃ" of his mantra,
> you should know that the aggregates are like an illusory
> city and sound is like a phantom's song.

When you perform a ritual of Yamāntaka, using his mantra with certain tantric words like "huṃ" or "phaṭ," you are supposed to imagine yourself as Yamāntaka, but not to generate deluded arrogance or aggressiveness. If you are arrogant with the understanding that subject and object and phenomena are empty, then that is all right. But, it is evil arrogance if you think, "Now I am the great, powerful, mighty god or wrathful deity; I can beat or destroy you." Therefore, when you are performing tantric rituals, you must always bear in mind that both the object that is being destroyed and the subject, the destroyer, have an illusory nature. You shouldn't think of the sound of the mantra as an absolutely real and powerful destroyer—that is the wrong view. Instead, you should think of it as an unreal or magical sound, almost like an echo. Whenever you perform wrathful or peaceful tantric practices, such as making offerings, you should first meditate emptiness.

> 35 Recognize the varied contents of your own mind as
> nothing other than phantoms. Like the mind of a phantom,
> your own mind has never existed at all, so leave it to itself.
> When you see ultimate reality, you will be truly free.

Discussions about emptiness can be very difficult to understand. In addition, different schools have different ways of explaining emptiness. Here the emphasis is on regarding whatever you perceive externally as a mental creation. People often have different evaluations of the same external appearance; some may think it beautiful, others ugly, some attractive, others unattractive. It's the same with the weather; one person may think it's hot, another cold. Some might find a certain food delicious whereas for others it would seem like poison. Whatever you experience, whether pleasant or unpleasant, is mostly your own creation arising from previous karma and your mind. In this sense things are principally mental appearances that can be experienced in varied ways. Therefore, there is nothing that can be identified as existing absolutely in an external or objective way. Objects and other phenomena are mental imputations based on their appearances. For example, in certain types of tantric practice everything appears pure; but for us, everything appears impure. Things are experienced differently based on different levels of consciousness or spiritual practice. Thus, you should think of things as magical creations of your own mind. Mental creations can seem perfect; you can mentally create wonderful worlds and elements, but such things don't exist objectively. Thus, this verse is from the mind-only point of view. The third line means that since things do not exist absolutely, leave them alone, don't hold them as real. The last line refers to seeing the real nature of everything as empty of inherent existence.

> 36 Some may arise as enemies and demons, but regard them not at all. Trample on attachment to self and aversion to others without conceiving of them in any way. View memory and perception like the wrathful Yamāntaka.

You should not conceive of hostile demons or evil spirits in either a favorable or an unfavorable way. If you consider them to be truly real, then you will have attachment and hatred. You should simply trample attachment, hatred, and discrimination under your feet. This is just a way of illustrating the attitude you should have toward such things—cover them with dirt and step on them. You should regard whatever is in your mind, whatever you see or remember, as having the nature of the wrathful Yamāntaka: in other words, things appear to be fearful, destructive, and full of anger, but in reality they have the nature of perfect wisdom or Mañjuśrī. Both Mañjuśrī and Yamāntaka have the same nature, which is understanding ultimate truth or emptiness. Therefore, all mental contents should be understood as naturally empty.

> 37 Once you are convinced that all living beings have been your parents, gather them together without hesitation. Free from bias, give them refuge in your compassion and impartially protect them with the two truths.

This verse makes two points: All living beings are equal because they are all empty of true existence and because they have all been our own dear parents. Thus, you should not hate or discriminate against anyone, and you should keep all sentient beings in your heart with love and compassion, not viewing some as close and some as distant out of your own attachment or aversion. You should protect them all with the two truths: the ultimate truth of understanding them as empty of inherent existence and the conventional truth of regarding all of them as your parents. Verse 38 praises these practices:

> 38 To train in this way is to follow the Sage's spiritual biography. If you act accordingly, the Jewels will burst into smiles and the Dharma protectors will naturally surround you. Know this well, children of the Sage.

If you make a habit of the practices that have been described in the text, then you will be emulating precisely the Buddha's life story. If you act in this way, the Three Jewels, the Buddha, the Dharma, and the Sangha, will be very happy and smile or laugh. All the buddhas and bodhisattvas will happily smile because they want sentient beings to practice in this way. They are pleased like a good father who sees his children behaving exactly as he wishes, and their smiles will burst out forcefully and spontaneously. If you behave in this way, the Dharma protectors, who have the duty to protect the teaching and its practitioners, will naturally come to protect you without the necessity of your inviting them.

The preceding is about what to do in the meditative session. The first two lines of verse 39 are about what to do *between* meditations.

> 39 I spit on the shameless way of life! Having considered the heedless life, I view it with disgust. This is the heroes' actual practice: part three of *The Elixir Made from Poison.*

Between your meditation sessions you may see all sorts of shameless things being done. You should spit on such things out of contempt; when we Tibetans see a bad thing, we spit. If you do something carelessly, without conscientiousness or forethought, you should view such actions as dirty and disgusting, like excrement.

This is the conclusion of the third part of the text. The fourth part is much longer; it is concerned with the way of serving the Buddha's teaching. This next section is a detailed refutation of the "nest of faults" or incorrect views.

> 40 Though you may be as perfect a monk as Upāli and as conscientious and handsome as Aśvajit, if you don't lead your parents along the path to enlightenment, you should trample underfoot the liberation of personal bliss.

Upāli was an arhat, a disciple of the Buddha who had very pure moral discipline; he never broke even the smallest rule of monastic discipline. Aśvajit, another very conscientious arhat, had such a beautiful appearance that when people saw him they naturally developed faith. These are the types of people you should emulate from the point of view of monastic discipline. The Buddha taught that it is necessary to take the monks' and nuns' vows, the rules of monastic discipline, and that these should be followed by the development of bodhisattva conduct and tantric practice. Therefore, at the beginning of practice it is important to control your behavior by taking vows and behaving with strict moral conduct, in order to be disciplined and calm and to practice for your own liberation. But even if you are extremely diligent and conscientious like these arhats, you can still have the fault of not leading sentient beings along the path to enlightenment. If you don't do that, you are acting selfishly, despite your careful, calm behavior and attractive appearance. If you don't lead beings along the path to emancipation, your liberation will be only for your own peace and happiness. This is senseless from the Mahayana standpoint; it should be "trampled underfoot."

41 Though you may achieve great expertise in the sciences and
delight in your reputation like a government official, if you
don't take upon your head the great burden of the teaching,
your reputation should be dismissed, like a madman's dance.

"The sciences" refers to both religious and secular disciplines. Someone who has mastered these sciences may be famous among scholars and ordinary people. It's good to have such expertise, and everyone likes to be admired by others. But, you also must take on the great responsibility of the Mahayana teaching to protect other living beings. The text says to take this on top of your head, which means very respectfully, like the Buddhist custom of respectfully receiving a holy book or image by placing it on top of the head. If you don't assume this responsibility, then all your scientific knowledge should be scorned, as you would dismiss the dance of an insane person.

42 Though everyone may honor you like a guru, if you do not
bear the great burden of the whole teaching but eagerly
pursue your own desires, the noble ones should spit on you.

Even if others respect, honor, and bow down to you as a guru, you are really only pursuing your own selfish objectives if you do not take up the burden of the teaching, if you do not work to spread the Dharma to all sentient beings. The great sages will spit on such behavior. Verse 43 discusses those with wrong views:

> 43 Though everyone may claim you are a good person,
> you are as terrible as a tigress who eats her young, because
> your egotistic view grew in the jungle of wrong views;
> the attendant protectors should destroy you.

Even if everyone believes that what you are doing is excellent, your behavior is wrong if it is impelled by wrong views. "Wrong views" can refer specifically to the egotistic view, or it can refer to nihilistic views such as that there are no past and future lives, no karmic cause and effect, or no possibility of achieving buddhahood. It is nihilistic to believe that the most important things are to enjoy this life, take care of your friends and get even with your enemies, and that to act otherwise is wrong or stupid. There are also wrong views about the permanence of the soul or self. Having such views is very dangerous to others, therefore they are described as terrible and frightful, like a tigress who wants to eat her young. Such views should be cleared away by the attendant Dharma protectors who protect the true teachings and destroy the false ones. These are a class of deities, some of them higher and some lower, who may have started out as harmful spirits but were later subdued by a powerful yogi, sage, bodhisattva, or buddha; then they were forced to vow that from then on they would never harm or hinder others and they would protect anyone acting in accordance with the teaching and working for the peace and happiness of living beings.

Verse 44 concerns religious practitioners who appear to be good on the outside but are actually deceitful.

> 44 Though you may wear the saffron robe and be of congenial
> temperament, there is no cure for a cat-like, vicious-
> minded impersonator of a holy person; you should be
> thrust into the mouth of the she-demons.

Even if you dress in saffron monastic robes, seem very calm and peaceful to others, and have the appearance of holiness, if inside you have an evil attitude, then you are being deceitful—like a cat who crouches on the ground very calmly and quietly before springing up to kill a bird or a mouse. This type of deceit is an irremediably bad quality, and the verse says that if you have it you should be put into the demons' mouth.

> 45 Though you may be the lord of tens of thousands, the light rays of your unruly mind's lust and hate pervade the ten directions, like Vishnu: You should be thrust into the mouth of Yamāntaka.

If you are the ruler of a great number of people but your mind is always disturbed by lustful, angry, and selfish thoughts, your behavior would be like that of the Indian god Vishnu, who is depicted as a warrior who fights and kills everywhere. The consequences of activities such as destruction and killing motivated by a mind disturbed by attachment and hatred are like light rays, in that they will spread everywhere, bringing war and suffering. What does it mean to put such things into the mouth of Yamāntaka? As we've seen, Yamāntaka is a wrathful form of Mañjuśrī, who represents the highest wisdom, which acts as the antidote to ignorance, the source of all evils and demons. Although literally the meaning is to put such a person into the mouth of the wrathful deity, the real meaning of putting such things into the mouth of Yamāntaka is that perfect wisdom should be utilized to destroy selfishness and hatred.

Verse 46 deals again with deceitfulness.

> 46 Although you may govern all with smiles and affability, you are reknowned as the chief of the faithless, causing your followers' defilements to increase; you should be thrust out of the den of the genuine vow.

People can appear virtuous, always smiling and seeming to help and protect their disciples, but in reality they may be deceitful and untrustworthy, actually increasing many of their disciples' internal afflictions rather than helping them attain liberation. People like this, who are famous as leaders, but in whom people have misplaced faith, should be thrust out of the nest of the real vow.

> 47 Though you have left home and passed through the door of the teaching, like a householder you still busy yourself with myriad activities and disparage all proper religious behavior; you should be destroyed by the sages' curses.

Even if you take vows and become a monk or a nun, you still may act like a layperson and run around engaging in a lot of secular activities and behavior that should be avoided, while disregarding serious practice. Such things should be annihilated by the curses of the great sages; this refers to the power that some sages have to destroy things with special mantras.

> 48 Though you wear the saffron robe, you do not guard your morals. Letting your fantasies run to lustful acts, you overestimate or deprecate the holy ones; you should be utterly destroyed by the ḍākinīs.

This verse is also about people who wear religious garb but don't guard their moral conduct. Instead, just like laypeople, they have thoughts about desirable visual, olfactory, and tactile objects. Their thoughts are continually and completely concerned with attractive things, and so they have no power to guard their mind and their vows. In addition, they may denigrate those who really take their vows seriously and criticize their activities, or they may praise bad people. Such improper activities should be destroyed by the *ḍākas* or *ḍākinīs,* meaning the male and female "sky-goers." These are certain kinds of high deities who can give protection or remove obstacles. Of course, the highest sky-goers are the perfect buddhas and bodhisattvas.

Verse 49 deals with the wrong practice of tantra.

> 49 Assuming the guise of a holy person in order to gain wealth, you pursue objects of sensual pleasure like a dog or a pig, claiming your actions as tantric and deceiving everyone; you should be thrust into the fire altar by the vajra-holders.

This is about tantric practitioners who appear holy but really are interested in gaining wealth. They run after beautiful things or attractive people, good things to eat and drink, sexual pleasure—all of the objects of the senses;

they are completely obsessed with sensuality, like animals. Externally they appear to be holy persons, but internally they are just like a dog or a pig. For example, there are certain kinds of tantric secret teachings that literally say, "You should kill sentient beings" or "You should have sexual intercourse." These are indirect, profound, secret teachings that have many layers of meaning: a provisional meaning, a final meaning, a definite meaning, an interpretable meaning, and so forth. There are some who claim that drinking alcohol, using people sexually, or even human sacrifice are tantric practices; that you can, for example, liberate human beings by killing them. All of these things can be performed under the name of "tantra" and are extremely dangerous to the person who is doing them as well as to others. There are those who proclaim such things to be tantra, but in reality they are deceiving everybody.

Tantra is one of the most powerful Buddhist teachings; if it is properly practiced, it can be a method for quickly obtaining enlightenment and helping many sentient beings. However, if it is misused it can be extremely dangerous. A person who misuses the tantra will go to the worst hell and suffer the most extreme pain that can be experienced, for eons and eons. Therefore these high tantric practices are called secret teachings. If disciples haven't reached the right level of spiritual development then the guru shouldn't give them these teachings but should keep them secret and only reveal them depending on a careful assessment of each disciple's mental abilities and potential. In Buddhist countries like Tibet, the guru and disciple live together in close quarters, and it's easy for both of them to know when the disciple is ready to receive tantric instructions. If the disciple isn't ready, the guru will give more basic teachings that will gradually prepare the disciple for the tantra. The disciple has to be patient and not want to jump immediately to the tantra because he or she thinks it's the best or most powerful teaching. "Secret" means the guru doesn't share the tantric teachings until the disciple is ready for them, because otherwise it is dangerous. If the disciple isn't ready, then instead of getting a fast and powerful good effect, these teachings will bring an equally powerful negative effect and be the source of evil. In tantric ritual there is a kind of purification in which you imagine yourself as the deity and build a mandala. Then, in your mind, you make a fire offering to the deity in the mandala. All deceitful actions, sins, and other negative things should be put into the fire on the altar; this is a very complex matter. In the verse, the Tibetan word *thab* means the fire altar for the offering. "Vajra-holder" refers to the tantric master who holds the bell and the vajra, symbolizing the internal state of the high realization of wisdom and compassion.

Verse 50 deals with the wrong utilization of emptiness.

> 50 You, the demonic impostor who, in the name of the
> Mahayana, disparages moral causality and deceives your
> followers with empty boasts, should be destroyed by the
> spells of the vow-keepers.

There are some practitioners who profess to being on a high spiritual level, above ordinary morality, and who claim that it is a Mahayana teaching to disregard karma and its results. They think that they can kill, steal, get drunk, and have sex for the benefit of living beings. However, someone who has a true realization of emptiness also has compassion and will only do things when they are proper. But people who do not have a true realization and think that emptiness is a license for every kind of bad behavior may also teach that to their followers. Telling people to disregard their family and not to be attached to their worldly possessions can be a way to steal their wealth. To behave like this is to act like an evil demon. A bodhisattva tantric practitioner should destroy such evil activities by means of mantras, out of love and compassion. This can only be done by a tantric practitioner who has the complete and pure tantric vow and the requisite knowledge and ability to conquer evil with spells. There are four types of tantric activities: pacification, extension, control, and destruction. Destruction is a wrathful activity that can even include killing, but it must be done only by a very high tantric practitioner in possession of the necessary qualities to ensure that it will be for the benefit of others. This is what is meant by "destroyed by the spells of the vow-keepers."

> 51 Your claims about mantra and the profound oral instruc-
> tion are of no benefit to the teaching at all, and your
> wretched verses are written out of your imagination. Thus,
> the holy ones should degrade you to the lowest class.

Some people claim to be teaching profound mantras and giving special oral instructions, when in reality what they are doing doesn't help the Dharma or other sentient beings. They may also write and publish books claiming to teach some profound tantric teaching, but these books may be badly composed and include weak lines and verses. Such books are destructive and should be publicly denigrated by holy scholars who have examined and analyzed them. In ancient times at the great Indian Buddhist university of Nalanda, scholars would gather to discuss a certain subject. Some of them would compose treatises on the subject to help others, and these books were sent to other scholars for review to see if they should be published. If they found the book bad and useless, they would fasten it with rope to the tail of a dog and send the dog to wander the streets with the book trailing after it in the dust. In that way the holy scholars would publicly humiliate the writers of bad books.

> 52 Even though you might help someone temporarily with something, like giving rice beer to a person with fever, if you should harm the teaching, you are a person of such pernicious usefulness that you should be thrown into the river.

You should renounce actions that may have a small benefit in a particular situation, if they are also harmful to the Dharma. The analogy is with giving rice beer to a feverish person; even though the liquor may make the person temporarily feel better, the alcohol will increase the fever and make the sick person much worse, possibly leading to delirium and death. Obviously, giving the person beer is the wrong kind of help. That type of wrong action should be gotten rid of, like throwing it in the river.

> 53 Base adepts with little education proudly consider themselves superior when they obtain the ordinary supernatural powers. Because they are not on any stage of the path, the wise should humiliate such deluded fools like dogs.

This verse addresses those persons who have achieved minor supernatural accomplishments but proclaim themselves great adepts. Such people, who actually have little religious education and do not know very much but claim to have great spiritual achievements, are false adepts. A real adept is a great sage who has reached a certain level of the inner path; you can't become a great adept without study and understanding. There are both ordinary and extraordinary powers or achievements, which are called the superknowledges. Ordinary powers come about through meditation techniques, such as calming meditation, which are common to both Buddhists and non-Buddhists. Ordinary lower beings as well as higher, superior individuals can practice and achieve a state of great calm that they can then utilize in a special kind of training to attain the superknowledges. There are six kinds of superknowledge: (1) the divine eye; (2) divine hearing; (3) the ability to see your past lives or those of beings equal to or lower than yourself; (4) the ability to see the future lives of yourself or of beings equal to or lower than yourself; and (5) the ability to read the minds of others, especially of spiritually lower beings. The sixth and supreme superknowledge is the knowledge that you have exhausted all defilements; but this can't be directly experienced until you have obtained complete emancipation.

So, although some people are superior to ordinary people because they have obtained one of the ordinary superknowledges, such as seeing the past or the future, or reading someone's mind, they still haven't achieved the supreme superknowledge. Such people may be conceited, priding themselves on having the supreme power, when actually they have realized only an ordinary one. They have not reached any of the stages of the path, because they have not studied and practiced, and so they lack the requisite knowledge to lead others, and they deceive the foolish people who follow them. According to the last line of the verse, such foolish and deceitful people should be humiliated by the masters and scholars as if they were worthless dogs. Americans may find this hard to understand since they consider dogs so precious. But in India and other parts of Asia, although a few dogs may be treated well, most dogs are strays that run around and bare their teeth at people, who shoo them away and throw stones at them to get rid of them. The line refers to this kind of attitude—treating these false adepts like you would a stray dog.

The topic we have been discussing is how we should relate to and serve the Buddhist teachings. To serve the teachings means to follow them scrupulously without disregarding any of the instructions. We reviewed extensive ways of attacking one's own nest of faults and the many facets of this subject—faults regarding education, practice, meditation, monastic conduct, and adherence to a vow. We saw that even Mahayana practitioners can have faults in their practice that they must discard. Many of the faults that impede practice spring from a selfish, egoistic mind-set; that is, you may engage in religious activity out of your own selfish fears and desires rather than for the sake of other sentient beings. From the point of view of the Mahayana, many things will go wrong if you engage in religious activities under the control of an egoistic and selfish view.

Verse 54 is concerned with the Prātimokṣa vow and the *vinaya* rules that go with it. Many of these rules concern avoiding injury to anyone through actions of your body, speech, or mind, because if you hurt someone you create karma that will impede your attainment of emancipation. Thus, the vow and its rules mainly concern your own welfare. However, in the Mahayana or bodhisattva practice, we completely give up concern for ourselves out of dedication to others. Since that is so, we are not always so worried about observing every vinaya rule and regulation. Your adherence to the Prātimokṣa may at times be beneficial to other beings, but at other times it may be harmful to them despite its great efficacy for your own emancipation. In the latter case, you must act mainly for the benefit of others; if keeping the vow restricts what you can do for others, you should not strictly adhere to it out of the belief that it always takes precedence over everything else.

> 54 When enemies rise up against the Buddha's teachings,
> it would be absurd if your pride in the excellence of
> the monastic vows stopped you from performing the
> authorized rituals for returning your vows and made
> you keep them in the face of the teaching's destruction.

The teaching of Buddha, the Dharma, is beneficial because it is the source of all happiness and peace for sentient beings, who all have been our mothers and fathers. The teaching of the scriptures and of the inner mental realizations should be disseminated in the world in a pure form. These teachings should not be allowed to disappear, for if they do, then the source of the spiritual path and its goals would be lost and there would be the potential for great harm to sentient beings. Therefore, when there are enemies intent on destroying these valuable teachings, you shouldn't disregard what is going on and think that the best thing is just to keep your excellent Prātimokṣa vow pure.

You have to consider which will have the more negative effect: keeping the vow or giving it up. Keeping the vow may result in your own emancipation, but it may entail danger for many other people. Thus, when there is a war against the enemies of Buddhism, you may have the ability to fight or do other things to benefit the precious teaching. In that case, if you are a monk or a nun, it is proper to temporarily return your vow to your guru with the proper ritual. Later, when the special situation has passed, you can retake the vow. Not to do that out of the belief that maintaining your vow is the most important consideration is wrong. Such behavior would be amazing in the negative sense, very strange and absurd. Verse 55 has a similar theme.

> 55 You may fear that if you put aside your monastic vows
> you may be born into an extremely wretched state of
> existence. However, anyone who does not destroy the
> demonic enemies of religion, those who are demolishing
> the teaching, is breaking their vows. The demonic enemies
> of religion must be utterly destroyed.

You may be afraid that if you give up your Prātimokṣa vow you will be born in a lower state of existence, perhaps in a hell where you will have to endure great suffering. Even if that were to be the case, not destroying the enemies of religion because of fear for yourself is in itself a violation of your vows. Those who destroy the Buddhist teachings, which are the only medicine for permanent peace and happiness for sentient beings, are enemies. Such enemies should be eliminated; the person who does not do so is almost like an enemy. This verse is thus similar to the previous one, but stronger in tone.

Verse 56 is concerned about killing an enemy for your own particular purposes using tantric methods such as mantras; such actions are wrong.

> 56 Ignorant people, driven by their afflictions and actions
> and without any regard for the teaching or for living beings
> will, out of anger, utterly destroy with magic spells the
> enemy who has injured them. To ask whether or not such
> people have broken their vows is ridiculous.

This refers to ignorant people pursued by their own bad actions and afflictions. People like this may not concern themselves with the Dharma or with others' welfare, but they may have great anger toward an enemy who has harmed them, and out of such anger they will try to destroy their enemy using mantras or other tantric techniques. Deliberating whether or not such people have pure moral conduct would be bizarre; it would be ridiculous to even consider the question because it is obvious that such conduct is wrong.

Therefore, the point of the preceding verses is that even virtuous religious activity, undertaken with an egoistic perspective, is completely contradictory to bodhisattva conduct. Such conduct must be attacked and removed; if it is not, it can be harmful to others.

The next subtopic summarizes how to practice with the buddhas and bodhisattvas bearing witness to your aspiration. Verse 57 shows that nothing should be done solely for your own benefit.

> 57 Do not engage in any self-interested action that the
> victors have scorned. Come what may, it is proper to
> carry out whatever has been praised by the victors of
> the ten directions.

"Victors" (Skt: *jina*) is an epithet of the buddhas; they will be displeased and unhappy at any of your actions that are done only for your own selfish purpose. On the positive side, you should only do things that please the buddhas, who are like loving fathers to sentient beings and so will hate anything that is done to harm their children. Conversely, they will be happy about anything that is beneficial and favorable to their children. Making the buddhas and bodhisattvas happy does not mean giving them offerings and then acting in a way that is harmful to others; this would be like giving a gift to parents and then beating their children. Therefore you should only perform the type of activities that would be praised by the buddhas because they are helpful to sentient beings.

Verse 58 tells us to practice in a strict way, to not take our practice lightly. In general, all practice should be performed in the strictest way, without looking to cut corners.

> 58 People of intelligence, know that all practices should be
> performed punctiliously. Whatever is opposed to the

> teaching should be rejected, even at the risk of your life.
> Injure no one and benefit yourself.

This tells us that all practices should be done meticulously. If there are two ways to perform a practice, you should always follow the stricter one and avoid any action that goes against the Dharma, even at the risk of your own life. Great bodhisattvas don't care much about protecting their own lives, but will always do whatever accords with the Dharma and is beneficial to others. Nothing we do, whether physically, verbally, or mentally should be harmful to others. If we act in this way it will also be beneficial to ourselves. You should also take some care of your body and life; since you serve others with your body and mind, you should maintain them suitably for the purpose of benefiting them. Śāntideva says that if you are doing good for others with your body, you should look upon the body favorably; if you are doing harm, you should regard the body as evil.

Verse 59 deals with distinguishing correct and incorrect practice.

> 59 While fools do not come to understand things even by degrees, they are clear and vivid to the wise. This is the heroes' actual practice: part four of *The Elixir Made from Poison.*

Ignorant people do not understand the difference between right and wrong or good and bad, even if they try. However, such distinctions appear very clearly and vividly to the minds of wise people or masters. If you want to understand things, then you must study—that is what this verse is saying. You will not be able to master a subject without learning, just by hoping that knowledge will come naturally or through some so-called meditation that doesn't involve learning, concentration, examination, and analysis. An ignorant person will not know what to do when a complex situation arises. But someone who studies and learns through experience will clearly see what is correct or incorrect. This person will have no qualms about doing the right thing or giving up what is wrong.

Now we come to the next main topic: the antidote that is produced by means of the union of method and wisdom. The main targets of the bodhisattva's practice are the self-cherishing attitude and the view of a real personal identity. The self-cherishing attitude means loving only oneself. The view of a real personal identity refers to the object of self-cherishing, which is holding the "I" or "me" as absolute, unitary, dominating, or supreme. The self-cherishing attitude and the view of a real personal identity are often compared to a king and his subject because they always act together. The next verses deal with getting rid of self-cherishing and the view of a real personal identity by means of the union of wisdom and method.

There are certain kinds of tantric practice in which you offer your body and everything you possess to evil spirits, demons, and animals. Sometimes in order to perform these practices, practitioners go to cemeteries and other fearful places where most of us are frightened by the sights and smells. We are frightened because of our self-cherishing attitude and view of a real personal identity, so in order to confront this fear and to fight against self-cherishing, a practitioner will deliberately go to such a terrifying place. There, with horns and bells, he will invite flesh-eaters, blood-drinkers, the snatchers of souls, and so forth, to come and accept his body. We have this kind of practice in Tibetan Buddhism; it is called "cutting" *(gcod),* where in your imagination you cut your body to pieces and give it to the spirits. Tantric practice works in a similar way to fight against self-cherishing and the view of a real personal identity. In tantra you "cut" these two attitudes and generate compassion and make offerings equally to all beings in the universe, whether they are wrathful or peaceful. Here the text is not actually teaching us how to perform this type of tantric practice, but it is showing us how to use a similar method to fight against self-cherishing and the view of a real personal identity.

In connection with this topic, there is the preparatory practice, the actual practice, and the conclusion. At the preparatory stage, we invite all the beings in the various realms of cyclic existence, those in the higher spiritual realms and those in nirvana.

> 60 May all the malicious and hostile hordes of evil ones, wherever they may be, come here to me! May all the trillions of flesh-eaters and blood-drinkers come here to me, a being of flesh and blood, today!

With this verse you invite all malevolent spirits and evil beings, especially the flesh-eaters and blood-drinkers, to come to you and drink your blood, eat your flesh, and gnaw on your bones.

> 61 May all the troops of gods, serpent deities, harmful spirits, heavenly musicians, titans, snake spirits, the numberless hungry ghosts who roam the sky, and the armies of retributive spirits come here to me!

This verse is also an invitation; besides the gods, there are certain types of invisible beings that you may not want to have around you, but they are always with you just the same because of the power of your previous karma. Sometimes they will harm you, at other times they will help. All creatures are surrounded by these types of spirits. In the materially developed part of the world people do not usually believe in these types of beings; they think that if you can't see them then they don't exist!

> 62 May the co-natal deities, the sages, the Bringer of Obstacles and Evils, the eighteen great demons, all the protective goddesses and assistant protectors, the Triple Refuge, and the troops of noble ones assemble in this place!

When the practitioners of cutting meditation and similar kinds of practices gather in solitary places such as cemeteries, they sound a trumpet made from a human thighbone, strike a drum, and ring a bell. Then they express gratitude and invite certain gods to come and be present. In this verse, we invite the spirits who attend each person when they are born and who follow almost like a shadow, as well as certain kinds of sages, spirits who bring obstacles or hindrances, malevolent spirits, and goddesses. In some cases you can make a deal with these malevolent spirits by giving them offerings or performing some action of which they approve; then they can become helpful. Such types of rituals are not generally known, but there are some great sages with supernatural powers who can perform them.

In addition, the verse invites the Three Jewels: Buddha, Dharma, and Sangha, and the mass of holy ones to come here. Finally, you invite them to sit down, just as you do when you invite guests into your home.

> 63 Thus, all who belong to cyclic existence or who are beyond it, after gathering in front of me as witnesses, should listen without hesitation as I deliver the great discourse that I have vowed to present.

This verse announces to the guests what you are going to do; it is a summons to all beings who are in cyclic existence or who have passed into nirvana or peace. Having been invited, they have come here as witnesses to listen to the great discourse you have promised to give. The first subject of the discourse is an explanation of what has happened in the past and what you are going to do from now on.

> 64 Through the good fortune of previous causes and conditions I have obtained this body that has the ten advantages. I rejoice day and night over this wonderful birth, so how could I not make use of this treasure of benefit and happiness right now?

We should think about our past karma and the causes and conditions that have produced our present fortunate situation, for example, sitting here and tasting the wonderful teaching of Dharmarakṣita. You have the eight freedoms and the ten positive endowments, which are explained in the *Stages of the Path* teachings. These involve conditions such as birth as a human being in a particular region. When you consider how wonderful it is to have your present life and to have obtained this human body, you will be surprised and rejoice in your good fortune. You will contemplate how marvelous it is that right now you have everything needed for spiritual development: being in a certain place, having a human body, possessing the necessary internal and external conditions. Therefore you should rejoice and think from now on, "Why not enjoy the benefit and happiness of this fortunate but impermanent body and mind?" Benefit can apply both to this life and to the future, because having a human mind can be helpful for accomplishing things in the future. So, we actually have an unimaginable kind of wealth; if we think about how to utilize and enjoy it, we will have real spiritual riches.

Verse 65 is about being in a situation where you have the opportunity to become ordained as a monk or to enter into a similar type of life.

65 Enter the homeless life with a pure prayer. Renounce your selfish desires and put on the garment of aspiration and engagement. Acquire the supreme thought and take up the burden of others' welfare. Enter upon the path and take supreme bliss as your nourishment.

To be ordained as a result of a pure wish or prayer is to go from lay life to the superior religious life. Whether you do this now or in the future, it is a wonderful thing. When you do so, you abandon your selfish wishes and put on the garment of aspiration and engagement bodhicitta. Here, being ordained doesn't refer primarily to departure from lay life to become a monk or nun; it refers to emulating the bodhisattva way of life and abandoning your own selfish desires. The analogy compares wearing the monastic robes you put on when you are ordained and wearing the garment of the Mahayana bodhisattvas, the two bodhicittas. When your mind is completely pervaded by bodhicitta, it is like wearing the garment of Buddha's life; this is called the supreme bodhicitta. Once you have obtained this supreme bodhicitta, then you take on the responsibility of carrying the load or burden of others by working only for their benefit. When you do that, you enter the Mahayana path and your nourishment will be like eating supreme bliss. It's like taking a trip away from home and eating some wonderful food on the road, rather than some coarse food; what you eat or utilize while bearing the supreme burden of benefiting other sentient beings on the Mahayana path is consummate bliss. It is blissful because if you are truly acting as a bodhisattva, you will rejoice over what you are doing.

Verse 66 deals with the way of chopping the self-cherishing attitude into pieces through tantric rituals. Chopping the self-cherishing attitude to pieces is analogous to cutting up a piece of meat on a chopping block with a cleaver; here our tools are wrathful tantric rituals. The deeds of a bodhisattva endowed with bodhicitta, that is, with love and compassion and the realization of emptiness, are not always peaceful. Bodhisattvas have an awesome responsibility to help all sentient beings, who are like their parents. To carry out the necessary work they engage in four types of activities: pacification, extension, control, and destruction. Sometimes destructive or violent activities have to be undertaken. This is why some buddhas and bodhisattvas are represented as wrathful deities, their mouths agape, with big tusks, holding weapons, and surrounded by fire; though they are motivated purely by love and compassion, the outward manifestations of their activity can vary from peaceful to wrathful.

Violent tantric practice is specific to the Mahayana; it is not allowed in the Hinayana. Because the tantric practitioner has the highest level of mental development and is completely dominated by conventional and ultimate bodhicitta, all his or her actions benefit sentient beings. That is why some of the protective deities can seem terrible, eating flesh and drinking blood. In wrathful tantric rituals, the view of a real personal identity is represented as a devil who is to be symbolically destroyed by burning or by shooting with arrows, or cut up with knives or cleavers. All of these are symbols of wisdom. The following verses illustrate this type of violent activity.

> 66 All the congregation that is assembled here, listen further!
> Since the savagery of the dark quarter is such, and the
> merit of the unfortunate is so, I shall not aspire to paradise.

What you are saying to the beings who are gathered in front of you is that since there are so many savage, evil things in the world, such as murder, theft, and war, and because unfortunate beings have very little merit and so experience all kinds of difficulties, you do not wish to be born in the pure land of Sukhāvati. Often, when people are feeling old and tired, they want to be reborn in some wonderful paradise. However, here we generate the resolve not to go to such a place, because we see all of the suffering and difficulties that are experienced by the unfortunate. To see that and to want to go to heaven is really not good! Thus, a bodhisattva has no desire to go to such a paradise. This verse shows their energy and resolve to work right here in the world to eliminate the hardships suffered by others.

> 67 There are infinite beings who have not accumulated the
> collections, and the suffering of those in the wretched states
> of existence is a heavy burden. When such is the career
> of sinners, I would not feel happy in a peaceful place.

We should consider that in this world there are so many unfortunate beings who have not accumulated any merit, and that in the lower realms of rebirth the hell-denizens, hungry ghosts, and animals have much pain and misery. Because this situation is so awful, we should want to stay right here to help sentient beings. Thus, we could not feel joy in going to some peaceful place.

> 68 For immature persons the antidote is easily subverted, and such is the plan of demons. Because there is no time to rest in this impermanent life, I would not feel happy dwelling in a solitary place.

"Immature persons" translates the word *byis pa*, which usually means children. From a spiritual point of view, common people who have neither the realization of emptiness nor love and compassion are considered like children even though they are fully grown. For this type of person, the antidote for suffering is not reliable; only those with a direct realization of bodhicitta actually have the antidote for getting rid of the afflictions. Even when immature people try to practice daily by giving charity, meditating, studying, and performing rituals, their bodhicitta, which is the antidote, is weak and unstable; it is easily changed into something else. In addition, the army of evil spirits has wicked thoughts and acts harmfully. Further, this life is not long enough to develop freedom from misery and suffering. Therefore, you should devote yourself to beneficial activities all the time. Don't be happy just staying in a solitary place—that would be a selfish thing to do.

> 69 The enemies who hate the teaching are many, and the adepts who have gone to a safe retreat are few. Because to outward appearances the situation in this degenerate age is bad, I cannot feel happy in heaven.

The teaching refers to the pure Buddhist teachings of the path to salvation, which should be respected, praised, and propagated. Scriptural teaching is the source of knowledge about how to get rid of what is evil and negative and how to attain freedom and peace. With this valuable learning you will come to understand how to practice the path to reach enlightenment; it is the only source of peace and happiness.

However, as Dharmarakṣita's verse says, there are many enemies who hate the teaching and its practitioners, like the Chinese communists in our time. Also, the number of adepts who have achieved high realizations and gone off to solitary places is quite low. Given the bad situation in this degenerate period, where the religious teachings are very weak and corrupted, it would not be a cause for rejoicing if we were to go to heaven or a pure land. A Mahayana practitioner would rather remain in this impure place.

Verse 70 is concerned with taking a vow to generate heroic confidence exclusively for the benefit of others.

> 70 Now, even if all the mighty ones in all the worldly realms were to rise up as my enemies, I shall, without the stirring of so much as a hair, put on my armor in this jungle of cyclic existence.

This verse says that even if powerful beings in the world, like gods and rulers, should all become my enemies and want to destroy me, not a single hair on my body will move. In other words, I won't have the slightest fear of these mighty beings. It is like going into a battle where there are so many enemies on the other side that you need to have a heroic attitude. Like soldiers in ancient times who wore armor to protect themselves, you should put on the spiritual armor of bodhicitta. Here, the enemy is ego-clinging, which brings with it the troop of afflictions and bad karma. The armor that protects you against these afflictions is the realization of emptiness and universal love and compassion.

> 71 Wherever infectious diseases may strike, or great plagues disrupt the world, I shall put on the great mighty armor in order to serve as a doctor or nurse.

This type of aspiration is similar to prayers found in the works of Śāntideva and others. When you acquire the necessary education and training and have the opportunity to work as a physician curing peoples' sicknesses, you can experience joy and happiness every day. In the morning you can put on your spiritual armor before going to the hospital or clinic; then, in every situation you can be compassionate, no matter how the patients behave, even if you are insulted and they don't listen to your instructions, even if they physically attack you. Regardless of others' conduct, you have to be a compassionate and loving doctor. This is a great religious practice; you don't have to sit somewhere in a corner of a room for many hours and think: "I am practicing meditation." Instead, you can be active and put all of your physical, mental, and verbal energies at the service of your patients. If you go to work without the proper feeling and attitude, thinking only about making money and not about curing your patients, most of your work will be wasted.

It is the same with nursing, whether you are a professional nurse with a degree or you work in a nursing home taking care of the elderly and sick; you should see this type of work as a great opportunity and be glad every day that what you are doing is not for yourself but for others who badly need your help. You need to be mentally and physically prepared to act skillfully, calmly, and gently toward your patients. You need to have compassion and to talk to them kindly. Even if you are exhausted by the end of the day, you have much cause to rejoice at what you have done for others. In doing such work, you accumulate much merit; this is the real practice of Dharma, the performance of bodhisattva activity. Thinking in this way, your fatigue won't matter and you will feel eager to get back to work the next day. Otherwise, you will brood about not earning enough money, about being reprimanded by your supervisor, or being ill treated by management, about nasty patients, and so on, and you will be more aware of your fatigue and reluctant to return to work. This type of unhappiness is created by the mind, by the stupid, selfish, self-centered view. If you turn in the opposite direction and learn these instructions, even though you may not be able to act completely like a great being, you will be able to do so partially. This in itself will be a wonderful thing.

> 72 When I have been kindly taking care of helpless persons
> and they savagely reject me with gross ingratitude, I shall
> put on the armor of the heroes who greatly help and love
> those people.

Often, when we are helping or taking care of someone out of kindness, we may not be able to do exactly what they want. The other person may become dissatisfied and treat us badly. At such times, we are accustomed to thinking how we've tried to help the person but they're behaving in such an ungrateful way, and so we become angry with them. On these occasions we should, out of love and compassion, try even harder to be of benefit to such people. We should realize that their behavior is due to their being under the power of the view of a real personal identity; this fantasy is their enemy and will bring them even more misery. Seeing this, we should make a special effort to be compassionate and patient with them and to figure out what we can do to help them. These are powerful commitments that will increase your heroism and confidence for future activities. When we are mentally prepared, we will be able to meet challenges as they arise. Our response might not be perfect; we may get angry for a short time, but then we will be able to respond with kindness.

> 73 Wherever terrifying man-eating tigresses lie in wait and hunt human lives, I will put on my armor without hesitation and go there for the good of sentient beings.

If a bodhisattva hears about a hungry tigress with cubs to feed who is hunting humans to kill for meat, he or she will run there joyfully, thinking about the great opportunity for giving his or her body to alleviate suffering. We have discussed this in connection with the story of the hungry tigress from the tales of the Buddha's past lives (verse 2). Though we may not be ready to exercise this kind of heroic intention, thinking about it can inspire us to sacrifice for the sake of others. Śāntideva has some stanzas that may help us understand this. He said (*BCA* 7.20):

> Then again, I may become frightened, thinking: "I must sacrifice a leg or an arm or something." It is merely through confusion, by not distinguishing between the grave and the trivial, that I become frightened.

All fears come from ego-clinging. When we begin religious practice, it isn't right to give up everything immediately—that would be insane. The purpose of these teachings is to train the mind; once it is properly trained and on the right spiritual level, there will be no problem giving anything away. If we don't examine the difference between what is important and what is unimportant in the light of the bodhisattva vow, when we come to apply the precepts, we will, from ignorance, think that we have to give up our arms and legs, and that this practice is too hard. The next verse (*BCA* 7.21) says:

> For countless millions of eons, I will be pierced, burned, and split open many times, but I will not attain enlightenment.

We have been born in the world again and again, as a human and a hell-denizen, an animal and a hungry ghost, and we have experienced many kinds of torments, such as being cut up, speared, and burned. These kinds of things have happened to us countless times but the experiences were valueless because they occurred while we were under the power of the view of a real personal identity and self-cherishing; the experiences were unwanted and we were unwilling to bear them because we were still attached to our body. It didn't get us closer to enlightenment or benefit others in any way, so the suffering was wasted. If, like a bodhisattva, we suffer these torments purely to benefit others, then we will attain enlightenment. As Śāntideva says (*BCA* 7.22):

> My suffering, which is for the achievement of enlightenment, is limited. It is like the pain of making an incision in the body in order to get rid of the pain of a debilitating illness.

In contrast to worldly suffering, which is immeasurable, suffering for the benefit of sentient beings so that they might attain emancipation has a definite limit. It is like having some injury or disease that is cured by having your body cut open through surgery, for example. You may have to have a vein cut from your thigh for a cardiac bypass or you may have to have a diseased limb amputated. This will cause pain and suffering but it has a limit, and it will put a stop to much greater suffering. Therefore we accept this suffering and even seek it out when we ask a doctor to perform the surgery. In fact, Śāntideva says in the next verse (*BCA* 7.23):

> All physicians eradicate illness through unpleasant treatments; since they destroy much suffering, you should happily bear small unpleasantnesses.

The Buddha gave teachings that people who are on the lower levels of the path can practice. As they go further, they are given more responsibility until on the superior level they get to tasks that seem almost unbelievable, but that great beings are able to accomplish. But, Śāntideva says (*BCA* 7.24):

> Such ordinary treatment is not rendered by the supreme physician; he cures innumerable chronic illnesses using very gentle methods.

In the next verse, Śāntideva tells us how the Buddha taught in a gentle way (*BCA* 7.25):

> The guide teaches us to give vegetables and so on at first. After becoming accustomed to this, later on, by degrees, we can even give up our own flesh.

The Buddha didn't say to give thieves all of your property, or to give away your parents or children if someone asks you for them, or to give your body to a tiger when you begin to practice. The time must be correct, and you must be on the right spiritual level. Later, you will have no hesitation about giving away everything. In the beginning, our selfishness is strong, but still we should give away whatever we can, like some vegetarian food. When we have reached the first bodhisattva stage and have developed bodhicitta, we will be able to give away even our own flesh. Śāntideva continues (*BCA* 7.26):

> When we realize that our own body is like a vegetable,
> then what is the difficulty in giving up one's own flesh?

I've presented these verses because Śāntideva's *Bodhicaryāvatāra* is the main source of the mind-training teachings. Śāntideva concludes (*BCA* 7.27):

> Because we have done away with sin, there is no suffering. Because we are wise, there is no unhappiness. It is wrong views that injure the mind and sinful actions that injure the body.

74 When all sorts of ill omens portending calamity cover the worlds in darkness, I shall put on the armor that welcomes them as auspicious signs of the conquest of the evil-natured enemy, ego, itself.

Verse 74 says: All of the undesirable things that appear, like fires, floods, and famine should be accepted and experienced as if they were auspicious signs heralding the destruction of the view of a real personal identity.

> 75 When the illusions of undesirable actions and afflictions are stirred up in the worlds, I shall put on the armor of willing acceptance in order to put an end to the life of ego-clinging.

Verse 75 describes the attitude of accepting the bad consequences of actions and the afflictions, in contrast to our usual egocentric reaction, which wants to fight against them and escape their consequences. This is another type of spiritual armor.

This concludes the section of verses concerned with tempering the heroic attitude. The theme of the following verses is that of removing any opportunity for the manifestation of what we are looking to get rid of, that is, the self-cherishing attitude. We do this by means of the antidote, bodhicitta, under the guise of killing, burning, burying, and cutting, which are wrathful tantric activities.

> 76 Destroy! Hurrah! Kill the Lord of Death! Burn up the life of the demon hedonism! Thunder down on the head of lazy indifference! Completely sever the ties that bind you to cyclic existence!

Ego-cherishing is considered to be a demon who directs all of your actions toward selfish, hedonistic purposes. The lazy attitude of wanting things to be easy for oneself without having to take on any hardship is also part of self-cherishing. We should symbolically throw knives and other weapons that make a thunderous sound of clashing and banging on the head of this lazy indifference. When we destroy the self-cherishing attitude, we will cut off all that binds us to cyclic existence.

Beginning with verse 77, the subject is the refutation of ego-clinging as a mistaken apprehension by means of the skillful use of the conventional logic of debate. The view of a real personal identity, or ego-clinging, is based on the misapprehension of an "I" and "mine" as real objects, like a king or queen who are put at the center of one's universe; this must be eliminated through logical proofs. Imagine a rock shaped like a snake lying on the ground: if you go out at night and run into it you might look at it and think it is a snake; you might even definitely believe that it is a snake. This is a completely wrong belief, but it can create great fear. However, once you clearly realize that the rock is not a snake, your fear will dissipate. It is the same with the view of a real personal identity; and similarly, it is why the main objective of Buddhist teaching and meditation is to gain the wisdom that destroys the wrong attachment we have to the ego as an object.

At first through logical inference, and then through direct perception, we have to understand that the ego does not exist as it is perceived to exist. While logic will allow you to understand this intellectually, you have to continually practice until you have a direct apprehension of emptiness, which will then extirpate that misapprehension from the root. The first step in this process is to argue about the view of a real personal identity, where we identify what it is we're actually refuting and ritually summon it as an enemy to be destroyed.

> 77 If we energetically seek the ultimate cause of our suffering
> here in cyclic existence, look up there in the palace of
> conceptual mind where King Ego dwells.

We are all suffering here in cyclic existence. If we look for the real source of our suffering and trace it to the root, we will find it in our mind, or in the center of our heart, as we say in Tibet. It is the egocentric view, the sense of "I" and "mine" that seems to sit in the center of our conceptual mind—like a king sitting on his throne, "King Ego."

> 78 When you have rebuked and fought him, what does he say?
> "I have existed from beginningless time; I pervade the
> inside, the outside, and the in-between. Ask the chief
> of the six senses whether this is true or false.

At this point the wise part of your mind will blame King Ego for all of the misery and suffering that he has caused you; this is a mental battle. Then the king will reply that he has existed as the ruler from beginningless time, and that he pervades everything, both internal and external. He says to ask the chief, in other words, mental consciousness, which is considered the most important of the six sense consciousnesses: visual, auditory, olfactory, gustatory, tactile, and mental. All of these primary consciousnesses are under the influence of the view of a real personal identity.

> 79 "Since your ego is your enemy, against whom shall you fight? Since your ego itself is the protector, whom shall you protect? It is the very witness of all that you have done and left undone. When you have tamed your ego, you shall be liberated.

The king continues his argument, saying that there is no enemy separate from one's ego or self, and since this is so, with whom are you fighting? Similarly, your own ego is your own protector, so whom are you protecting? Since the executive, observing ego is the witness of all that you do or neglect to do, once you have controlled this ego, you will be free from all of the problems caused by unhealthy attitudes and behavior.

> 80 "When someone is tamed by another, there will be a struggle; in such a struggle the number of sinners will be immense. It is certain that there is no chance of liberation for those who lust and hate. Therefore, nonconceptual yoga is bliss."

This seems to be a continuation of the argument of King Ego, of the view of a real personal identity. Even though it appears to be wise speech, we will see in verse 81 that it is not. Verse 80 says that when you try to control somebody else it will lead to fighting, arguing, and sinfulness. There will be no opportunity for liberation for people who are lustful and full of anger. Therefore, according to the verse, bliss lies in nonconceptual meditative absorption, in remaining in silence and solitude, without attachment, hatred, or conflict with others.

Verse 81 is the reply from wisdom. The subject of this verse, according to Geshe Losang Tamdrin, is the simultaneous removal—under the guise of casting spells, burning and burying—of the two extremes of eternalism and nihilism through the sovereign logical reason, that of dependent arising.

> 81 Ah! What can you say to that speech? Kill the life of clinging to existence! Burn up the life of clinging to nonexistence! Crush the chief, the demon ego-clinging!

Here there is an exclamation of amazement at the extreme position that was articulated by King Ego, namely, that there is a permanently existing self. Here we are commanded to destroy the belief in such an ego. However, after you do this, you may be led to believe that there is no ego at all, that the person doesn't exist in any way at all; this would be to fall into the other extreme, that of nihilism. This extreme of nihilism must also be eradicated. Nihilism is dangerous because it can lead people to deny that there is even a conventional self that accumulates the results of karma or goes to nirvana. The command to kill and burn these extremes uses the violent language of tantric rituals; what it means is that we are to use the main weapon, the supreme logic of dependent co-arising. That logic helps us to understand that there is a conventional self that exists dependent on causes and conditions, but that there is not an *ultimately* existing permanent self. The self ultimately responsible for our holding extreme positions is the demon ego-clinging—therefore we should destroy it. It is right to have a negative attitude toward the view of a real personal identity, since this viewpoint is the cause of all of our misery. In order to get rid of this attitude, we produce a kind of synthetic anger, which should not be confused with the kind of anger we ordinarily feel toward others, for the latter is unwholesome and is produced by our ego-clinging itself.

Verse 82 is about how the personal self gets mixed up with mental consciousness, and a phenomenal self gets mixed up with the sense-consciousnesses. We see, smell, hear, and taste, and then we believe that the objects we perceive are real because they are experienced. In addition, we believe that the subjectively experienced self is equally real. So this verse establishes the selflessness of person and phenomena in connection to what is presented to the various consciousnesses.

> 82 When the chief, mental consciousness, is not tamed, there
> is the danger that King Ego-Clinging may lead it astray.
> When the chief, mental consciousness, is tamed, vision
> and so forth will be destroyed along with the chief.

This is a difficult verse; it says that among the six forms of consciousness, the primary one is mental consciousness. Therefore, since it is always involved with ego-clinging and the perception of objects in the wrong way, it is the one that must be controlled or subdued. If you don't subdue it properly, then King Ego-Clinging will lead it like a dog on a leash. If this happens, all of the sense consciousnesses will be led to falsely believe that objects inherently exist. If you purify this primary mental consciousness, then the senses will no longer incorrectly apprehend their objects. Although the verse literally says that the visual and other consciousnesses will be destroyed, it means that their incorrect apprehension of their objects will be destroyed.

> 83 Therefore, you should tame mental consciousness, and form, sound, smell, taste, and the rest will cease to be. "I" and "mine" will cease to be, and King Conceptualization will then lack a basis.

Thus, we should control the primary mental consciousness. When we do this, all the other forms of consciousness will themselves cease to seem actual. If you do not understand that mental consciousness is empty of inherent existence, then the objects of the other consciousnesses—form, sound, and so on—will also appear to be independently, objectively real. When this is understood, the apprehension of a truly existing self and of external things as belonging to that self—"my house, my family, my friends"—will also disappear. Holding to "I" and "mine" is referred to in Buddhism as "the wrong view that the destructible aggregates are the ego." The five aggregates, or *skandhas,* that make up a person—physical form, feeling, perception, and so on—exist only for an instant and then change. They are impermanent and dependent on many causes and conditions, which is why they are called aggregates. There is nothing solid or permanent about them, yet our mistaken conceptualization imputes to them something absolute and permanent. The apprehension of a real "I" and "mine" comprise two forms of this mistaken view, and from this mistaken view come pride, attachment, hatred, and all of the mental poisons. When all these wrong views are banished, there will be no conditions to form a basis for the existence of the "king" of these false conceptions, that is, the ego.

Verse 84 is concerned with first recognizing that the logical predicate, emptiness, is free of elaboration, and then establishing a subtle form of conventional existence.

84 When you have spoken to the king in this way, you will know that conceptual construction is inherently free and is the ultimate reality. The six senses are false, like a magical elephant. Subject and object are false, like a phantom's deeds.

Once you have understood emptiness as explained above, then you will realize that all false conceptualizations are free from any true existence. At that time you will be released spontaneously from these conceptualizations; they will vanish, and you will recognize them as the sphere of ultimate truth, the *dharmadhātu,* meaning that they are ultimately empty of any inherent nature. Thus, the true nature of all conceptualization is the sphere of ultimate truth. The perceptions of the six senses will be seen as false, like a magical elephant that does not exist in the way it appears to exist. The same applies to the basic dualism of the perceiving subject and the perceived object; they will similarly be recognized as false, like the deeds of a magical emanation. The emanation appears to be a real person, but it isn't; its activity, like all phenomenal activities, is false. There are many such analogies in Buddhist scripture: a magical creation, a reflection in a mirror, the moon appearing in water, and an echo—these are all examples of the illusory nature of phenomena as we perceive them.

The following verses show that powerful analysis pursued for a long time will lead to the understanding that emptiness and dependent co-arising are one; this understanding is arrived at through "wrathful activity." Now, if emptiness and dependent co-arising are identical, when we look at a person, a house, or a river, we should see emptiness, shouldn't we? But we don't, because things that appear due to dependent co-arising are conventional truths, and emptiness is the ultimate truth, which is difficult to apprehend. For example, this table here, and I, myself, are conventional truths, not ultimate truths. The ultimate truth of the table and of myself is that we are both empty of ultimate existence *because* we are dependently co-arisen.

85 Such being the case, extirpate conceptual construction! Since there is neither subject nor object, transform the egotistic view into space! Since there is neither "I" nor "you," transfer attachment and aversion to the innate!

Because the nature of all phenomena is empty and dependent, we should completely root out the false conceptualization that grasps appearances as truly existing; such conceptualization has no foundation. Nor is there a truly existent subject or object. Thus, the false view, which holds to a substantially existent personal self and a self of phenomena, is transformed into space, meaning that it becomes empty. Believing in a real "I" and "you" leads to attachment and hatred. By seeing that "I" and "you" do not truly exist, attachment and hatred are put to rest.

> 86 Remove the shackles of high and mediocre intellect, which,
> like rabbit horns, are neither sharp nor dull. Unite into
> equality everything worldly and transcendental, which, like
> a barren woman's child, is neither clever nor foolish.

Usually we discriminate between people: we see ourselves as superior, our friends and relatives as intermediate, and other people as unattractive, inferior, or even as enemies. But this is just like talking about the sharpness or dullness of rabbit horns, which of course don't exist at all. Discriminating between people in this way is a kind of bondage that keeps us tied to cyclic existence. We should release ourselves from this type of bondage. Everything in phenomenal existence and beyond it, meaning nirvana, should be rolled into one, like rolling many threads of different colors into one spool of thread or merging many different tributaries into one river. This means that in an ultimate sense, all phenomena are equal, because they are all empty of inherent existence, in the way that a barren woman's child cannot be said to be either clever or foolish. This is why in the Perfection of Wisdom sutras many negatives are used: "There is no samsara, there is no nirvana, there is no form, sound, smell, taste, bodhisattva, disciple; there is no buddha, no dependent co-arising, no four noble truths." This is spoken from the point of view of the ultimate sense, because of the lack in these phenomena of an inherent existence.

> 87 Release into the great middle all arising and perishing,
> which, like the hair of a tortoise, is neither short nor long.
> Unite into a single ultimate all conventional phenomena,
> which, like an echo, have been forever empty.

Just as we cannot talk about long and short tortoise hairs since they do not exist, the phenomena that arise and perish, which we *do* experience, do not exist in the ultimate sense. Thus, everything should be released into the great middle, which is the Mādhyamika or centrist view between eternalism and nihilism. Similarly, even though we do not recognize this at first, all conventional phenomena are naturally empty from the very beginning, like an echo. Once we understand this through logic and meditation, all of the conventional phenomena that we have mentally divided up and given different names and attributes to will be seen as having the same nature: that is, as being empty of inherent existence.

Verse 88 is the conclusion, which Losang Tamdrin calls "a song of joy on the perfection of analytical understanding, a dance of rejoicing after hard work."

> 88 Ah, ah, the nature of non-arising is like space. Ee, ee, the body of non-perishing is free from discursive elaboration. Oṃ, oṃ, having recognized it as the ultimate body, may the compassion of the Compassionate One sustain us.

The nature of all things is non-arisen like the sky; the Sanskrit letter "ah" is symbolic of this non-origination. There are three bodies of a buddha: there is the essential body of a buddha's perfect emptiness; the form or emanation body, which is created to help sentient beings and can be seen by humans and other lower beings; and the enjoyment body, which can only be seen by bodhisattvas. These bodies are imperishable and free from all false elaborations. The third line is concerned with the dharmakāya, the essential body or the ultimate reality of emptiness. Sometimes the other schools of Tibetan Buddhism, like the Nyingma and Kagyu, understand the dharmakāya in a slightly different way; they say that everything is of the nature of the dharmakāya, or that whatever appears is a reflection of an ultimate, pure mind. This is more a Yogācāra viewpoint, which holds everything as the nature of pure mind and says that once we realize this, all the impurities will disappear. The text concludes with the prayer that once we have realized the ultimate truth, we will be sustained by the compassion of the Compassionate One, Avalokiteśvara.

Index

About Wisdom

Wisdom Publications, a nonprofit publisher, is dedicated to making available authentic works relating to Buddhism for the benefit of all. We publish books by ancient and modern masters in all traditions of Buddhism, translations of important texts, and original scholarship. Additionally, we offer books that explore East-West themes unfolding as traditional Buddhism encounters our modern culture in all its aspects. Our titles are published with the appreciation of Buddhism as a living philosophy, and with the special commitment to preserve and transmit important works from Buddhism's many traditions.

To learn more about Wisdom, or to browse books online, visit our website at www.wisdompubs.org.

You may request a copy of our catalog online or by writing to this address:

Wisdom Publications
199 Elm Street
Somerville, Massachusetts 02144 USA
Telephone: 617-776-7416
Fax: 617-776-7841
Email: info@wisdompubs.org
www.wisdompubs.org

The Wisdom Trust

As a nonprofit publisher, Wisdom is dedicated to the publication of Dharma books for the benefit of all sentient beings and dependent upon the kindness and generosity of sponsors in order to do so. If you would like to make a donation to Wisdom, you may do so through our website or our Somerville office. If you would like to help sponsor the publication of a book, please write or email us at the address above.

Thank you.

Wisdom is a nonprofit, charitable 501(c)(3) organization affiliated with the Foundation for the Preservation of the Mahayana Tradition (FPMT).